A FORMULA FOR GETTING RICH:

A guide for personal change and to easily make a fortune from scratch

Sergio Chiti

Index

Dedication --- 1

Biography of the author--- 2

Foreword -- 3

Introduction --- 6

Part I: The potentials of the subconscious and the cycles of success

Chapter 1. Breaking the Covenant with Lethargy ------------------------------ 10

Chapter 2 Why we should take this path-------------------------------------- 14

Chapter 3. Princess Perseverance and the Ogre------------------------------- 17

Chapter 4. The wizard of your own success ----------------------------------- 19

Chapter 5. The mantras of success-- 22

Chapter 6. The Potentials of the Subconscious and the Children of the Mind --------- 25

Chapter 7. Closing the Doors on the Past ------------------------------------ 34

Chapter 8. Change -- 37

Chapter 9. The Cycles of Success-- 45

Chapter 10. What to do when you have your dream in your hands ---------------------- 48

Chapter 11. The Circuit of Success -- 53

Chapter 12. The Short Circuit of Success ------------------------------------ 55

Part II: Our experience around the world

Chapter 1. Beyond borders --- 60

Chapter 2. The emerging business world ------------------------------------ 65

Chapter 3. The path to a profitable enterprise ------------------------------- 69

Chapter 4. The Way of the Dragon and the Way of the Turtle ------------------ 73

Chapter 5. Ending a stage. Searching for a new world ---------------------- 77

Chapter 6. Our profession enslaves us -------------------------------------- 80

Chapter 7. Vicious Turtle Circles --- 82

Chapter 8. Debts --- 85

Chapter 9. Breaking every paradigm --------------------------------------- 87

Chapter 10. Analyzing our environnement. Banish envy ----------------------- 90

Chapter 11. Opening Doors -- 96

Chapter 12. Pursuing a goal -- 99

Chapter 13. Our Peruvian history: between pisco and the Limacause-------------- 104

Chapter 14. Arriving on Aztec soil -- 109

Chapter 15. A new stage in México Lindo -- 116
Chapter 16. The Spanish Dream --- 127
Chapter 17. Between Two Seas -- 132
Chapter18.Purelife -- 138
Chapter 19. Is there an ideal country to invest in? ------------------------------ 141

Part III: The road to success: how to achieve it step by step

Chapter1. The secrecy of the commercial project --------------------------- 145
Chapter 2. The first step, selecting the location ---------------------------- 154
Chapter 3. Building the Commercial Society ------------------------------- 156
Chapter 4. The Business Plan --- 159
Chapter 5. The recommended office --------------------------------------- 168
Chapter 6. Recruitment --- 170
Chapter 7. Business Induction -- 184
Chapter 8. Keys for the Professional Salesperson of a Salesforce Unit ---------- 189
Chapter 9. Training Manuals and Operating Modes ----------------------- 194
Chapter 10. Commercial and motivational management ------------------------- 199
Chapter 11. The Sales Success Script ------------------------------------- 203
Chapter 12. Organizational and working outline ------------------------------ 211
Chapter 13. Taking care of details in the organization ----------------------- 217
Chapter14. Goals and Competition -- 223
Chapter 15. Motivational plans. Your own multilevel from scratch ------------- 226
Chapter 16. Administrative functions -------------------------------------- 239
Chapter 17. Initial Investment and Fixed Business Costs --------------------- 242
Chapter 18. Interaction with the Corporation and its Directors ----------------- 244
Chapter 19. Implementing a successful corporate policy ----------------------- 251
Conclusion --- 257

Dedication

To my greatest inspiration and strength in life to keep going at every step, which is my wife and partner Natalia; to my beloved children, even boys, Augusto, Antonella Angelina, and Emiliano Valentino. I hope that this book will be a compendium to follow in their lives, I feel as if I have written it for them from the first day, that is why the love I put in it and that I want to transmit to them in every paragraph so that they can forge their destiny based on these lines; to my father, Sergio, a fighter; to my brother, Hernan, a military man, and in memory of the one who preceded me in the family as a writer of one hundred and sixty seven books, my great grandfather the commander Alfredo Chiti (18781956), Pistoia. And for all those fighters and entrepreneurs of the business world. For all of them, these are the pages where I bring together all my experience based on mistakes and successes so that the reader can find that path of greatness where dreams come true.

Sergio Chiti

Email: schiti7@gmail.com

Biography of the author

Who am I? I was born in 1964, of Italian origin. I studied at the university with a degree in Tourism. Married with two children. When I was very young, I was a sales manager for prestigious tourism companies. I developed high impact exhibitions, such as the first Ex pofútbol in the world in 1999. I was one of the pioneers in implementing the knocking door system with the salesforce in the mobile phone industry in Latin America. In the 2000's I established companies in countries like Argentina, Peru, Costa Rica, El Salvador, Mexico, Panama, Colombia, and Spain. I was the number one distributor of two of the largest multinationals in Mexico until a kidnapping attempt led me to settle in Spain for a short time. Then, in Panama, I managed to conquer 15% of the cell phone market among the four brands operating in the country. In 2011 and 2012, at the opening of the market in Costa Rica, I was hired exclusively by the state company among two hundred local applicants to stop the entry of the two new communications operators in the context of the opening of the market in that country, a mission that was achieved and where, between the two, could only reach 5% of the market that first year. I have trained more than 100,000 salespeople around the world. I am a lecturer, business consultant, currently, I work in ecommerce, among other activities.

Foreword

This book summarizes the experience of more than twenty years in the development of companies, in sales organizations in eight countries of Latin America and Europe, with worldwide known companies, and where I approach in each chapter what I consider will help you to achieve the objective proposed in the title: to get to know the formula to become rich, even the philosophy that this entails and from where we will start. It is a guide that will help you achieve the destiny that every human being has been assigned, and that is abundance in all aspects and senses of life.

Each chapter will be a step by step, a compass that will guide you to achieve that goal. It is a life philosophy based on experience and a proven methodology to develop business and achieve fortune around the world based on one's own business experience in countries with very different idiosyncrasies and wherein each one of them the same marketing system and philosophy were implemented.

All this spiced up with strategies that I will propose in these lines and that were implemented developing organizations where we could decipher the secrets of combined techniques of network marketing and knocking the door, very effective in the commercialization of services or products and that led us to concretize the goals that we proposed in every occasion with companies as dissimilar as the most important multinational of security of EE. The most important security multinational in the United States and worldwide, the most important mobile phone company in Latin America or the number one in Germany, known worldwide, or state owned telecommunications companies, among many others, achieving invoicing in dollars of six to seven figures annually and monthly.

I will be presenting concepts and operational modalities for you to implement in your race to the top. Also, in this journey, it is necessary to manage subtle energies that act in pursuit of the goal set, energies that are mobilized along with a whole philosophy whose implementation begins with the positive word exercised repeatedly, like a mantra based on the thought that gave its origin, causing that big bang in our mind, directing that energy with passion and precision, like an archer to his target, to achieve the desired result always and what part of educating our subconscious with those mantras of attraction.

"Mantra" is a word that comes from Sanskrit, one of the oldest documented Indo European classical languages, used today as a liturgical language in Hinduism and Buddhism, as well as being one of the twenty two official languages in India. All the references to the oldest Sanskrit texts that have survived to the present day were transmitted orally for centuries until they were written in medieval India.

That said, the Sanskrit word "mantra" refers to sounds syllables, phonemes, words or groups of words which, according to some beliefs, have some psychological or spiritual power. "Mantra" comes from the sum of two Sanskrit words, "man", which means 'mind', and the suffix "tra", which could be translated literally as 'to release'. In conclusion, the mantra is an instrument to free our minds.

On our way through these countries, we have achieved successes based on this philosophy. Many authors, when we read a book, encourage us with their words to improve our thoughts and transform them into positive ones, such as The Power of Now, by Eckhart Tolle; Manual of the Winner, by Suryavan Solar, Ask and You Shall Be Given, by Esther and Jerry Hicks; Evology, by Jaume Banchs Lopez; of course, Rhonda Byrne's Secret and the whole series of The Magic, Hero, The Power, You Can Heal Your Life, by Louise L. There; Discover Your Unlimited Potential, by Cynthia Kersey; The Law of Attraction, by Dr. Camilo Cruz, and the famous Think and Get Rich by Napoleon Hill, among many others.

My idea is, in this book, to go a little further, providing the formulas so that, starting from a positive state of mind, thanks to the mantras of success and the strategies that we will expose, we walk step by step, developing a scheme to reach the state of happiness that economic and spiritual wellbeing offers us.

We have achieved with our company, with only one office, to invoice millions of dollars as distributors of cellular telephony with recognized companies and with electronic security systems with the number one brand worldwide.

Pioneers in Latin America in dividing into small sales forces and deploying them in different areas raked daily and to which we put their names, product of my experience   in selling tourism in the '80s, where I implemented the same scheme based on achieving better performance of the sellers and a more compact and effective organization; To do so, I divided my sales force, composed only of salesmen until that moment, without any hierarchy, into what I called "salesforce unit" (UFV), all of them hierarchized in different levels and awarded according to their achievements with tangible and intangible prizes. We included training and daily coaching.

Today companies in Latin America knock on doors with this scheme implemented by us in those years. Then we coupled all the experience gained in the U.S. multinational from 2000 and moved it to the area of mobile phone companies in the mid90s in Argentina and early 2000 in Mexico, which then implemented it throughout Latin America, sometimes with relative success and other times with resounding failures of distributors who wanted to start without knowing where to start or believing that it was easy to organize and man age. We were part of those pioneers.

4

This book was created as a guide, a GPS system, the treasure map to follow to obtain the goal and wealth that every human being should legitimately aspire to, developing healthy businesses and providing quality employment to those who help us fulfill our dreams.

We can say that we first create wealth and then write down how we come to achieve it based on a concrete and unvarnished experience, directly to the heart.

Anyone who has savings and does not know what to do or where to go in his life or wants to start a new business is a commercial director of a multinational or is related to the world of sales, I hope that this book will be your inspiration.

My wish is that I live this path from a new and real perspective so that it will materialize in hard cash. It is not my intention to remain only in good suggestions and words, which always help, but do not materialize success.

My motto is to move from motivation and the project to concrete facts in order to reach the top that each one of us considers as an individual and entrepreneur.

I know that after reading it you will surely try, and I guarantee that you will succeed if you follow the map I drew. You don't have to have a lot of experience, you don't have to be a scholar, a professional, a university student or have a large amount of money to start, the important thing will be to take action.

What I will bring you in the first and second part is a philosophy to keep in mind all the way; they are techniques and strategies to follow, tested to develop a whole project leading to wealth, victory, joy and money, easy and quick to learn, based on a wealth of experiences and funny stories that will help you to know how to move, to overcome obstacles, to arrive intact and easily to victory. Tell me if you wouldn't be tempted to follow that map and start the search as soon as possible, wouldn't you?

Introduction

"Man finds God behind every door that science manages to open.

ALBERT EINSTEIN

Dear readers, this is your travel guide, your GPS. My name doesn't matter much, what matters is you. By reading this book, you have chosen the route that will lead you to your dream destination. Be ready to leave and fasten your seat belts, because this one has many up and down curves, it will be a journey full of adrenaline until you reach the top. The one I will tell is a long road of more than twenty years. It is a true story about my business experience, where I had falls and climbs, monitoring the results, correcting mistakes that I repeated as if everything I had learned from nothing had been useful, always with blind faith, with a burning passion, with perseverance that is proof of everything and of all the negative and envious people, who do not lack on the road.

If you wish to embark on this journey, it will be like a game, that of life itself, which understands the realities of an investor and entrepreneur in search of the most precious treasure: to achieve victory in his beloved projects. This story is about getting into the fascinating world of business and how to achieve the expected and dreamed of results. We will travel together in the right direction, step by step, pointing out successes and mistakes as we walk through different countries, cultures, and individuals. By following this path, I guarantee that you will be able to obtain the happiness that money, in large part, buys, where we must also understand that success is a process that begins from a position of the joy of the spirit.

If you think money is bad and dirty, you should read this book so you know the ways it can be obtained and then judge whether you were right. This is just a civilized means of exchange that allows us to self-fulfill in life, allows us to enjoy every moment, brings the world closer to our hands by traveling to cities and places we never imagined we would visit, brings us closer to culture, extends our lives, takes away stress, and allows us to enjoy more time with our families. In short, it gives us the time to fulfill ourselves as people. Time is the most precious good that money can buy, or who is employed does not give his time and capabilities to a third party in exchange for a fixed monthly salary, working for the dreams of this?

Only in sales do we get a bonus for our time invested, which is proportional to our real effort and is usually very well rewarded. It's a different kind of job, it's motivating, and it catapults us to personal success because of the dynamics that it contains in whatever field.

Most millionaires have gone through the phase of the good salesman, then the good manager, to culminate with their own enterprise, which was born from intuition, that instinct, that animal sense of smell that some development in their lives to capture the winks that the universe offers us through messages that we must know how to capture thanks to the development of our hidden faculties in our subconscious.

If you have not been able to achieve all your goals, read this book, because I will show you, based on many of my own experiences, that it is possible to realize yourself professionally in a year or two by applying a specific philosophy of life and strategy.

If you are a person who has tried everything and has phrases such as "Money is not for me, it's difficult to do it, as it comes it goes" or "only the corrupt do it, I'll never get out of this situation, I'd better keep smoking and drinking alcohol to forget about the problems, total, life is like that", "life was cruel to me, it's my parents' fault, it's God's fault, it's my lack of education, I'm not attractive, I'm fat, ugly, skinny, I resent life", etc. And there are countless excuses for not acting courageously in life's circumstances, you are the one to keep reading this book.

Starting a new life by applying simple concepts and risking our time in a new project with little investment that you can dispose of by requesting, for example, a loan or looking for a partner, an investor to whom you can sell your project, is not bad at all, it is well worth it to be able to experience that satisfaction that provides the comfort and freedom of action that allows us to self-realization. Ours were years of effort, but a lot of enthusiasm, and I speak in the plural because in this adventure my wife accompanied me as a partner in everything.

My intention is that when you finish reading it will know how to do it easily. If you don't think it's easy, you should read this book, because you are wrong. Making money honestly is easy. And I didn't do it just once by chance or by appealing to luck, but I repeat ed it on other occasions, other economic moments, with different products and in different countries, as you will see below.

It is so easy that it depends on how intensely you experience your dream to make it come true. Everything we think becomes our reality whether we want it to or not, it can be something negative or positive. Every thought is inevitably materialized. A thought is something material, even if we do not touch it. It has form and color, if we see it in our mind and strengthen it with blind faith within us, it will be a matter of time to touch it. It's as simple as that. The greater the intensity with which we carry out our thought, the faster the result will be.

How many times have we thought, or rather dreamt, of obtaining a significant figure that we see, generally, as unattainable? Sometimes we think that it is an optical illusion to obtain a good six digit figure and, in short, we think we are not made to obtain it. Maybe we think that a million dollars is a very high figure for one and we think that it is only for guys from the financial centers, from the stock market, bankers, great artists, sportsmen, gentlemen related to power or simply lucky. Nothing could be further from the truth. Everything is closer than you think.

Let us remember something important: everything we see as unreachable is because we believe it is there, far away, and will be unreachable. It is like the world of a blind man; he sees nothing, but the things there are in front of him, but he is nullified in order to see them. If we bring it closer to our minds, we will see it as possible; therefore, it will become more attainable.

If we see it mentally and desire it with a firm passion, immeasurable love, with the certainty of obtaining it and we consider that the path is the right one even if at times it turns zigzagging or we stumble in the attempt, nothing matters knowing that we are advancing; once we have it in our minds, it will be a matter of time and organization to have the abundance in our pocket and to have fulfilled our dreams.

Part I

The potentials of the subconscious and the cycles of success.

Chapter 1: Breaking the Covenant with Lethargy

"Just as we do not have the right to consume wealth without producing it, we do not have the right to consume happiness without producing it.
GEORGE BERNARD SHAW

Ninety percent of the world's population, and perhaps more, has a blurred vision today. They cannot see clearly. They do not realize that their problems are created by themselves because their vision is clouded by the pollution that surrounds them, which is nothing more than negativity, envy, bad habits, lies, among others, and which is found among those around us every day.

What you call problems are just lessons because life is an educational process, a school, and a university at the same time, which depends on challenges and which goes from birth to old age.

I rely on statistics to develop the concept of what I call world blindness. The distribution of wealth, for example, in the world's leading power, such as the United States, is as follows: 10% of the population owns 71% of the wealth, while only 1% of the population owns 38% of the wealth and 40% of the population gets 1% of the wealth. According to the UN University's World Institute, 85% of the world's wealth is shared by 10% of the population. To be in this select group requires a patrimony of approximately sixty thousand dollars and, if we have more than five hundred thousand dollars, we belong to the richest 1% of the planet. I once read that, if all the wealth were distributed in equal parts, in a short time it would return to the same hands. We wonder why.

We see people who work from dawn to dusk to get a salary that is usually not enough. We see societies destroyed by poverty without hope.

This is both a cause and an effect of the negativity engendered by the places where we develop and their cultures of poverty, which envelop every individual at every step of their lives. The negative vibrations that surround us and in which the whole of society is immersed are obviously responsible for this mental prison, as the numbers attest, where 10% of the world's population lives steadily and the rest watches it on television and in celebrity magazines.

It is easy to get out of this vicious circle and free our mind, it is a whole mental issue, and only mental, to start vibrating in another frequency, in that which vibrates that 10% of the world's population.

Some are real problems that we ourselves attract into our lives and, at other times, are concerned that we believe will happen and that never, in the end, do happen.

Given the lack of positive results in our economic life, the best option that finds part of that 90% is to get comfortable as vegetables, watching how time slowly slips out of their hands, thinking about getting a salary at the end of the month and that leads them to find another one and another job in order to be able to gather a minimum of money that will be enough just to survive, pay the mortgage for thirty years and the car for another ten, and the cycle repeats itself month after month, becoming slaves of our debts.

My view is that slavery was not abolished in the NINETEENTH century; in my view, it took another, more intelligent, and more comprehensive course, which would this time include all the races of the world at the same time.

We don't know if this scourge of those times, which has been repeated, has appeared on purpose, as the conspirators who put forward countless theories in their blogs argue, or if it has occurred only because of a lack of calculation on the part of the financial world that governs us economically, to the point of making us believe that we have everything figured out: house, car, vacations, and life in instalments instead of the crazy life, as the famous song says.

In my opinion, that world has surely gone away now in these times we live in, just as it had gone away in the 1930s. Our blindness has reached such a point that we have been driven by a culture that tells us how to live from a young age and how we should worry about contributing to some fund or corresponding box to obtain our retirement at the end of our monotonous lives.

It would seem that, from the beginning, we have projected ourselves not to achieve the financial stability and the superlative economic progress we deserve so as not to be thinking about a miserable retirement marked by the policies of the day as a means of salvation in our old age, as if in all that time of working life we did not aspire to anything more than the collection of an eternal basic salary that makes us feel secure, although miserable.

And that is why we invent negative feelings that also bring us a series of illnesses, especially spiritual ones. In this way, we seal our fate out of fear, we convince ourselves when we reach adulthood that everything should be the same, without major shocks, poor but safe, without any risk, mediocre but conform and other similar phrases or self-imposed negative cultural mantras.

There is so much negativity that certain phrases are transformed into negative mantras that are transmitted from parents to children, parasitizing our societies with negative concepts, contaminating the minds of our young people.

I remember that in Spain there was a negative mantra that can even be heard in the media, which is the following: "How envious I am of such a person or situation". "Envy" is the preferred word for outlining a feeling towards others, which is part of the daily vocabulary of most people and is said as an innocent word when it is not. How different it would be to say, "what joy your progress, your good luck gives me", to bless the other and never to envy him.

Envy delays and postpones those who exercise it. The reason that we encounter failure at every step responds precisely to these kinds of feelings. Therein lies the origin, without a doubt, and I say this from experience because I have seen it in an infinite number of people and friends.

This is a cultural detail that should be changed, since it is a negative word that seems innocent, but hides a lot of misfortune for those who say it and for those who receive it. With these negative mantras, our thoughts are formed, although always, in each of us, there persists that spark that lights the fire at some point in our lives, and some of us change if we want to.

Thus, we come to see that part of that 90% of people want change and know that it is possible; that is why many times political parties that talk about change are voted for with enthusiasm.

Today, some of us are astonished to see a large section of the world's population defeat ed, immersed in their comfort, which I call "the turtle's lair", in which the shell that covers them, which protects them, is so large that they prefer to remain in that position before taking risks and coming out of their lethargy.

I think it's because they don't know, nobody explained to them how to do it or they don't know a mentor who will support them and help them develop their potential, which we all have without exception.

It is there, in their inaction, where resentment begins towards life, society, or themselves, shutting themselves in their world of the blind and sharing with others of their same condition those contagious viruses that spread around the world and kill more people than the flu, AIDS or global warming. These viruses are the comfort and indifference to life, to others, and even to the ecological reality of the world we live in. Nothing matters to us, first and foremost, we are indifferent.

This also translates into a lack of passion for the work they do, a lack of commitment to the society they live in, the company they work for and the planet they inhabit, a feeling of laziness that invades them, that same anguish that never ceases to down our throats at some point in our lives when we have lost our magnetic north.

That feeling of not knowing how to get out of the pit, that uncertain future, a life without meaning, without emotions, a path to I don't know where, and there begin the desperate paths that lead to drugs or alcoholism and so many others.

At the last extreme, we find the one who has already surrendered and says: "I don't care about anything", and others more mystical, in their own way, prefer to blame God for all their hardships or say: "I wish, God wants it that way". Etymologically, this word comes from the Arabic; "OJ" is 'to want' and Allah, who is God for Muslims, and I always wonder why God would not want it. And yes, as all religions agree, God is a God of love who sometimes puts us to the test not to condemn us, but to teach us to walk and to advance on the path of triumph, towards happiness, as long as we are humble of heart. We do not understand this either, but only blame him.

When the sermons of any religion speak of the humility of heart, we always tend to interpret it as poverty and economic scarcity, but, it speaks of the heart and the will that we should have. God does not want us to live badly, bitterly, depressed, or resentful, much less without feeling love for anything or anyone, not even for ourselves. All this is the cause of the hardships we have had to go through and which we inflict upon ourselves as a self-destructive punishment which leads nowhere but to a life of failure.

One of the objectives of this book is that we exterminate together negativity and thoughts in that sense. Thinking positive or negative takes the same effort, so why do we tend to think negative sometimes? It sounds silly, but only we can bring about change, and God will always respond favourably to us.

Chapter 2: Why we should take this path

"Knowing your life purpose is scary too."

DANIEL HABIF

In short, if your life has been plagued by bad business or social habits, forget about them forever.

It is important for the achievement of the promised goal to be in harmony with the law of good works. These support only those who do good. They are laws that are not seen, but they are there, as well as the law of gravity, only exist.

For example, if you don't prioritize payments to your employees on time, evade taxes, or if you sell to nonexistent or poor quality customers or forge documentation, stop that at once and turn the page, that's not the way. Change now! The sun is behind the change, I guarantee it. If you do wrong, the consequences will always be the same. Your failure will be repeated over and over again.

Once, Maximo Pradera said these words: "The most important changes in my life have taken place in moments when I thought that everything was lost". There are plenty of examples of people who changed when others were retiring but ask about Ray Krock, the founder of McDonald's, who started the restaurant chain at age 52 when many are thinking about retirement, or Colonel Sanders, who founded KFC at age 65.

In my early years as an entrepreneur, I thought I had learned all the theories and ways of selling, and that's when everything changed. Life took other paths, in which it was difficult to apply what I had learned, an endless number of turns that led me to polish the method that I present in the following chapters, based on my experience through several countries getting into the marketing of different products, such as credit cards, home alarms, mobile phones, tourism, exhibitions, television programs, Internet portals, advertising postcards, and even gastronomy.

I accumulated all these experiences one by one and perfected them until I achieved this material that I want to share with you today about how I managed to invoice my first million dollars with a sales organization in one year, investing relatively little, about fifteen thousand dollars at the time, and repeating it year after year.

Also, in this way, I met other distributors in the American company, who also made that first million and started with only five thousand dollars borrowed and a computer. However, after a year or two, they had far exceeded their expectations in sales commissions!

Our biggest investment will be our enthusiasm, plus a small sum. On occasion, the CEOs asked us to help other agents in the same company, which we gladly did. A few took advantage of what was passed on, and almost got stuck in their old ways, capriciously held against any logic, and were unable to obtain the development they were seeking for their company.

The whim of holding on to old sales methods made them fail. Others tried and succeeded, many entrepreneurs believed that higher commissions or salaries could make them sell more; however, they only ended up frustrated and without sales, and those salesmen, who with us had many sales, there made fools of themselves due to lack of motivation, restraint and good payments.

We always saw and in all places that, in any country where we were going to invest, we were immediately taken as distributors, and in a few months, we gave the expected results.

This made me think that, if so many directors and businessmen were constantly trying to copy our methods and they were not succeeding, it was because they were not doing it properly since we were not advising or transmitting to them the detail of our culture, structure, and methods due to lack of time since we had to dedicate ourselves to our company.

It was then that I felt it would be important to write this book that would transmit our concrete techniques and in detail so that I could help other entrepreneurs to carry out a business project that would serve to develop a healthy company from every point of view, and thus change the economic life of many people.

Because we want to emphasize this sales thing. It's simple; let's assume that in life everything becomes a sale. And sales are everything in life.

A lawyer, a doctor, an accountant or in short, any professional must know how to sell their services; those who succeed in doing so far outnumber their colleagues.

The sales are emotional in 50 % and we use the technique in the other 50 %. Luck does not exist; everything that happens to us is previously projected in our mind and God and the laws of the universe deliver it to us.

Let's keep in mind that to be a good entrepreneur we must first be good employees, good salespeople, good managers, and good at customer service.

In a second instance, after having gone through other previous experiences, a salesperson can access a leadership environment, which is when he or she assumes the responsibility of overseeing a workgroup. This experience is like climbing the first step or obtaining the first degree to reach our graduation, which will be to be able to undertake our own business project.

If you were not able to go through these previous stages as a sales professional, either because of any circumstance in your working life, in this book you will find a guide to develop a successful sales company as well.

Everything in business life is about to cause and effect.

There are parameters to be followed and we will explain to them so that you do not make the mistakes that make an entrepreneur a compulsive loser.

The main cause of always ending up a loser, in my experience, is to leave the ship early believing it is sinking without even persisting in repairing the dam age or correcting the course.

Everything depends on that friend that, sometimes, we leave aside and that guarantees us the way to reach our objectives of triumph, that very noble princess called perseverance.

Chapter 3: Princess Perseverance and the Ogre

"There is no security on this earth. Only opportunity."

GENERAL DOUGLAS MACARTHUR

The princess is our Dulcinea del Quijote and in our case, it is called Perseverance. We must see her that way, as a princess, and not as a witch. We must be knights and never let go of her hand, even in moments of distress.

We abandon it one step before the final victory almost always, a mute moment of time where everything seems to have been lost and silence, together with disorientation and discouragement, always prevails. It is a second before we step on the last step to open the door that leads us to the hall of the triumphant. It is forbidden to leave it, that is the first slogan. The story of a life is forged by stumbling and transforming theories into practical ways of embracing goals.

Perseverance, the great silent friend of this journey, takes us by the hand. We must not let it go, even if the strongest wind on earth is blowing, because after the storm you can be sure that the dawn will always come and the sun will shine; that long awaited moment that life promised us the day we were born.

Life is an endless number of trials in which, sometimes we lose, and sometimes we win, but if our north is firm with perseverance, the wind is blowing from behind and the sails are fully deployed, we will surely reach the destination that we plot in our minds in that magical moment of inspiration wanting to embrace our dreams, and I assure you we will reach them if we pursue them beyond the sea of circumstances that surround us, without giving up, with the security that comes from having blind faith in our project.

Hernan Cortés had to sink every last ship in his fleet because his poor, heroic Spaniards wanted to run away in front of the incredible number of warriors the Aztec empire had. Cortés burned his ships so that no one would retreat. And I think he did it because he himself doubted that one could have such a forceful result as the one, he achieved. I think he did it to silence his own fears, history tells us that thanks to his alliance with some fifty thousand indigenous sworn enemies of the Aztecs he achieved his goal.

His move seemed, at first, suicidal. Today no one would remember him if he had left for Spain with fear as his burden. It would be just one more anecdote lost in the Archive de India's in Seville. But something must have beaten within him that a shocking event would happen, and that life would smile on him. He knew that with five hundred men alone he could not. His being felt like a raging fire that threw him towards a conquest almost impossible to imagine.

Not only was Cortés' a struggle for conquest, but for survival itself, where there was no room for that uncomfortable passenger that is fear. If perseverance is a princess, fear is the ogre of the play that is presented in the theatre of our very lives.

That's our game today. We are afraid of conquering new horizons, of what they will say, of closing a sale just because they say no and we feel that this is a missile aimed directly at our low or no self-esteem.

We are afraid of failure, of money, of change, of sickness, of laughter, of the success of those closest to us, for we do not know how their triumph will affect us, afraid of the night, of the dark and of not knowing how to make money. Fear is defeated with love, joy, and faith, I tell you with firmness and conviction.

Love for what we do, for those around us, for our clients, for the project at hand; without love there is no force for change, we would not exist in this world from the moment that life arises from the love between two people.

And faith is that which moves mountains, as Jesus would say in his parable. Faith in ourselves is the first condition because if we do not believe in our potential, we could hardly transmit our objectives to those who accompany us. In short, faith in the positive conclusion of our projects must be beyond our strength.

Chapter 4: The wizard of your own success

"80% of success is based on simply insisting."

WOODY ALLEN

Many think that by entering college, studying hard, and receiving a piece of paper they will get the success they desire and will be welcomed everywhere with open arms. A piece of paper that says we can achieve personal fulfilment through our profession. What do they think?

Since we were children, during our academic formation, they began to inculcate and teach us a culture of science and history, among others, that for practical purposes are of no use to us in our life of economic development and only add anecdotes that we do not know how to channel for our own experience to make a destination of abundance related to money.

Moreover, the study centers to which our parents sent us are full of teachers with a vocation for teaching, but who in their lives did not experience a business transit and did not generally achieve their economic goals, perhaps I would say that famous 90% of whom we were talking about. How am I going to pretend that these very worthy people teach us a lot of important things, but the most important thing is not, which is economic survival, how to achieve economic realization and success in what we propose or how to project our dreams and make them come true with a philosophy of life that points to happiness and joy.

I think that studying helps in the basics, but in educational institutes, you will rarely see a successful entrepreneur teaching how to perform in economic life, which is what really matters once we leave the institutes and find ourselves in a competitive and demanding society, where everyone seeks to reach the zenith in business or profession, while others only aspire to survival, that is the difference.

Imagine a world of entrepreneurs. Imagine a world of salespeople and everyone applying sales techniques to perfection; hunger would disappear and trade between countries would grow along with their GDPs. If there were more sales professionals, the social explosion, the strikes, the union marches would be a thing of the past. If there were more successful entrepreneurs, businessmen in the field of product distribution, the great fortunes would increase hand in hand with an endless number of happy and fulfilled employees.

Here we go on the practical side, that is, giving it the form, the method, the day to day technique, the necessary secrets, in short, all the knowledge of how to do it, the knowledge of how to start up a serious project to reach income levels of over a million dollars after one year. We will move away from theory to enter the real world of business and how to get out of it as little as possible but decorated with the star of plenty.

A lot has been written about positive thinking, about self-suggestion, about revealed secrets, there are even those who talk to aliens or something like that and pass on to them their teachings on how to get everything you want, like the one about the marriage of Esther and Jerry Hicks, Ask and it shall be given to you, learn to manifest your desires, about Uranus. All of them are books that fill my library and are very recommendable, even the one about the aliens because it has very positive and encouraging words.

All of them comprise a compendium of important teachings to keep in mind, but that, in short, leave a good taste in our minds without indicating to us with certainty the scheme to follow, the steps to develop, where to get a business, what to do or how to do it and develop a business scheme. In short, it is not the objective of them; their objective is to instill in us a change in thinking and acting. But once this is achieved, the question we ask ourselves is where to start then.

From these pages, I am going to give you the passport you were looking for and to the princess called Perseverance to delight you during the journey with her presence. What more can you ask for? Good company on an unusual journey. A practical guide that will be developed in part III with real applications in the field of business or large corporations to develop a practical organization along with a change of idiosyncrasies in the mind that can come to realize us in abundance.

In our case, we have applied it in the field of telecommunications and electronic security, with the most important company worldwide in this area. In this context, we have obtained the kinds of honey of success. As I said before, it is a real story that we had to live. It is not a fantasy, nor have we gathered countless entrepreneurs to tell us their experiences, which, in general, leave us only halfway through, since it is difficult to reveal all the secrets in a brief interview. We are not disciples of magicians, nor are we going to talk about the chronicles of a fantasy world. This is as real as you are if you apply it with common sense, enthusiasm, and faith in the project.

You will be the wizard of your success, the one you always wanted to achieve. That world that your dreams always tended to. "Life is a dream", argued Calderón de la Barca; we can add that, as long as we want to reach the top, dreams come true. It is us and only us who are responsible for carrying them out.

They will experience it. We will travel to various countries on Earth where we have developed and tested these schemes. Different markets, different cultures, which gives us the certainty that these business actions lead to one single place, to the goal we set for ourselves anywhere in the world. We will analyze the best options together with their characteristics, where to invest, and be able to develop your business project in countries and cities of the world. We will put on the table the steps to follow to install your company and your dream in the world and within the reach of the market. No one is a prophet in his land, according to the Bible, and I believe that we will be able to start our story there, later, traveling around several countries and developing companies in them.

Chapter 5: The Mantras of Success

"No one does badly for long without being blamed for it."

MICHEL DE MONTAIGNE

To obtain what we call success, we must first educate our mind, and the easiest way is to convince our subconscious of what we want to achieve so that it, in turn, transmits our desire to the universe. From our experience, we will use certain mantras that lead to success and a complete strategy that we will explain below.

The Sanskrit word "mantra" appears in Hinduism for the first time in the Rigveda in the second millennium, meaning 'instrument of thought', 'prayer', 'supplication'; over whelming word.

It is to experience mental liberation with words that crush all negativity and envy that arise like stones carried away by a river in its flood or the so called waico for Peruvians, which are deposited in our path.

This is what happened to us in Peru, where we met what a waico was on one of those nights when, with all our illusions on our shoulders, chasing our dreams, we were on our way to Lima from Santiago de Chile for the opening of a new branch and we came across this obstacle, a waico, which is a waterfall of water on the road and which deposits stones from the landslide on the way. What was our reaction at that moment when a dense layer of water covered the small road in a mountainous area in the south of Peru? To go ahead with resolution, without looking back, shouting and repeating a mantra to give us superhuman strength on that journey. And we went through it.

In Tibetan Buddhism, every mantra is recited to identify with every aspect of the enlightened mind. For example, the famous mantra Om mani padme hum corresponds to compassion; the mantra "om" corresponds to the creative sound of the universe and the beginning of existence. Furthermore, according to tradition, a mantra has no effect unless it is authorized by a teacher who is backed by a particular lineage that goes back to the Buddha himself, that is, it was successfully applied by someone who achieved results, a teacher like the Buddha.

They also suggest that a mantra can be left written or waved on flags, producing the same spiritual benefit as if it were spoken.

In psychology, this term, mantra, is the repetition of words by the subject in or der to fix and reinforce a circular thought. A circular thought is when we don't stop thinking about things and even at night, we are like this; it is like a passion for that idea or dream that we cannot detach from our mind.

In Eastern thought, life is circular, everything that goes returns. A thought, a feeling, a desire, a dream, love, good wishes or bad; everything returns, everything is part of cycles that repeat, just have to wait the time it takes to return that thought in material or spiritual form to oneself.

Everything is reborn. If we break up with our partner, if we do badly in our company, if we break up with a friend, it will finally come back with another face, otherwise, but those feelings we had of falling in love or of motivation with our projects or the good times with those friends or lost partners, they will all come back one way or another, life does not end in a bad period or a lack of love, we just have to have perseverance and patience, being receptive and open to new life experiences where there is no room for the fears that parasitize us.

We must bury the past, because every time we remember those moments, those images of the past we bring them into our present and they invade our mind with toxic thoughts that belong to the time tunnel, and it is not necessary to give them life again, we must bury them definitively.

Everything returns in a positive way because it is part of our nature, to vibrate in a positive way, as long as we are vibrating in the same frequency as those things that we wish to return, and to help us in this task, there are certain positive phrases or mantras that will make our wishes concrete in the here and now.

Mantras contain very high vibrations which, by repeating them for a specific purpose, with a certain vibratory frequency, that is, by putting passion and deep feelings into them, have the power to focus the mind and produce the changes we desire.

By concentrating on a mantra, our mind becomes free and lets the meditation flow into what we are affirming.

The mantras of success contain creative energy through the sound they emit, while they vibrate generating positive energies, so they generate focused change where we direct that mantra, whether it is changed in health, in our appearance, in our economy.

Working with our intuition, we can create our own mantras, those that resonate and vibrate at the same frequency as our essence. Thus, I came to create my own mantra that helped me to materialize our dreams at an economic level and keep us in a positive vibration. He himself says:

I deserve, decree and obtain success, wealth, victory, joy, health, and money in abundance, which come to me easily, in expected and unexpected ways.

It is the combination of words that we will use daily to infect our subconscious with what is necessary to advance along the path of abundance.

By repeating the mantras, we will free the mind, bring it back to the lost virginity in a mound of negativity.

We will repeat it aloud or in our mind, it could be in the bus, in the car, taking a walk, any time and place where we need to clear our mind and influence it with positive thinking and inject it with that dose to keep the desire we aspire to high.

Chapter 6: The Potentials of the Subconscious and the Children of the Mind

"I was convinced that if you think small, you are still small, and I didn't in tend to be!"

RAY KROCK

Luck

The children of the mind are those that are established as true in our thoughts, they are states of our mind; some heal us, others sicken our subconscious. Some are good and others not so good, as in real life children. Among them, we can find luck, criticism, faith, doubt, visualization, action, imagination, patience, enthusiasm, concern, meditation.

First, we mention luck, which is nothing more than a vibration corresponding to the dominant state of thoughts.

Thus, if these are oriented to the opposite side of luck, that is, the negative side of your moment of anxiety, you cannot create opportunities for luck in your life. And, consequently, if you are not presented with opportunities for luck, you cannot take advantage of them.

Why? Because he thinks negatively, he thinks the worst instead of the best. It takes the same effort to think one way or the other.

The only antidote to your problems is to practice positive mental visualization.

Being less critical of others is part of the solution. The favorite sport of the masses who develop negative energy is criticism and gossip.

If he criticizes others, the true personality that must arise from the repetition of positive mantras that infect the mind in order to free it cannot be manifested.

Focus your thoughts and energy on your goals. Don't waste time criticizing, think about your future, your life, which is more important than that of others.

It's hard to let go of all those energies that make you doubt. That is why changes will not come as quickly as they should if we do not correct our negative tendencies. It is as if you were driving on a motorway where you can go at a hundred and twenty kilometers per hour in peace and only drive at forty kilometers per hour.

Doubts start from being afraid of the unknown, and these fears stop us from acting and getting the victories that are waiting for you.

Doubt is the opposite of faith, and faith is nothing more than the firm confidence that the invisible things we hope for will come to pass. Faith goes hand in hand with positive visualization. If you wish to free yourself from the thoughts of doubt that limit your progress, you must practice visualizing the things you desire. There is a mystical definition of faith: "Faith is possessing in advance what is expected. Possession in advance is only achieved through visualization exercises.

This visualization is achieved by closing your eyes and imagining inside you the person you would like to be, the life you would like to live, the things you would like to possess, the children you would like to have with the person you love and that you visualize with love in those moments.

Then you just have to wait for your wishes to materialize. Once we project them, once we determine them, we achieve them. Once we see them in our minds and feel them with deep emotion in our hearts, it is only a matter of time before they materialize in our lives once we take action.

The only problem most people have in their lives in doubt. Doubt dies, it fades away before faith and love, which transforms hearts, and the weapon that these two uses, the one that destroys doubt, is called passion. Passion for our dreams and projects.

Moving out of the comfort zone is vital to materialize our thoughts. This zone is a prison of the mind that only we impose on ourselves; therefore, we can take the key that is found in ourselves and open our door, that is, our mind. Success, wealth, victory, joy, health, and money are within your reach.

The point is to dare, the world is one of those who dare.

We must not be afraid of making mistakes and we must act without hesitation, with passion. You must be fully aware of all the unlimited potentialities that are in your being.

You must nurture that potential, that security on a daily basis; life is, above all, a matter of choice, in short.

Therefore, you must choose and have a concrete idea of what an ideal day and life would be like and apply what we call visualization.

Until you have defined your ideal, your objective with precision, your subconscious cannot work on its realization. So, take some time to reflect.

Practice every night, at bedtime, the visualization of your ideal. Stick pictures representing your dreams and ambitions on a blackboard in front of your desk and look at them as if you have already achieved them.

Knowing each other is good, controlling each other is better. Never worry, always take care. It is by means of mental exercises that you will acquire the power of the will, and it is by means of these exercises that you will conserve it. Do not allow fears or doubts to paralyze you; they only limit you and destroy everything.

What you should do, decide to do it today and now; what you have decided to do, do it now; what you have done, do it now.

Don't slow down your ascent because of a useless burden, formed by pride and self-sufficiency. By following this advice, you will respect the law and elevate it above yourself. Forget your egos, trample on your pride, which only slows down the arrival of success; bite your tongue three times, as one of my Italian grandmothers used to say, before revealing your secret dreams.

Human beings have a tendency to reject change and to change their habits. The German philosopher Nietzsche said: "Without music, life would be a mistake". Nothing could be truer.

Music has a truly magical power to raise our subconscious and psychic vibrations.

That's why I listen to music every day.

Themes such as Vivaldi's Four Seasons, J. S. Bach's Brandenburg Concertos, or Mozart's 21st Concerto are used in fast learning centers, such as language teaching laboratories because their hearing stimulates intellectual faculties, memory, and concentration.

Folk wisdom says that the true treasure of a human being is his activity. If you consider your activity to be boring, unrewarding, or forced, then it produces negative energy and the psychic blockage feeds itself somehow. This leads us to reflect on this fundamental notion that sees the outside world as the representation of our inner thoughts. If you understand this, you will be aware that you must change your thoughts in order to change the outer material conditions.

As a general rule, you should put enthusiasm into everything you do. Even the smallest things. By sacralizing your actions, that is, by giving them a higher meaning, you will make enormous progress in developing your potential. There is a form of the disorder that predominates in the thoughts of those who are not yet enlightened, as if they find it difficult to focus their spirit on a given subject.

The first thing is that it could bring more mental clarity in the definition of its goals and objectives. To do this, write down on a piece of paper all your objectives and everything you would like to achieve. Once you have written this list, you are going to prioritize, from highest to lowest, these objectives and goals you want to achieve. So, at the top of the list, there has to be your priority objective. It is on this objective that you will have to focus all your thoughts.

To focus your thoughts on this goal, I advise you to read this priority goal aloud several times a day as if it were a mantra. Keep in mind that, for the time being, you should only focus on one goal at a time.

Once you have established what your priority objective is and read it several times a day, at night, before going to sleep, practice as always, the positive visualization of the realization of this objective. Stop believing that things will never change. Apply this rule now and, I promise you, everything else will come.

Concentration is fundamental to success, and it is necessary that you develop your ability to concentrate, to focus your spirit on a concrete task.

One of the important laws of metaphysics is the law of action and reaction. So, to get something, you have to act. Nothing is born out of nothing. It is through action that things are accomplished.

Thought and desire are only two precursor elements of success. Only action allows the materialization of a thought, a project, an objective. So, you have to look for that force of action. I know thousands of people who have exceptional potentials in themselves, but despite this, they do not manage to achieve the life they desire.

It is not that they do not have the necessary means, but simply that they have never put into practice the strength of action, of the will to act and to transform things. That is why you must apply your will to action from today onwards on specific objectives. Set yourself challenges. Look up, do not be afraid to dream or to accomplish great things, because you have the capabilities.

That is why in this book I go one step further than just being a compendium of good advice, and in the last part precisely I move on to the options of various actions that we must take on the road to the realization of our desires for wealth, victory and joy, through undertakings that we can prove to be able to set in motion and advance towards those objectives confident of obtaining the results that I offer in these lines.

I conclude, in my opinion, that the power of imagination is stronger than the power of reason.

"Imagination' means 'creating images' or, in other words, imagination is nothing more than mental visualisation. And this is very important. Your rational spirit somehow dictates that you cannot do this or that. Instead, by the power of imagination, you can get anything you want. That is why it is necessary for you to visualize the realization of what you want to achieve. Imagination rules the world.

You must visualize the scene of being surrounded by a full life, imagine how you would feel in that state of consciousness as if you had already reached it, surrounded by an image of prosperity, full of light, where your dream has already been reached and you are enjoy ing it, feel it, touch it in your mind, smell the harvest of triumph, put all your senses into action imagining those moments of joy and victory.

To practice this exercise, you should wait until the last moment before falling asleep. When you feel sleep coming over you, form that mental image in your spirit. You can also help yourself by having a blackboard on your desk, office, or place where you relax, and on which you write down what you want to achieve with passion and love. Have pictures of the house and car you want to reach, pictures of the places in the world you would like to visit, pictures of the children you would like to have.

Repeat this mantra: "What the mind is capable of conceiving and believing I can achieve. Realize that you have unlimited power and that now is the time to express it to the outside world.

If it is difficult for you to remember the mantras, it is the same effect to record the phrases and, with headphones, to repeat them in your ears; thus, it facilitates the assimilation which should, like a sponge, absorb your subconscious. Write down all the positive phrases that come to mind and repeat them, you will know within yourself which ones you need.

You surely know this metaphysical law that says: "You shall give, and you shall receive". By wanting to give and share, you place yourself within reach of good fortune, manifesting the generosity of your heart. Those stingy people hardly find the train of happiness. Very few manage to acquire wealth. Most live a life of misery that creates its own idiosyncrasy. Those who are stingy do not love their neighbors, nor themselves. He is a person who is ill with doubts, fears, who does not believe in himself or in others. The miser is a being who has earned hell on earth, he will never be happy. The one who does not share the universe will not share his goods either.

Originality is a sign of success. There are no limits to what you can achieve. The only limits are those set by your mind.

But you also have to know how to be realistic. Truly, you can achieve everything thanks to the powers of your subconscious. But keep in mind that the changes you desire will only manifest through action.

It is good not to set limits on the level of success you expect, but you must provide yourself with the means to achieve it.

If you act, you'll break down all the boundaries! Miracles require patience. Patience is the only key to positive personality restructuring. Rome wasn't made in a day.

First, you have to get rid of that inner shell. Impatience makes it impossible to assess the effects that are actually occurring. So, you have to realize the virtue of patience and perseverance.

Focusing on the solution and not on the problem is a condition for strengthening patience and obtaining perseverance.

For this, some true anecdotes that history gives us.

When NASA began launching astronauts into space, they discovered that pens would not work without gravity or zero gravity because the ink would not go down to the surface where you wanted to write. It took them six years and $12 million to solve this problem. They developed a pen that worked under zero gravity, upside down, underwater, on virtually any surface, including glass, and in a range of temperatures from below freezing to over three hundred degrees centigrade. And what did the Russians do? The Russians used a pencil!

Another case was that of a hotel magnate who traveled to an Indian city for the second time a year away from his first trip. When he arrives at the counter of a hotel inferior in stars to those of his chain, the employee smiles at him and greets him, saying: "Welcome back, sir, it's good to see you back in our hotel"; surprised in a great way, since, in spite of being such an important person, he likes the anonymity and it would be difficult for the employee to have such a good memory to know that he was there a year before, he want ed to impose the same system in his hotel chain, since that simple gesture made him feel very good. On his return, he immediately put his employees to work on this issue to find a solution to his request. The solution was to find the best software with face recognition, database, special cameras, response time in microseconds, employee training... at a cost of approximately two and a half million dollars. The magnate preferred to travel again and bribe the hotel employee to reveal the technology he was using. The employee did not accept any bribe, but humbly told the tycoon how they did it. He said, "Look, sir, we have an arrangement with the taxi drivers who brought you here. They ask him if he has already stayed at the hotel to which he is bringing him, and if he has, then when he leaves his lug gage here at the counter, he gives us a signal and that is how he earns a dollar.

The conclusion is not to complicate our lives with fancy solutions, we must always find the simplest way, focusing on the solutions and not on the problems, or rather, not to worry, but always to be concerned.

The last step is to have confidence, is to have faith in your possibilities. There is a brightness that shines deep within you and it is the enthusiasm that we must polish. Enthusiasm means, in Greek, 'to have a god within', 'to be possessed by God'. You know well that nothing can resist divine power.

This "divine" power is in you. You are able to move mountains and perform "miracles".

Enthusiasm arises in an instant when one least expects it; inspiration appears to give way to enthusiasm.

A new song, an idea for a new project, a dream that inspires a business, etc.

Now, it is you who must take the reins of your life. No one can do it in your place. Only you have that power. What I am trying to tell you, perhaps clumsily, but from the bottom of my heart, is that until you decide once and for all to face life resolutely, you cannot get what you want. It is time to look to your future and the things you want instead of thinking about everything that is not working in your life.

If you wait until all the ideal conditions are in place to be able to decide if you do some thing that will go in the direction of realizing your projects, you will do nothing.

After having mastered patience, he must move into an active phase and take possession of his inner powers.

The strength is in you, it is an act of faith that at last you have confidence in yourself and claim your right to abundance. The "psychological" blockage usually comes from negative mental programming. When one does not have a good image of oneself it is because of that negative programming.

You always have the solution, no matter what the obstacle is. And I would like to point out that this negative programming also comes from you and your environment. Consequently, you undoubtedly evolved in a negative environment in your childhood or adolescence.

Starting to improve is part of an open mind to the outside, to the challenges we face, to the changes, to the communication, and to the desire to learn new things. Breaking negative paradigms is the solution; these are those thoughts that limit us, that we have as wrong models to follow.

Breaking the boundaries is how you will advance to victory. Do not stop, to advance is to add wills around you, is to summon followers, is to invoke the universe.

The process of transformation always begins in the most intimate part of the being, we feel it in the soul, and it is transformed into a new entrepreneurial spirit that manifests

31

itself in our world. We project that force that infects the world. We must never lose sight of the goals we have set, much less worry about events that will not happen beyond our minds or inevitable situations.

Worries are part of these psychological blocks. Concentrating on the things that one can change in life and not wasting time on worries that are out of one's field of action and out of every day, worries about things that will not happen, being mentally present in the day to day is a condition sine qua non to be able to advance in the daily becoming in order to be able to undertake.

His will power must be concentrated on the things of the present, because only by acting in the present can he guide the future.

This is equally valid for the past. You have no power either in the future or in the past.

Instead, you have the power to act in the present to guide the course of your future.

Many parasitic thoughts tend to control your life, to make you doubt your self-confidence. We must first identify them; once you identify those parasitic thoughts, ask yourself if it is in your power to change this thing or that which is tormenting your mind.

"If it doesn't happen, it's convenient", says an old saying, so we should turn the page and continue with renewed strength and not attract old situations to our present, because it would be like giving life in our present to those past torments or future worries when, in reality, we have no control over them.

Even if sometimes the mere idea of acting paralyzes you, don't forget that you have the positive energy. Thinking about the past and what might have been generates unnecessary worry and only exhausts the mind, killing the entrepreneurial spirit.

It is fundamental to meditate accompanied by the mantras of positive thinking, which we must practice. Reflection is part of that meditation, meditating on times, things, people, paths and strategies to take. Meditation produces miracles.

Meditation is a mental exercise that consists of analysing things in depth.

Have you ever thought about a bottle of wine, for example? The story begins on the day the vine was planted and bore fruit, where time, sun and water did the rest. Then came the harvest by the hands of man, the selection of the grapes, the process of fermentation, then the oak barrels, time gave it its tannins, whose juice was decanted into a bottle beautifully adorned with its qualities, to finally be transported and arranged on the shelves of a luxury restaurant or in a supermarket to reach your table and served in a decanter for this purpose, until it releases all its aroma and flavour in a glass and is tasted by whoever consumes it.

To meditate is to see all possible aspects of a thing, an object, an event, a person. It is exactly an exercise in mental reflection. It is advisable to practice it frequently.

The only truly important things to be found on the outside are ideas and interaction with others.

You will simply need a pencil and a notebook, cards or a blackboard for each month, so twelve pages, twelve blackboards or twelve cards will suffice. For each month, write down your objectives, your goals, your hopes, etc.

Then reflect on them and write them down, because remember that thoughts are forgotten and words are carried away by the wind, while what is written remains forever.

Chapter 7: Closing the Door on the Past

"Tell the world what you're trying to do but do it before you say it."

NAPOLEON HILL, *Think and Grow Rich*

Leaving doors open means not being able to let go of your past or live today satisfactorily; there are plenty of examples in terms of love or toxic friendships that you do not close the cycle out of fear, out of doubt, that you think they might come back and it would be different this time. So, we must ask ourselves why return. Do I need to clarify anything? Do I need to clarify anything? Silences that invaded moments. Or maybe words we didn't say?

When the past calls, don't answer; what they think of you doesn't define you, it's just an opinion and opinions change. A plane is safe at the airport, but it was not built to stay there. Your current situation is not your final destination. Don't judge, better understand. Today's pain does not compare to the future joy that we must project immediately and that will come when we least expect it, as if by magic. One should not focus on the difficulties, but on the possibilities ahead. We must not let the vicissitudes that are presented to us change their goals, their moods or their dreams.

If the strategy fails, changing it is the best option, but do not abandon the path. Never have a plan B or dream B at hand, for it will then be the plan that will be realized, for we have not focused all our energies on plan A, and so we are dispersing without realizing our priority goal. If we have a plan B it is because we do not trust fully, blindly, with passion, in our plan A.

If our present, our friendships, partners or acquaintances do not feed our spir it, do not add up, do not bring happiness or love, letting them flow is the most convenient and the only thing we must do to be able to continue on the path of positive mental attitude, which we must cultivate to reap the successes with confidence, with passion, with firmness, without looking back.

We should not stick to businesses where passion and love have already faded over time if they are not turning out as we wished because of the circumstances.

No one is against anyone, the world continues to turn; only your mind can turn against you, opinions and positions always change. Therefore, clinging to a negative idea is suicidal.

We must look at things from another angle, everything happens for a reason, but we must always consider that it has been for the better and never for the worse, because that is what happens when we vibrate positively. All the attachments that were holding us back fade away and we must let them go, let them flow away. If they do not let us go forward or no longer add anything to our life that we want to create from happiness, we must let them go.

Even if these attachments keep us in a status quo, they are useless if they do not mobilize us. Because of the fear that a new situation offers us to face in that future that we believe is uncertain, we believe that we should not continue. We must know that leaving this attachment aside and, in the past, the present and the future will provide us with better things to live and experience than what we had with this attachment, the same one that held us back and no longer contributed anything.

It is not only in business that this rule is given. I have also applied it in love, and I have obtained very positive things that have happened to me.

I remember that I had a toxic girlfriend that we will call M. After two years of a tortuous relationship, those relationships that no longer contribute anything or feedback, I met another girl that I did like, and I wanted to start something new with her. Because of my attachment to Me, I was reluctant to let her go, and because I didn't want to let go of that relationship, negative things happened in my life.

I never knew what M said to that other girl when he was able to reach her by phone to get her to run away from me in a relationship that was just beginning. Besides, she stole all my furniture saying that she had sold it only for a hundred dollars, paintings and gold and silver items, leaving me without all the memories of my loved ones. Even my grandfather's violin came into the supposed auction of my house held in only one hour and without my presence, and many more negative things he inflicted on me that would be extensive to relate. Those are the consequences of attachment to something that no longer adds up in relationships or business. Shortly after, another woman appeared, and my life changed dramatically. I immediately cut off my relationship with the abovementioned M, despite the cries and scandals, even harassment from her of all kinds. With that firmness, the real results are obtained. Today that relationship that I started after M gave me my two children that I have today and more than twenty years of happiness.

Making a firm decision and knowing how to let go, let go of those things or businesses or people that are toxic on the road to happiness is fundamental to advance in our goals in life. I have seen in one of my ventures, which was the gastronomy, where many entrepreneurs in the field cling to places that have gone out of fashion because they do not dare to let go. The fear of "what will I do with my life from now on without my famous restaurant" invades them, the current reality that clashes with the expectations already lost, where one finds cooks who do not measure up, with worn out dishes and tablecloths, with chairs to be repaired, debts with suppliers who can no longer sustain themselves, hours that one no longer enjoys with the family, since one must be in a box that each time bills less to avoid robberies, and a long etcetera.

There is life after every failure and life in abundance. Failures are part of success, it would be the school to achieve success, you overcome them, you give the test and that's it, you move forward.

Life is too short to wake up with regrets, negative feelings, or memories that are bad for us. If someone or some situation hurts you and is toxic, it is time to let go of what does not make you happy. It is no longer worthwhile to continue with topics that are perished and do not bring positive things into our lives.

If you convert, your environment will change too. No matter if a hurricane is wreaking havoc around you, you must take control of everything you can control.

When things seem to be falling on you like hail with stones the size of a golf ball, it may be that everything is settling down to give you a surprise; there is no need to feed fears or negativity, your way of thinking conditions you and sculpts the personality of what you are and what you will become.

Chapter 8: Change

"Happiness consists in agreeing on your thoughts, your words, and your deeds."

MAHATMA GANDHI

Changing the perception of the events that surround us day by day is key. When our desires and expectations are not fulfilled is when one experiences negative emotions. You are the one who decides and chooses whether you will be affected by the negative daily events that you cannot control. Most people allow themselves to be consumed, feed on the negatives, and that can make you sick and is contagious; you can quickly go from euphoria to sadness or anger.

We must obtain from within us a clear idea of what the desire will be like, the goal we want to reach, and once it has been realized, how we will feel.

We must sculpt a mental map of it and then capture it, as if it were a painting, on a canvas that is our future life. To do this, we must write in great detail all the steps and strategies that we must implement to achieve our goal. Your thoughts should be oriented only towards the goals, thus filtering out all the parasite thoughts and moments that could dis turb you. Even to keep away any toxicity from our surroundings, people or circumstances, such as thinking about debts, ex partners, envious friends, etc.

To give meaning to life, don't waste your time doing a job you don't like, that you don't enjoy, you will never be able to develop as a person doing something you don't like. Success, wealth, victory, joy, and health are things that come easily when you love what you do and maintaining patience in the face of delays and inconveniences is of vital importance.

Fear weakens, paralyzes, depresses. You should never be guided by what others think. Don't let them pollute your days full of joy and hope. Just listen to your heart, your hunches, your intuitions, and then follow them. They are inspired by God and the laws of the universe are with you.

You must take control of your life before you can start on the road to success. He is solely responsible for the things that happen to him. I remember I once started a very fancy restaurant in Panama. I hired several chefs with supposed experience. After a while, none of them worked out, nor did they make the grade, causing me to lose customers and my business to fall into disrepute. Sometimes, through personal work on social networks, I managed to call for an average of five hundred reservations per day, and they did not correctly calculate the production or did not want to do it; I could never know for sure, and there were six chefs plus assistants, where each one charged about fifteen hundred dollars.

It was then that I understood the excessive attitudes of the protagonist in the series of the Englishman Gordon Ramsay when he went crazy in the face of such ineptitude. In the beginning, I left them in their positions for a while, because I felt sorry for them. Then I blamed them for not generating customer loyalty. Until I took control of this situation and decided to kick them out of the restaurant and put together a new team of cooks. I want to say with this as an example that to have pity is the worst feeling and advice that exists and, above all, in business.

Without decisive decisions in front of someone who does not give the expected results, we will never reach the top in business. We must know how to get out of our environment the people who are not good at the task at hand, we must have zero tolerance for attitude problems, that is, knowing how to get rid of personnel who are not competent is the key to moving forward in business.

Taking control of your life is precisely about feeling responsible for the things that happen to you and not blaming others for our lack of control and making the right decisions.

To achieve complete happiness, you must meditate once a day for at least fifteen minutes and do a sport that you like, such as running, walking on the beach or in a park, playing ping pong or soccer with friends, but moving is key to completing the process of change.

Be your architect. Make your life marked by the decisions you made and not by those you didn't make, move your energies, and decide to take a stand, always move forward, never backward.

The important thing is the time and the way we abuse it. We are concerned about the appearance of our body, where we spend time and money to dress it, pay for expensive surgeries, and only realize as we approach adulthood that the body is only an Armor that covers what is truly perennial and important: our inner self. This Armor covers our personality, thoughts, beliefs, intentions, feelings towards this world. We must have within that Armor some combination of all that can change our world around us.

This is why giving love no matter what you receive in return is fundamental to the realization that endless rewards will come your way, even success in business, for by giving love you receive more than you thought you would.

Being faithful to your thoughts and feelings is fundamental to achieving victory. Releasing that which delays or is harmful is key.

He is always recognized sooner or later, simply when he feels that it does not bring him anything, bothers him, or takes away his energy and time or sees that it induces him to bad habits.

You should always talk about positive topics, do not contaminate yourself or let others do so with your negative words or gestures. Avoid the news, visualize your projects becoming a reality, be grateful, do not try to change the world, change yourself and you will see that the rest will change through your ex ample.

What you think, that's right, is projected and everything will manifest in its proper time; believers say in God's time, it is best not to press.

In my case, when I took a couple of years to travel around the world and visit some thirty five countries, they were years full of economic success. We organized the company, set the guidelines, participated in the main decisions, and selected our top managers with great confidence.

Then we started traveling at a rate of every three months. We would visit Europe, Canada, or the Caribbean for pleasure on a cruise or by renting a car and staying in beautiful castles, the Fairmont hotels in Canada. We never pressed our success in those years, and everything just happened. It was not well understood, but there it was, month after month, the production we had scheduled. Our minds were a bit flying and our minds were a bit on the company, but without stressing, that's when we knew the most about the words "victory", "joy" and "money in abundance". We read motivational books as we discovered the world.

Not rushing time and maintaining a hint of indifference really makes a difference in life.

I remember when the American security company's main sales slogan was: "Relax and have fun". They even put it on coffee cups.

That's what we did, we followed that advice and got the results we wanted. When at other times we were consumed by fear, we were torn by worries, we were liquidated by our moments, by anguish, we could never see success, much less know the peace that comes from sweet victory in business.

Therefore, my advice based on experience is not to rush the times, it is good from time to time not to worry about tomorrow or wait anxiously for it, to stop demanding the reasons why this or that, but simply to let time and energies flow according to our thoughts and be proportionally equivalent to the peace we manifest within ourselves.

We must learn to relax and have fun with what we do, to have a moment of reflection with ourselves, meditation is the key; and those who would like to go a little further, to pray to whomever we please according to our beliefs. God always listens, but he has his times.

Contemplating life and not having life contemplate us, experiencing patience so as not to get frustrated, is an important key in this game, letting life amaze us, admire us, shock us with its days.

Everyone is responsible for their actions and we must face them with courage at every step. Let us not be taken by surprise, let us lean on the antonym of confusion, let us place ourselves at the base of the mountain that we must move. This base, which is the faith that we carry within us, is that force that must drive our thoughts imbued with feelings of passion so that they contain all the energy necessary to be able to move circumstances towards what we desire with love.

That faith that sweeps away fear is that powerful and determining force we need to realize ourselves. The most important person in your life is you, and that is how you must face the situations that come up every day like a summer storm.

Abandoning the past is an unavoidable condition, whenever you invoke it as a negative mantra, it will return, so you must bury it to rise from the ashes. What is the use of focusing on something that no longer exists, that has vanished into the harvests of time? That they were scattered on the road, and already trampled on those moments, realize that they returned to the earth and fertilized your effort and suffering to bring you to where you are today.

Every moment, every minute and hour were the creative impulse to bring us to the realization of the projects, as long as we do not let ourselves be overcome by the stings of fear.

Bravery and courage are what life demands to propel us forward. Faith alone is not enough; everything is a shake of life and joy where the right ingredients must be mixed in the right measure to achieve the permanent taste of success. Your opportunities present themselves here and now, never in the past.

This is the moment, as you read these letters. Give yourself a chance to change things and define your future, what you want to do, is here and now.

Let's ask ourselves this question: what work would he do for free, even if no one paid him a penny? Well, there you have your future, the moment you an swer this question.

That which we love, which will lead us to success. That which he desires so much that he would do it for free: there is his victory.

The same thing that people close to you told you that you could not do, because it was not for you, and that you better follow a standard career or become employed in some job that would give you stability, the same stability that many sought throughout their lives and, unfortunately, retire from those monotonous stable jobs that we always detest doing to end up with a miserable retirement that does not even cover the remedies for any condition.

I was listening to the other afternoon on the radio to a young man who said that to pay for his studies, he worked in a taxi for years. He finished university and then went on to do a master's degree, but after that, he was still driving the taxi because of the lack of opportunities. Unfortunately, in the houses of study, they do not teach us how to earn money once we graduate and how to materialize our knowledge for the realization of our dreams so that we can realize ourselves as people and professionals earning money in abundance.

We must never embark on a path, a profession that we do not love only because of what our friends, our families, our partners expect.

This pressure creates a fear of disappointing others and not meeting their expectations by ignoring our own.

The engine of your life is you and only you define your wellbeing. Therefore, do not be paralyzed, let it flow, bless your reality, giving thanks is essential, even if it is the least bit, because you will receive in compensation more than what you are grateful for and, at some point, you will become a snowball of good things that will happen.

Everything implies teaching, do not despise those moments, always be grateful for the teaching and start again; everything evolves and transforms according to your thoughts and where they are directed. It is like Aladdin's lamp, rub your head and thoughts will arise, and they will trace their path and become reality.

If they are positive, they will quickly manifest, and fortunately, if they are negative, it will take many of them for something bad to happen.

Nothing happens by chance, luck does not exist, it is all part of what generates its interior. Never back down, never give up, no matter how many times you fail, the important thing is to have the courage to start again if necessary. In my case, I failed several times and counted fifteen times in my life since I was eighteen years old, that is, fifteen dreams, fifteen frustrated hopes, fifteen buried life projects, fifteen momentary passions, and from the fifteen I got up and reached victory. Everything is a path that we must travel until we reach our goal and then start a different path to keep our dreams high. We will always be motivated to continue reaching higher financial goals and then, at a certain moment, we will realize that we must reach our spiritual goals, which entail other higher states of consciousness. Many people only stay in the first economic stage and never know the benefits of the next stage and become only consumer beings.

If with the first or second failure I had become depressed in my youth, giving in to vices to drown my sorrows, I would surely not be writing this book, nor would I have wonderful little children, even growing up, I would not even have the love of my life by my side or the economic stability that I enjoy today.

On this path, there will always be bad investments, bad decisions, impulses that make us make mistakes. We must return again and again until we define that which we love with passion and which will stabilize it for the rest of its life. Thus, we find thousands of examples in history of willpower being put before fears and failures.

If one seeks different results, one should not repeat the same life ritual, we should always seek alternative paths to reach different consequences. Let us keep in mind that emotions are only strangers that stay for a moment, pass by, and leave. The positive ones propel us to the sky, the negative ones sink us into hell.

Happiness is the daily attitude that we should seek with just a smile in front of the mirror watching a funny movie, reading a book that inspires us, having a pleasant chat among friends, hugging a child or our partner with love, taking a morning walk and watching the sunset. There are different moments that we can look for to find those that we should capture in our hearts, those moments that lead us to the happiness that will positively drive our actions.

We must infect our spirit with these balsams that inspire us and seek them out at every moment of the day, the rest will follow.

At these times let us not think about tomorrow or yesterday, they are two days that do not count. Only today is important and what we do today will be what we harvest tomorrow.

Each day is sowing; either we snowstorms or we sow the calm that will give us the peace of soul and spirit to assume the attitude we need to face the circumstances that are presented to us.

Let us never compare our lives with those of others, for they have nothing in common. From the moment we are born, we are all different, and that is why judging delays, and nobody knows how the paths of others have been in the past to judge them in the present.

I know that fear consumes and delays travel. Once we let go of those fears, those people will appear who throbs at our very frequency and enthusiasm. They are waiting in that dial tune, in which we have to position ourselves to find that dream partner, those coworkers or partners who drive our dreams together.

As a contemporary Church saint of the TWENTIETH century, Father Pio di Pietrelcina, said: "You must have unlimited faith in the divine goodness because victory is certain. Victory is always certain if we seek it with zeal and excessive passion, as when we fall in love and feel that we cannot live without that person.

The fear of loneliness is one of the great fears we face, which has no foundation, because it is a wonderful opportunity to start to know yourself and, from there, from that point of self-knowledge, project yourself to find those who are worth having at your side and who deserve to share their experiences and their life vibrating in the same energy.

The fear of poverty, of lack, of misery, is very close to those moments where we must start again, at that moment when everything becomes cloudy and we think we are touching the bottom.

We should only be grateful for every moment and opportunity that presents itself to add more than what one is grateful for and multiply the positive energies around us, even in the face of any negative circumstances that may arise, giving way only to positive experiences.

Another great fear that afflicts us is the fear of falling ill. I have in mind a great bestselling book by Louise Hay, You Can Heal Your Life, where she recounts the consequences in the body of negative thoughts and resentment for not letting go of the past, which manifest themselves in wounds in the subconscious that are transformed into illnesses.

Another important fear is that of death, the same fear that has accompanied us since we were born; we are like a river that flows into the wide sea and must be overcome as a form of a cycle that ends and then is reborn. We must face it with the real hope of starting another cycle that is defined as eternal and that so many prophets, philosophers, and scientists have demonstrated the existence of that life that is beyond this one.

What we treasure in this life is what we will take with us; therefore, the import ant thing is to cultivate in us the best, and I sum it up in doing good no matter who or what we expect in return. It is that which will serve us to transcend and here, on this earth, to access those keys and ciphers that open the doors that the universe keeps secret and that pour out on us its laws of abundance that we deserve and that, at birth, were promised to us.

Taking the time to heal the wounds of the past is fundamental; the minutes of the day are like small dewdrops that our existence must take to heal those wounds inside.

Time consumes our passions of other moments, it rinses our tears, it is a fire that burns our sorrows and makes them ashes so that the gale takes them be yond the ocean and sinks them into the icy waters of the past.

Only there must they remain forever, without the possibility of a return, so that we can

project our existence towards the life we set out to live.

Some of the phrases that inspired me in my childhood and, in particular, was a book, that of The Little Prince, of which I share with you some to reflect on and finish this chapter that seemed to me to be appropriate as a corollary of the same.

It's crazy to hate all the roses just because one pricked you. To give up all your dreams just because one didn't come true. The beautiful thing about the desert is that anywhere there's a well hidden.

You should have judged her by her actions and not by her words.

Sometimes, we have to put up with caterpillars if we want to enjoy butterflies.

Here is my secret, which could not be simpler: only with the heart can one see well, the essential is invisible to the eyes.

Walking in a straight line you can't get very far.

It is much more difficult to judge oneself than others. If you manage to judge yourself correctly, it will mean that you are a true sage.

Chapter 9: The Cycles of Success

"Thinking is the hardest job there is, maybe that's why there are so few people who practice it."

HENRY FORD

Confucius, with his immense wisdom, said that "a journey of a thousand steps begins with a single step". It is the same as the goals one pursues. There will always be a certain uncertainty as to the objectives one pursues when one begins a journey.

By defining the objective very precisely, we will be able to visualize its realization and thus outline the written strategy, carrying out the realization of its goal. To do this, we must break down the main one into small objectives to take one step at a time. This is essential for success.

A happy person is not one who owns millions of dollars or the most beautiful things. A person is happy because he knows that all the riches, all the things, and the material events are only the reflections of his inner being.

It's what I call "the mirror". The people we meet in life are, in fact, like mirrors that reflect what we truly are. We attract what we are subconsciously. That is why it is important to work on our inner self with motivational phrases or mantras emphasizing what we want for our life, and it is important to cultivate our thoughts. It is of utmost importance that we do not judge others, because when one considers that such a person dislikes him because he acts in one way or another, he does nothing but judges himself. Because others reflect, in fact, what we are. To focus on not judging things or people because it is harmful to the mind and for thoughts to be directed towards the positive.

To receive what one expects from others, it is very useful to take the first step and it give before expecting to receive it in return. We must try to go towards others, we must try to communicate, be interested in their lives, and be generous; this inevitably attracts wealth.

To start taking the first step, you must ask yourself the first question: what would be the ideal day in your life? Perhaps, deep down, you are not able to find the exact answer. Perhaps you feel like a bee going from flower to flower not knowing which one to choose. Life is first and foremost a matter of choice. Therefore, you must choose and have a concrete idea of what an ideal day, an ideal life, would be like. Until you have defined your ideal, your objective precisely, your subconscious cannot work towards its realization.

Take some time to reflect on all this. Visualize your ideal life from your ideal day. Maybe we live in a comfort zone and, as the word suggests, we are very comfortable there. But that zone leads us to be off, it's the zone of denial, it's living in denial, it's being in the shadows, blind but comfortable, alive, breathing but in the cemetery ahead of time. We change our time that will no longer return for the coins that a miserable minimum wage gives us in a common job where we cannot develop our potentials as in sales and achieve goals and profits always dreamed of but not achieved.

Time is worth gold and lost time is irretrievable; therefore, let us take care of it as the most precious gold because, if we do not, when we look back at the age that awakens our critical consciousness and we have to self-evaluate our life until that moment, we may regret having parasitized in that comfort zone that we imposed on ourselves and meditate on how much we did not do.

Examples are the anecdotes we cannot tell our children because we will never live them, the many trips we will not be able to take, the unique experiences we will never enjoy, the exotic restaurants we will not taste, the fashion we could not wear, the shows we will not enjoy, the Disney we did not know, The Rome or Paris that we did not visit, the New York or Hong Kong that we did not visit, will be the Swiss or Patagonian lakes that did not excite our pupils, will be the best matches of our favorite sport that we could not manage to see or that World Cup that we always promised ourselves and that we never managed to reach. Could it be the love of our life who left because he couldn't stand our comfort zone anymore, because we couldn't afford to go to a movie or a dinner we couldn't afford? Could it be that sunset on a Caribbean beach or on the steep shores of Amalfi or Capri that we will never get to enjoy?

That will be everyone we will refuse because we do not change our residence and are always located in our comfort zone.

Where you are born, how much money you have, or the titles you hold do not determine your success. It is only determined by the higher power, which is driven by that fervent desire to succeed. Discovering that which attracts us so much as to set out on the path is what will arouse passion, will ignite joy, will be doing what one likes, and not by a commitment to anything or anyone.

The protagonist is, without a doubt, his dream. He who we intuit, think, meditate, he who is born of the heart. The same one that arises from thinking about what people need, to relate his dream to the needs of the market without ceasing to be faithful to himself, not to the world or to what they will say. Not postponing even one of your dreams is the basis and taking the first step means "today".

"Everything that happens is convenient," says an old phrase from Zen Buddhism, so we should not give way to anguish in the face of the stumbling blocks we are exposed to every day. Knowing how to change course, knowing how to let go of what does not compliment us, whether it be a job or a relationship, is key to moving forward.

Great fortunes were made in sales. Unfortunately, few are those who know the secrets of sales. And when I say sales, I don't mean going out with a folder under your arm and knocking on doors, but rather creating a network or sales organization to get richer faster.

Most people sell their time for money, that's what I call employees who don't want to go beyond their comfort zone. Other people do know what sales all are about or have a sense of it and know that the profits are determined by you and there are no limits on that.

Your skills and motivation are worth and priced very high, much more than a professional degree. Companies today are looking for skills, intelligence to solve situations, and a lot of motivation. Companies do not look for problems when hiring someone, but only for solutions. We must always sell profits, selling is the key to wealth. Most of the rich started as salespeople or organizing a sales structure or marketing network.

We in Mexico set up a sales organization in one month for a cell phone company. With only one office and twenty salesmen the first month, we got four hundred and four eighteen month postpaid plans, while the second month was eight hundred and eight, and the third month, 1296 new clients, billing in commissions half a million dollars. That was just in the first three months. Yes, you can! It's a possible mission, it's just to propose it, to have the dream to earn that money, and put the plan on the table.

To generate wealth, we must create processes and marketing networks that sell as if it were an industrial production chain where the processes are so oiled that with just a few hours of daily monitoring and coaching everything fits naturally within a context of motivation and professionalism that explodes into productions beyond our imagination, following a plan of action. This process should allow us to sell constantly without stopping the machines.

If we meditate, if we relax, if we look for joy, a state of happiness as prima facie of everything or starting point, the solutions will quickly arrive. Thinking, feeling, and then acting, is also worth that of "cogito, ergo sum", 'I think, therefore I am', by the philosopher René Descartes.

For success, we must prepare our minds, train them. We work better without stress; therefore, we must get rid of everything that produces it, characters, situations, debts, memories, and bad thoughts.

Chapter 10: What to do when you have your dream in hand

"Fear is suffering that produces the expectation of evil."

ARISTOTELES

Concentrating mentally, having the final vision is what activates the energy of the universe, and everything begins to flow, money appears, people appear, and even the right employees. The bigger the dream, the more interesting the path becomes, and the more money are made. By activating the joy in ourselves, goals are achieved. The goals are daily, one by one, we must map them out day by day.

Our joy is proportional to our positive results, the victories, and triumphs that we obtain. Even weight gain comes from stress beyond our diet. Practice joy and you will see those extra pounds go away.

The results in sales must be daily by default. How many doors or calls a salesman makes and conversations he conducts will be proportional to the result of hot sales. We must never cool down sales, nor our dreams, nor put them in a freezer because of any ad verse circumstances that may arise. Progress is the watchword.

Let's explore only the daily joy with simple things, listening to your favorite music, reading a book, watching a movie at the cinema, preparing a special dinner for your friends, planning a short vacation, just stop and contemplate a landscape, meditate, pray if you think it is necessary.

The slogan for sales and distribution partners of the world's largest electronic security company was: "Relax and have fun", and I would add today: "Get excited and feel light".

The doubts that fears generate begin with the lack of energy, and this begins when we stand still. The key is in moving; let's do what we like, let's do an activity, let's visit friends, doubts paralyze and delay our dreams.

The opposite of our joys are our negativities and excuses; never listening to people who tell us that we cannot or who tell us that they are just silly, unrealistic dreams, that is, what we know as toxic relationships.

It is too easy to question others about our suffering; wouldn't it be better if we each questioned ourselves and saw how much guilt we have in our failures? How many excuses do I make every day for not seeing the light of truth? How many excuses do I make each day for not seeing the light of truth? How many excuses do I make each day for not seeing the light of truth?

To say "I'm no good, I'm no good, I can't, I'm not capable" is to say "no" always, without risking too much, without going out of the comfort zone, is to remain closed in one's own weakness without counting on the power of the inner strength that we all possess and that is stronger than one's own weakness.

It's just taking action, even if we're scared. The bravest men in history have always had some fear that can only be overcome by the decision to take action. Problems are not solved by blaming others, but by each of us taking responsibility and assuming it.

The opposite of our dreams are the fears of failure that boycott us, fears of losing that security that comes from a minimum wage from a tedious job or trying to convince us that everything in the country we live in is already done and there are no more opportunities.

Lack of self-confidence oppresses us and from this comes anguish. What we must eliminate are the complaints, the blaming of oneself for a past that will not come back, the resentment, the constant moaning, the excuses for not do ing, the anger and the rage towards our closest environment; blaming others for what happens to us is devastating, trying to convince ourselves that we are a victim of the circumstances and not assuming our mistakes.

The next step is to mentalize the subconscious, to make belief, culture of your dream, to plant it there so that it blooms, reprogramming it, because it will be the only way to be able to be reborn from the inside.

If doubts appear, cut them out as I explained, seeking at that very moment the joy in that which pleases you; advancing one step on the ladder to the top every day, however small, is a fundamental part of the journey.

A daily schedule with small goals to meet should be made; crossing them out as you get them is a very good exercise. I, in my particular case, used liquid paper for this. Today I manage the agenda on my cell phone and I erase those small or big objectives achieved and I prioritize them, it is very hygienic mentally to adopt these gymnastics for the brain and inner peace that will lead to a significant satisfaction at the end of the day by the daily objectives achieved.

Let's make a slate of our dreams and their scope. Let's write and paste on it pictures of our future car, our future house that we wish for, our children, our future trips, the life and wishes that we definitely want to obtain.

This will help us to visualize more easily. We must visualize the whole process and the specific result, we must acquire that conviction that it is already real in our life, we must feel it with our five senses, smell it, touch it, look at it and imagine it.

From spirituality, or rather from within our spirit, thoughts emerge at some point as a spark of inspiration, as a hunch; from there we must reach the new attitude before this revelation and thus reach the stage of enthusiasm and achieve living within your dream and by your dream.

To do this we must develop the courage to escape from the comfort zone. In my case, this has always happened to me; when I realize that I am entering that comfort zone and I feel that I am getting bored, I start again. Maybe I'm a compulsive entrepreneur, I guess.

Life is movement, life is achieving goals, life is first conquering inner spirituality and then going for money in abundance. Money is a manifestation of the wealth that resides in each of us. With conviction and action, fear disappears. Getting started, making a commitment to advance daily is the condition. Taking action by following our intuition is the key.

When we're overcome by an intense hunch, we get a message. I have several examples in my life. The first one that comes to my memory is the one my wife had, she was always of having many hunches, it is a gift, it is a coincidence, I do not know, I just know that it is like receiving messages from her angel to decipher.

Once, when everything seemed to be falling apart in our environment, in our company, since a new director had arrived in Mexico in 2006 with the slogan of halving the distributors' commissions, she, my partner, in a crossroads between offices, in our four storey headquarters that we had in the pink zone of that city, told an administrative employee to communicate her with a cell phone company that was beating in her heart to request a distributor. I told her not to waste her time, they would never take a company that had just sold alarms that was my paradigm. She insisted, I did not object, in fact, I think I sketched a smile laughing at the fact with sarcasm.

She got the meeting, soon we were signing the distribution and, after three months, we were the first in sales in the whole country, invoicing two hundred thousand dollars a month. Unbelievable, but real.

If the plan doesn't work, we must change our plan or strategy, but never our dream.

The path of the dreamer is lonely and silent, his dream must be a secret until he reaches it, knowing that people have power in the mind, envy exists, bad vibrations too. And they are like radio waves which disturb your good magnetic field which vibrates in positive.

50

Obstacles will always exist; they shape us for success, they will forge us like the metal in the forge or like the gold that must pass through the fire to get its shine. In the face of obstacles, we can only rely on perseverance, faith, patience, and vision.

We stumbled once, twice, and even three times over the same tests until we learned the lessons that straightened out our path. Many also give up before the last effort. Visualization is the "language" of the mind, the way to communicate with the subconscious and influence it for success.

The importance of valuing each moment of the present is fundamental. Acting in the present with enthusiasm is when you can go faster to success and personal fulfilment. Success means radically changing the way you perceive the different things in life.

To wish with the passion to overcome all doubt. Dreams must have direction, that is, a guide to go through, a process in which to focus all our goals and a purpose, that is, to tell the subconscious what it is for.

Our environment shapes us from childhood onwards, and from there emerge the beliefs that determine us and, from them, the fears that dominate us. The family programs us for good or sometimes for evil in the sense of prosperity, and when we try to break the meld, we become the black sheep of the family. To succeed means to move away from the established, to find the passion, and to throw oneself into the void.

Did you know that Meryl Streep won eighteen Oscars after being rejected at the King Kong film audition because she was ugly, she was told, of which I disagree? That drove her to infinity. Imagine if Meryl had been blocked and distressed, whose eighteen Oscar statuettes would be so coveted?

Psychological blocks are a kind of lock, a lock, which precisely blocks our inner energies and prevents hidden potentials from coming to light. Many times, negative subconscious energies accumulate during childhood, adolescence, and adulthood.

We have to know that victory is a mechanism that is based on failure and success, alternatively. Making mistakes is how we learn and how we can correct the course we are on. This is not a vision of the spirit or the mind, but a strictly scientific and metaphysical reality; thanks to the errors, we progress and evolve.

Life must be understood as a kind of play in which we play a role, the main one.

According to the Hindu philosophical principle, material life is nothing but a conscious dream. For this, mental visualization is fundamental.

Visualize the person you would like to be, the life you would like to have, the things you would like to possess. Victory and money are nothing more than outward manifestations of your inner self.

Imagination means creating images or, in other words, imagination is nothing more than mental visualization. There is your rational spirit that dictates in some way that you cannot do this or that. Instead, by the power of imagination, you can get anything you want. That is why it is necessary for you to visualize the realization of what you want to achieve.

The law of attraction is a phenomenon whose existence is well established. Buddha was one of the first to speak of the law of attraction. He said: "What you have become is what you have thought. And in the Bible, it is expressed in these terms: "You shall reap what you have sown. Gandhi defined it as: "Keep your thoughts positive because they become your words. Keep your words positive because they become your behaviours. Keep your behaviours positive because they become your habits. Keep your habits positive because they become your destiny. And Voltaire, the French philosopher, summed up the law of attraction in these words: "I have decided to be happy because it is good for my health.

Worrying means 'taking care of yourself in advance'. However, there is no point in worrying in advance, because the only freedom of action you have to influence your future is to act in the present. Acting is the antidote to this poison; in the face of the worry that debases the soul, we must take the necessary measures in the sense of solving the problem; to worry is to increase the negative emotional charge.

The watchword is to care, not to worry. The quote from the French poet Boileau, "undertake your work twenty times over, polish it without ceasing, and polish it again," means that only in the things you work tirelessly do you achieve personal fulfilment.

Chapter 11: The Circuit of Success

"We don't like the sound they have, and besides, guitar music is out of **fashion.**"

DECA executive who rejected The Beatles in 1962

The diagram below is the flow of how one meets success or how, failing that, one gets lost along the way. It is a circuit that we must go through loaded with positive energy that starts from the choice of the place where we are going to develop our company, be it a country, a city, a neighbourhood, where each one has a certain energy and frequency implicit.

To do this, before we start, we must eliminate worries, remove the harmful thinking that causes us to think about debts, doubts, and fears. Then we will be ready to begin the circuit that leads us to crown ourselves with the laurels of final victory. It won't matter where we were born or whether our parents had money or not, nor will it matter if we are professionals or study a short career or none at all; they are all factors that are not sine qua non for achieving this. We must be aware that it will be a lonely and silent path so as not to arouse the envy of those around us. Dreams are always dreamt in secret.

We must feel passion for what we will undertake because this ignites the spark of joy in seeking that which attracts us where dreams are intuited; it is an intense hunch straight to our mind from the centre of our heart.

At that time, we must not put it off, but think about it and meditate. Knowing that we are on the right path when we would even do it for free simply because of the passion that comes from being in touch with that work that we would start from that light that lights up in our mind as the first phase of inspiration. To do this, we can make a list of our preferences to have a point of support to develop our business idea and passion. To do this, we must stop and meditate, listen to music, and breathe a breath of fresh air.

Meditate on what the market needs, search for a niche in it. In this whole process, we must know that it is a happy adventure. The bigger the dream, the more interesting it will be to achieve it. To feel it with the five senses becomes a condition, to define it with precise and specific words becomes inevitable to give it life from the ink.

What comes immediately afterward is the visualization of the dream come true, because it will activate the energy of the universe and the laws that govern it. It is also a trigger of joy, which we must feed with simple things. The work must imply as an indispensable partner to happiness, the complaints drive away from the good that is directed to our life, we must feel light of all weight that overwhelms us, and this is achieved by reprogramming our mind with daily positive mantra exercises, sowing with them the subconscious with the seeds of their dreams.

We will have to foster a culture of our success by living in it as if it were already a concrete reality because in truth it already is; if it is a culture and is firm in its mind, it is an absolute truth in this dimension. We know that from the spirit is born the thought and then comes the word to our lips, and from it arise the positive and negative affirmations the complaints. Affirmations create our experiences here and now and from them come the beliefs that create our lives for good or bad.

Our thoughts arouse passions, for they carry with them the power of feeling. Therefore, the most powerful slogan is the big bang of our mind, precisely to change the state of mind to positive, because at that moment the frequency of vibration changes and generates the enthusiasm that we need as gasoline to mobilize our destiny.

From emotion is born joy and from those positive thoughts are generated the positive words that unfailingly attract actions in that same sense and generate passion.

Getting started attracts courage, generates commitment and conviction that eliminates fears. The frequency of vibration magnetizes and attracts everything that vibrates in the same tune as us; therefore, by magnetizing our subconscious we magnetize our future and everything happens only in an instant, just as in an instant we are born or die, we fall in love or make decisions, also in instant positive changes happen. When that explosion of positive ideas and thoughts generated by our change of poles in the circuit of our mind appears in our mind, the change of vibration in our being is produced. In conclusion, success starts with the joy of the spirit.

Chapter 12: The Short Circuit of Success

"Let us look more to the fact that we are the parents of our future than the children of our past."

MIGUEL DE UNAMUNO

The environment shapes us like the wind and the sea sculpt the stones over time. It is there that fears, and beliefs arise. It is a heavy flow where the circuit that leads us to success is broken. One of the fundamental factors from which we start is the lack of positive attitude that triggers this short circuit with success, and this lack of positive attitude appears because of the lack of love for ourselves and our environment.

Love is an antonym for hate, envy, boredom, disappointment, frustration, criticism, guilt, thoughts of revenge. That's the explosive cocktail of our short for success. Reacting to circumstances negatively generates worry, regrets, negative frequencies and vibrations and, at the same time, is a factor that degenerates into a spiritual illness that comes from strong negative emotions that we experience in the circuit of life, promoting stress and fears.

Despair generates more negativity, and we see this when we think negatively about money or success; we will see that these do not come into our lives and we begin to experience shortages. If there is a lack of money it is because there is more negativity in thoughts than positive feelings and it becomes the lack of passion for what is being done. It is there where the ghosts of worries appear, and I say ghosts because that is all they are most of the time, we live worrying about things that will never happen.

The solution is to change the direction of what is being done because if not, those ghosts paralyze us; by being afraid of failure, we boycott ourselves. On many occasions, we are even afraid of ending up in toxic relationships without realizing that they are just fictitious stabilities that we create for ourselves as true.

We are afraid of losing our jobs, our health, our savings, our security, and even our freedom. It is a swarm of fears from which doubts and excuses appear, such as: "Everything has already been invented", "there is nothing else to innovate", "I am too old for this or that", and a long list.

From this swarm are born the lack of self-confidence, the complaints, the faults, the resentments, and the lamentations. We must let go of that which does not add to us, that which does not bring anything positive into our lives, that which leaves us without energy.

Feelings such as envy, jealousy, or resentment are things that hold us back in life on an economic level strongly. A sales coordinator in Panama once told me a phrase that I made my own time later, as I could see when I focused on discovering that clumsiness in some people. He told me: "When a person is envious, everything in life fails him, he does badly in love or business, in work or relationships with people. All his plans inevitably fall apart because he does not vibrate precisely in the frequency of love.

To cut this short circuit that we may experience at some point in our lives, we must walk step by step and advance one step at a time, conquer a daily goal, even if it seems small.

Never talk about the problems because one is anchored in them, take care of them and write them down one by one and solve them and cross them out in the agenda of our lives; we should not think about what we do not want.

Suffering and lamenting bring only negativity that we must fight at that moment with good music or outings to walking, to the cinema or just walking in a park. We must always take care of the internal dialogue, what we say to ourselves, prohibiting us from talking about debts, doubts, complaints, etc. In short, walking lightly provides openness of mind and creates new places where we can shelter our best thoughts and the development of projects.

In today's society we are used to transmitting more messages and negative news as if they filled our hearts for a moment to hear them and then to address more negative issues than positive ones; it is like a spiral from which we cannot get out. Let us know that the obstacles that are presented to us form us, sculpt us for the future like fire melds gold. Negative feelings always multiply and must be stopped with faith, patience, and constancy in projects.

Let's be specific about what we want to achieve, write it down and define it, describe it with words, awareness takes away the power of negative feeling; therefore, let's imagine the pleasure of mastering thoughts and emotions, thinking about good times, performing an action that completes us spiritually every day.

The circuit of success

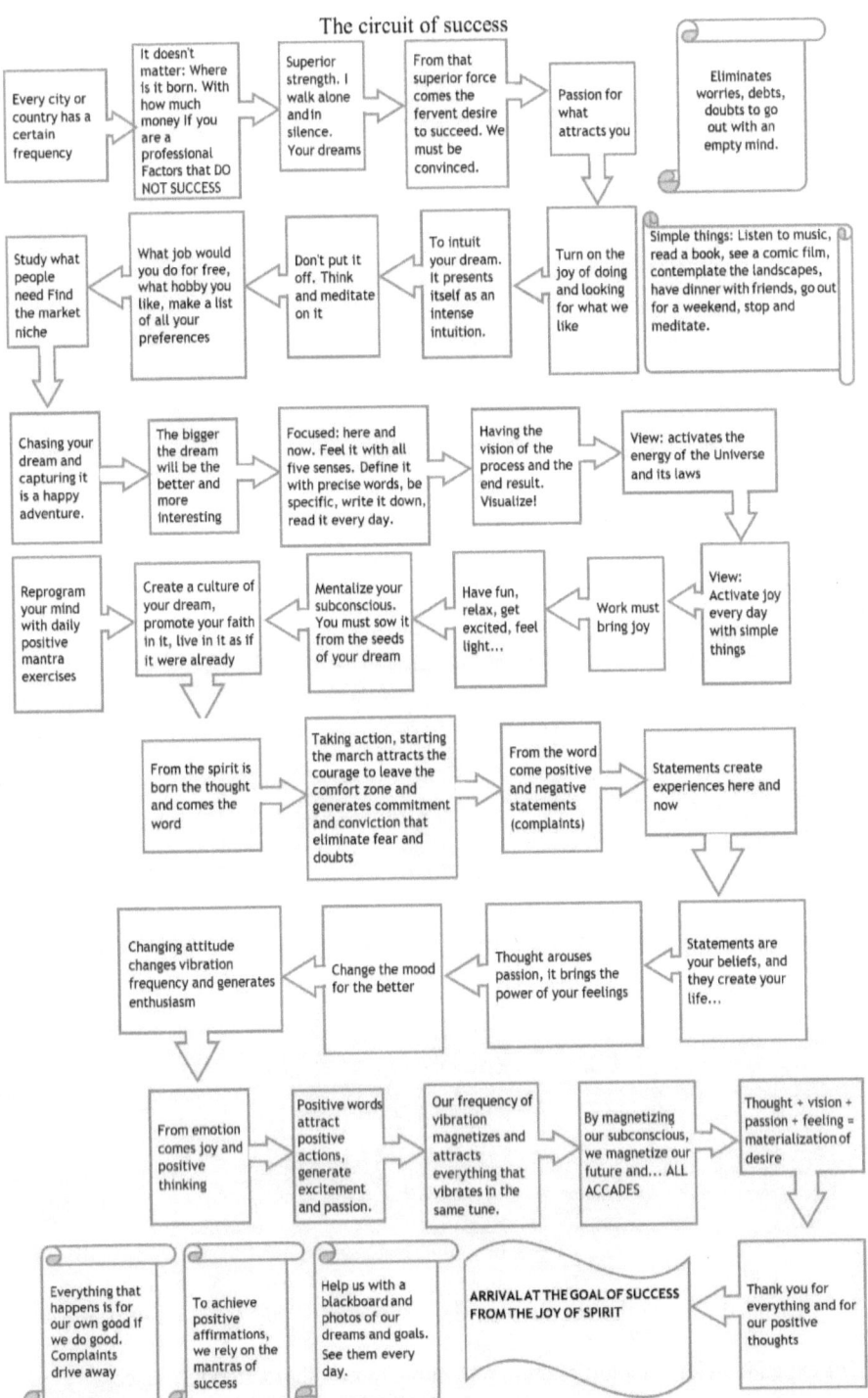

Every city or country has a certain frequency

It doesn't matter: Where is it born. With how much money If you are a professional Factors that DO NOT SUCCESS

Superior strength. I walk alone and in silence. Your dreams

From that superior force comes the fervent desire to succeed. We must be convinced.

Passion for what attracts you

Eliminates worries, debts, doubts to go out with an empty mind.

Study what people need Find the market niche

What job would you do for free, what hobby you like, make a list of all your preferences

Don't put it off. Think and meditate on it

To intuit your dream. It presents itself as an intense intuition.

Turn on the joy of doing and looking for what we like

Simple things: Listen to music, read a book, see a comic film, contemplate the landscapes, have dinner with friends, go out for a weekend, stop and meditate.

Chasing your dream and capturing it is a happy adventure.

The bigger the dream will be the better and more interesting

Focused: here and now. Feel it with all five senses. Define it with precise words, be specific, write it down, read it every day.

Having the vision of the process and the end result. Visualize!

View: activates the energy of the Universe and its laws

Reprogram your mind with daily positive mantra exercises

Create a culture of your dream, promote your faith in it, live in it as if it were already

Mentalize your subconscious. You must sow it from the seeds of your dream

Have fun, relax, get excited, feel light...

Work must bring joy

View: Activate joy every day with simple things

From the spirit is born the thought and comes the word

Taking action, starting the march attracts the courage to leave the comfort zone and generates commitment and conviction that eliminate fear and doubts

From the word come positive and negative statements (complaints)

Statements create experiences here and now

Changing attitude changes vibration frequency and generates enthusiasm

Change the mood for the better

Thought arouses passion, it brings the power of your feelings

Statements are your beliefs, and they create your life...

From emotion comes joy and positive thinking

Positive words attract positive actions, generate excitement and passion.

Our frequency of vibration magnetizes and attracts everything that vibrates in the same tune.

By magnetizing our subconscious, we magnetize our future and... ALL ACCADES

Thought + vision + passion + feeling = materialization of desire

Everything that happens is for our own good if we do good. Complaints drive away

To achieve positive affirmations, we rely on the mantras of success

Help us with a blackboard and photos of our dreams and goals. See them every day.

ARRIVAL AT THE GOAL OF SUCCESS FROM THE JOY OF SPIRIT

Thank you for everything and for our positive thoughts

SHORT CIRCUIT SUCCESS

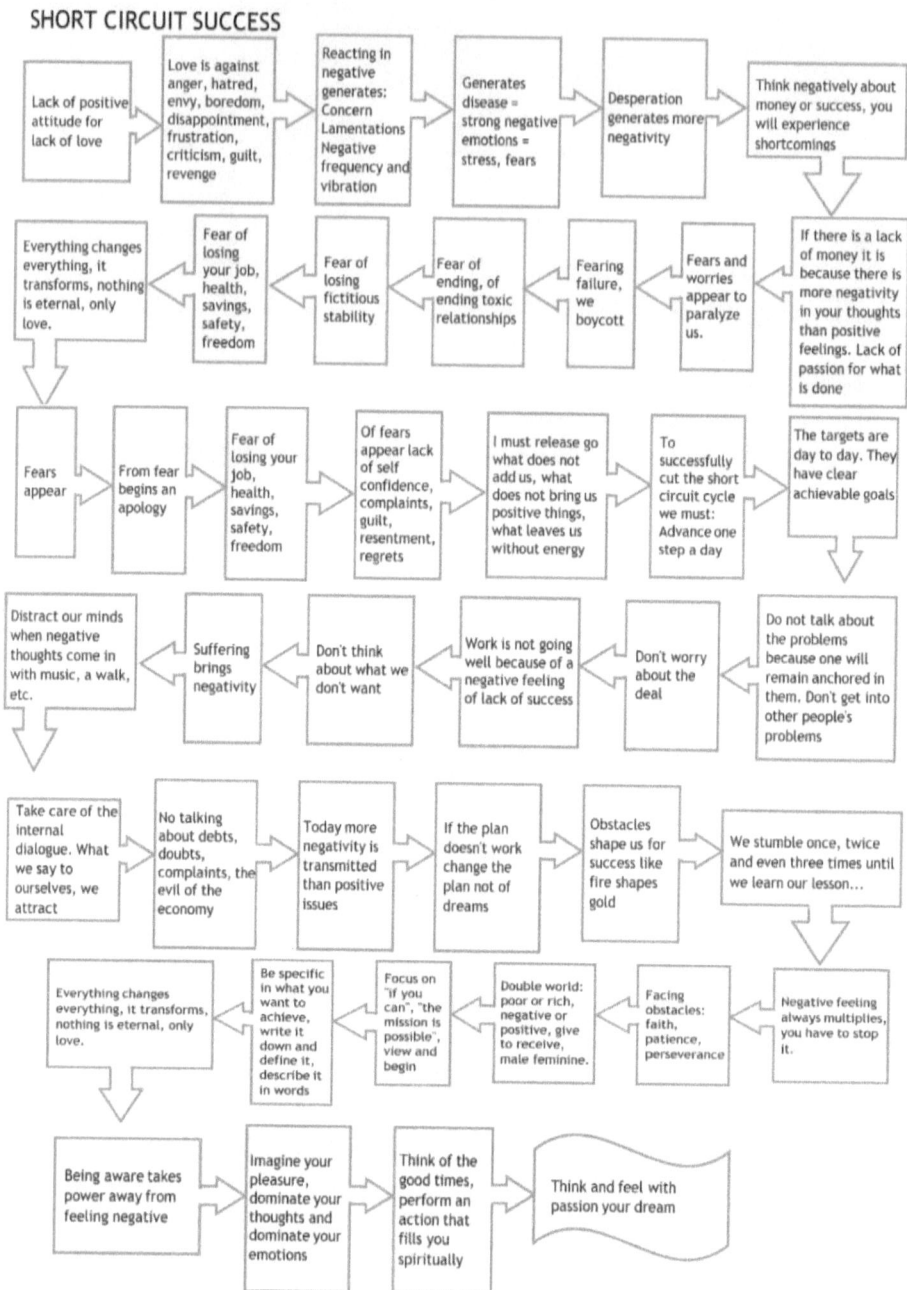

For expanded view of the circuit of success go to https://bit.ly/CircuitOfSuccess

For expanded view of short circuit go to https://bit.ly/ShortCircuitOfSuccess

Part II

Our experience around the world

Chapter 1: Beyond Borders

"I'm always cheerful, that's the way to solve life's problems."

CHARLES CHAPLIN

We knew more than thirty five countries in fifteen years and did business consulting for multinationals in eight countries in Latin America and Europe. In them, we confirmed our theory that it is possible to do business where one projects, or rather, where one feels comfortable with the local people, the cities, the currency, and the governments that drive those economies.

The latter is very important to note. Imagine doing business today in countries dominated by social and economic chaos or in places where there have been recent natural disasters, and it would not be possible to develop our company in those kinds of places where foreign investment is pursued.

The economic costs of our project are the following: the cost of living of a car, the rent of a hundred meters at a price that does not exceed seven hundred dollars or euros, that the purchase in the supermarket does not exceed one hundred and fifty dollars or euros with a full cart, where a trip to a restaurant is not once a year, but every weekend, where gasoline is at a good price and a tank is filled with fifty dollars or euros, where consumption taxes do not exceed twenty points and income is maintained at normal percentages and not un reasonable for growth, where the labour part is flexible and the basic salaries are low to be able to pay the appropriate social security and thus leave us space to pay important prizes to the production and not big sums to sustain unproductive employees, where the initial tax burdens allow us to begin to undertake with little capital and it is easy to register a company in a local chamber of commerce, among many other issues that we should take into account at the time of choosing our life project.

I explain that our average employees in terms of prizes earned more than a thousand dollars and their coordinators earned around four thousand dollars a month, while the base salary we paid did not exceed three hundred dollars, and thus the payment of social security became affordable, but all of them were productive, generated wealth for the company and, therefore, in the mirror provided them with lives never imagined when in their countries the income of 90% of the population did not exceed those three hundred dollars.

Where credit abounds, foreign investment, and a large expanding market with cities of more than two million inhabitants are potential for our development.

Our business was focused on the sale and distribution of products or services for large international companies. If we feel that the industry, we are in does not inspire us, we should not continue, or even begin; we should be truly passionate about what we are doing. Passion moves the world. Without it, everything is mediocrity and nothing we do will make sense.

Our concepts can be applied in all areas, but our experience advises us to look for the attractiveness to our essence in the country or city that more beats us in the heart, with products that entail a massive consumption and satisfy the needs of the market.

In our business trajectory, we have entered as official agents of major brands, also in the assembly of events and exhibitions, advertising campaigns, gastronomy with four restaurants, marketing, youth tourism, communications, electronic security, training, and sales coaching. All of them were faced with a minimum investment, a lot of dedication and passion to achieve the desired results.

We discover in each one of them that, as long as we act with the same passion we have used since day one, every fledgling business tends to grow exponentially at some point if it is well developed, organized and thought through.

Business organization and planning have always been my forte, the organization, training, and motivation of sales, an issue that I am passionate about and where passion cannot be allowed to wane because of the unbridled pace that our method of working involves. In my favour, I always had the unconditional support of my wife, who was my partner in each project and ended up being the alma mater of them and who, with great expertise, gave the strength that sometimes the team lacked to continue in the worst moments of their existence.

We must transmit to our team strength, organization, energy, and concrete objectives. We must apply hardness when it is appropriate, added to the good leadership of the leaders who accompany us, which will be of fundamental importance, since they are the ones who will transmit our idea to the rest of the structure, which will make it materialize in concrete results during the whole working day.

We saw across the different countries and cities that all people had the same training, motivation, and driving needs lacked clear production goals and did not know how to de fine or convey what the north of the company was.

Sometimes envy appears in the environment, the boycott of those we trust the most can also occur. It seems as if dark energy envelops the scope of development of our projects.

A very strong feeling that, unfortunately, affects more than anything else and that comes from the minds of the people around us, who send missiles loaded with envy and bad energy that are more harmful than a ninth degree earthquake and that we must eliminate as soon as we detect the character of our environment.

That bad energy is comparable to a pyroclastic cloud full of negativity and darkness that descends the slope of the most feared volcano, covering all its projects at more than a thousand degrees. As a corollary, we must isolate ourselves from negative characters, however close to our feelings we may have once considered them; they are what we call toxic employees.

Avoiding Harmful Relationships

Many times, it is not only a few employees, friends or family members who damage our environment, we can also find our ex partners, who can be the most harmful and have the strongest opposing wishes. If one is unprepared and his mind is not going through a good positive moment, our contact will certainly be almost lethal. In such cases, we must cut off that unhealthy relationship. There is no point in keeping it on a friendly level, as it can harm our goals of making a fortune. We will have plenty of time to make a better match as a couple or as a friend.

That is why it is a business priority to always keep quiet with everyone, and even more so when money is smiling on us. Those we once considered our friends were the first to wish us ill in others and the first to try to boycott our most expensive projects.

I don't say this without knowledge but from pure experience. Always, in every project, there was someone who wanted to frustrate our work. They seemed to be characters sent by some strange dark force that one cannot control, but who appear there without invitation. We must know how to deal with friends or relatives whenever we are undertaking business. He who envies you does not seek to get your money, wife, or life of luxury that you hold, but wishes that you no longer possess those blessings and are ruined; in short, he wants you dead, that's how real he is. That's how the envious think and they meet more often than you think on the road to success that we all seek.

The engine of our misfortunes is always the envy of our closest relationships. They are always close because someone far away who does not know us hardly, if he does not know anything about us, let us give him that chance against us; we will always find them as scavengers of our energy around us.

Feelings of great frustration prevail in many people around the world, and this generates that bad feeling in the face of the success of others. Please, do not misunderstand my words, there are also wonderful people, and we have been able, fortunately, to know them, but we always had to hide what one did in the economic face of the untimely looks of strangers, because we never knew for sure with the quality of the person with which one was going to meet ahead.

We must know our friends for a long time to be able to open up without prejudice; therefore, it is advisable never to comment on their business, much less their success. This is my advice.

Talk about football, art, cinema, tourism, whatever you like, but never about your projects, your work, or the money you earn.

In the 1990s

In the 1990s, I discovered a more practical and less vulnerable business niche. It was the professional retailing of products such as cell phones or alarms, partnering as distributors for large, world-renowned companies. This was our quantum leap in the business world.

Our greatest satisfaction, without a doubt, was obtained there. This is how we achieved not only our first million dollars but many more, which allowed us a very great mental and emotional stability.

We discovered that it's not the same to go out with your brand as with one already recognized in the market and imposed on people's minds; the effort to grow fast becomes much lighter, and that's how we took speed in the race to the million we had mentalized.

I want to take you there, to the triumph that awaits us like a sweet lover with open arms after reading and highlighting this book. Take it as a permanent consultation organ. I assure you that any man or woman, professional or not, with or without studies, from any part of the world, with any religious or political belief, will be able to achieve the goal that we propose just by implementing the proposal that I make in this compendium of my personal experience and that which I gathered in other entrepreneurs throughout my life.

It wasn't all rosy at first. Blows and stumbles abound, but for those who do not know failure they will never be able to glimpse success, they will not know the difference, they will not be able to distinguish the path, they will not know the traps they will encounter in a not too distant time. Likewise, I can assert that when a business works it does so from the beginning, in the first six months; if not, we must rectify our course and perhaps know how to let go of it; otherwise, we will enter into a senseless whim that will lead us to the underworld.

I'm talking about the first six months when we'll see some light, unimpeded, where it flows like the flow of a river.

Our first mission is to banish the pride that debases us and brings us closer to transforming ourselves into beasts. Our second mission is the conformation of our work philosophy, which is to know how to listen to our customers and employees, their concerns, their dreams, and expectations.

Projecting internal marketing before an external one is key. That is, selling the idea first to our people so that our people know and are passionate about transmitting the company's commercial policies and achieving the expected results and goals projected daily.

Let us know from the beginning that we have two types of customers of the same tenor, one internal and one external: our employees and our customers. If we do not apply internal marketing to our employees and sell them our idea first, it will be difficult for them in turn to sell the idea in its entirety to potential customers.

This is just a preview of something very important that we need to develop to get the results we are looking for in this book.

We must get deeply involved in the processes with perseverance, adding a sales strategy that, in our beginnings, we still did not know in detail and we were guided more by instinct than by anything else, as it happens to the common young entrepreneurs.

This is why 95 % of entrepreneurs fail. That is also why I wanted to write this compendium, along with anecdotes drawn from our real experience, to alert you to the pros and cons you may find, wishing to incorporate some data to improve their current projects, if by those circumstances of life are embarking on any business option at this time.

Chapter 2: The emerging business world

"Things don't change; we change."

HENRY THOREAU

Our experience in different types of business concerning sales is that it led us to perfect the methods that we present today. Going through the student tourism, with my scarce twenty one years I achieved sales productions of two thousand to five thousand passengers for three prestigious companies in the '80s.

It was sold in a kind of tender. In each school, we had to present our product in front of at least five other companies every night, and sometimes in front of ten different proposals, and so try to convince about a hundred parents per meeting that my proposal was the best often. Then, in 2003, I repeated my youthful experience in other destinations, such as Cancun and the Riviera Maya, which are truly a paradise. We decided to tempt the Mexican student market to take an end of year trip to the Mayan lands. We did this by copying, in part, the Argentine and American spring break scheme.

The business is to hire a charter of modern buses that, in this case, made the trip from Mexico City to Cancun in twenty four hours. Then select the hotels, which in this case were all inclusive five-star luxury hotels at fifteen dollars a night per passenger at that time. The payment for the promised tours and discos had to come out of the options sold by the coordination staff during the twenty four hours of the trip and convince the ticket holder that taking options was their best option. When they arrived in Cancun, the coordinators would come down with the money in hand. They were paid their 10% commission and the rest was used to pay for excursions, discos, and the contracted options.

It is an excellent project to implement in countries where this culture does not yet exist. The costs are low for transport and hotels and, above all, in low season; the rest of the ser vices are paid for with the optional ones and the profit is important, as long as we sell to a minimum of one thousand passengers, which would be at the rate of thirty passengers per course, resulting in about thirty schools. We can say that there is a profit margin of up to 40% of the cost of the package. Another interesting niche for a very fashionable incursion is the travel of fifteen years celebration.

One of the first business projects in which I glimpsed good money in Argentina was the sale of cell phones and their rental to tourists or businessmen who stopped in the country. To do this, I planted brochures in all the receptions of the hotels in Buenos Aires and handed out juicy commissions to the concierges of the hotels so that they would send me clients.

That's when the cell phone fever started. We had a group of so-called professional salesmen of all ages. Our first contact with the cell phone world was in 1996. At that time, I didn't have the necessary vision, I didn't know how to wait, I didn't have enough perseverance that is needed in any project and, for a personal matter, I decided to end that successful project.

After a break of almost a year in business, I entered the field of exhibition organization. I invented them or copied them from other countries and gave them my personal touch. That's how we made about five exhibitions of great impact.

We imagined a title, a theme, we looked for a database similar to the theme of the exhibition, we put together the plans, we hired the place where the exhibition would take place, the security, the cashiers, we contacted the owner who would have the panels, the lights, the carpet, the posters that would identify the stands and the external billboard, We implemented an advertising action plan that consisted of sticking posters on public streets social networks did not exist yet in the 1990s , some mentions in TV programs, promoters on public streets, advertising in newspapers and magazines or giving away tickets.

In the meantime, an own organization was looking for potential exhibitors to sell them from the nine square meters the spaces to display their products. The most successful I invented and that has importance until today was Expo Football, which unfortunately I did not patent in 1999 and I did not accept an offer of partnership by a large television network in the world of sport.

At the end of that year, a friend from school and ex partner in some project appears, a great businessman whom I always appreciated to a great extent, but that with the passing of the years and his circumstances and my travels we moved away. He came to us talking about an American electronic security company that paid approximately eight hundred dollars for each new client, to whom was given, as if that were not enough, the equipment and installation of an electronic security system free of charge and provided by the same corporation. Meanwhile, the client was only required to pay a monthly monitoring fee of no more than forty dollars. That was the turning point we were hoping for.

We had, at that time, an office of one hundred meters in the middle of the centre and a small group of exhibition sales. I began the search for someone who could share our destiny in this opportunity as a partner given the lack of experience in this field.

I heard that other acquaintances in the tourism field had already put up their distributor. One of them, a former tourism promoter of mine, associated with another acquaintance who at that time owned a tiny candy store in a neighbourhood of the city, together they had set up an office of no more than fifty meters with only two desks and a borrowed computer.

Between both partners, they did not reach the five thousand dollar investment, which was also borrowed, as I was told years later in Peru.

It was like with the famous Spanish commander in Mexico, Hernan Cortés, because they had burned their ships and we had lit our torches for such an event, nothing to lose, everything to win, we were practically starting from scratch.

After many doors were closed to us, we found a man we called Doctor, who was a golf fan and very kind as a person, who had a small electronic security agency in the area of Pacheco, in the province of Buenos Aires.

At that time, the American multinational, the country where it arrived, bought the client portfolio of companies in the electronic security sector and made them its distributors. We had two exhausting months until we could convince him to accept the sale of his client portfolio and take over the distribution by partnering with us.

We would set up the sales organization and infrastructure and the Doctor would have the technicians, his company, and his experience in the field of electronic security. We signed an agreement and that's how we started. There will always be a sponsor to invest in our dreams. This is called "leverage" in business if you do not have investment or knowledge in the field. You just have to insist and never give up. So did the greats in their early days, Steve Jobs or Bill Gates.

We only had one loyal showroom sales manager whom we will call Juan, a loyal employee, but his style had nothing to do with this type of sales we sensed. He was a dinosaur in a coat and tie, very formal, a young executive. We also had a secretary and some salesmen. Our dear Juan had the project to start with his archaic style visiting companies and doing telephone marketing. We were not convinced by all those options, so we decided to separate the waters: he in our old office of one hundred meters, and we in a new one even bigger, in the central area, on the square of the congress of the nation. With the Doctor, we decided to buy in instalments two SsangYong and Mercedes vans for twelve passengers, both in silver grey. We were very excited.

Emotion is an unavoidable requirement to start any business project, to have the emotion to begin, to know that it is the right way, not to take a step back and remove the ballast of negativity that we may have in the environment and from those who do not want to change the business culture with us.

Juan saw a low level of the type of sale we wanted to carry out and those people we wanted to take, without experience, with too many youths and without important studies in some cases. We, on the other hand, saw in them people tired of losing, thirsty and hungry for success, wanting to get out of the pit, to take the world away from them, to have someone pay attention to them and to be able to show all the potential locked up in their guts. They were just looking for an opportunity.

Without knowing much about the product, without any training from the multinational, because at that time their trainers were at the top of their agendas, we had to implement, based on our experience, a new model of sales organization that until today has been ad opted in almost all Latin America by mobile phone companies to sell door to door. Without realizing it, we were pioneers and put their hierarchies to this organization. We invented the idea of dividing into small sales forces and deploying them in the field in different areas covering coordinators with two supervisors and four account executives each, and all of them hierarchized at different levels and rewarded according to their achievements with tangible and intangible prizes.

The trainers were surprised by our versatility in managing the sales force and the novelty of the system. Once a month we implemented a weekend training in different tourist spots of the country. The American company, for its part, gave us some very basic manuals that contained the ABCs of what they were looking for and had tried for years in the United States and which gave them good results. We discovered that it was very similar to what we were implementing empirically, and it was giving us very important results.

Chapter 3: The Road to Profitable Enterprise

"Before you change others, change yourself. Clean your window to see better. Pay attention to the negative cause that has made you suffer, not the one that has offended you. The cause is the programming, it was put in you since you were a child, you are not to blame for that, neither is the other".

HENRYANTHONY DE MELLO

What do we call a profitable company? It is that which, based on our effort and concrete objectives, can give us an economic and spiritual benefit from work well done. In our case, we were able to obtain this benefit by joining the electronic security project in Argentina.

It was a time of continuous growth, where our dreams came true and we finally found a place, a space where we could develop freely to put into practice all our experience in sales.

We always started our company by making what I have called a smart selection of our staff, placing an ad in the main newspaper or web portal of the country where we were. We modified this type of ad over the years.

They were all of such impact that they filled our offices with rows of potential future vendors a hundred meters and more in length. And then, with the advance of technology, we began to publish by putting up just one email address. The number was climbing to a thousand resumes on average curriculum vitae.

That was our quarry from which we extracted the raw material that we then polished with training sessions day after day. After the announcement, came the selection of the coordinators and supervisors, to whom we kept a week and a half in training. It is important to maintain that first line of leaders for at least a week and a half in intense training, because it will depend on it to gain their confidence and align their minds with the objectives we want to achieve, because they will be the source of inspiration for the salespeople and will be able to transmit to them security, stability, confidence and clear goals.

Maintain motivation at all times

We have set up a scheme of commissions and tangible and intangible awards to an unbeatable sales force in Argentina. There were five vans mined with highly motivated sales elements. In that first office we had, in the training room, for the first time, a table football game. It was very motivating for the time between the sales training days or before them, and also while they were arriving at the office every morning with a cup of coffee in between.

Today we can also aspire to have a PlayStation or something similar, since these motivators create positive vibes in the office and have fun in the mornings, before work. That's what it's all about.

Without fun there is no success possible. A job where there is no fun and smiles tend to fail. We must have coffee, empanadas, sandwiches, cookies or whatever you and your budget can afford for breakfast every morning, but we must never lack a positive mental attitude and, therefore, a fun work environment where a good work climate, humour, a smile, good music and a feeling of re laxation abound before the daily sales challenges.

We must never transmit tension to our environment for the sake of results. They should be seen as a natural process that we easily reach every day. The day's sales achievements will come on their own, without pressure. The healthy pressure will be given by the same daily goal you impose, accompanied by important prizes.

Fear doesn't attract sales; it drives them away. Nerves and bad pressure also, everything must happen naturally.

The pressure is exerted in the daily personal interview monitoring each element that makes up the sales force. There, pressure is exerted by explaining the need for the daily result in their lives.

Every commercial sales element must be convinced of the product and that the objectives are easily achievable. Where they are suspicious and think they are difficult, it is all over. The first person who should see it that way is you. The method is not to put pressure on yourself for results or to instil fear in those who do not reach them, as this creates a boring and unreliable working environment.

I remember that initial group was a wonderful group. We were congratulated by the coaches at the American headquarters, as we had never received any training, but even so, it was the most joyful and productive sales force among the more than forty distributors that the corporation had at that time. This was also reflected in the high production we achieved month after month. In addition, we had organized with the announced scheme of the sales force unit (UFV) at a rate of one per truck.

That's when we thought of starting to implement training trips and award dinners for achievements. It was one trip and dinner a month. When we held the latter, those who lived farther away and were single, we would stay at a very modern four star hotel on the corner of the office in the Plaza de los Dos Congress in Buenos Aires, so that the next day we would be on time for a new journey full of incentives to achieve the goals set. All this created an extraordinary motivation. They had their company t-shirts on, and the mystique was overflowing. From there our model of competitive development of the 3M was born, where the strength of the brand must be sustained with the strength of the mystique, and this, with the strength of the mind. The strength of a brand is an emergent of what the people of a company do for it. On this depends their attitude and aptitude, their desire and their ability.

Brand is differentiation, positioning, loyalty. Mystique is commitment, sense of belonging, will to win, awareness of cause, understood and shared vision. The only sustain able advantage over time is service and customer care.

Our fundamental axiom has always been: "Our people first, our network's people, so that our people know and want to make the customer feel that he is our priority". We apply successful internal marketing. Investing in talent is the key that leads to good results.

On the monthly training trips, it was very common for us to leave from the work area itself, in the two Mercedes vans we had. That is to say, because of their motivation and their own decision, they kept on selling in the area until late at night. From the area we would leave to train in some tourist place far from the big city.

We would have dinner and then, already in the vans, good music would play until the arrival. The good mood made us cry with laughter, nobody slept until we reached our destination. On each trip we took some secretaries with us to organize the details of the training. We would leave on a Friday and return late on Sunday with our minds recharged.

These trips were only for team leaders and for those who were emerging in this area. During these trips, we gave out some prizes, set objectives for the next month and proposed how far the company and each of them wanted to go.

We aimed at the most ambitious dreams by committing them one by one. We swore to each other like medieval gentlemen our goals, and everything ended, as usual, in a fashionable local disco and we saw with astonishment that they did not take off the company logos that they wore in caps or clothes; they went dancing, we would say, in the company colours, a matter that the coaches of the headquarters could not believe such fanaticism for the brand. Everything was incredible, sales were rising like the tide on a full moon. The groups were like a brass band that sounded to the rhythm of the sales and the good work environment, their magnetic north, was full of positive energy.

It all came to an abrupt end in 2001, when the famous corralito appeared without warning in Argentina, stripping all bank savers of their life savings, on the pretext that otherwise they would have to close all the banks, and costing the succession of four governments in the same year, leaving the economy and confidence of that country destroyed.

Only two hundred dollars a week were allowed to be withdrawn from the banks, and imagine in our case, with more than fifty employees and the fixed and cash expenses that the operation demanded, it was impossible to go ahead, so I went to ask for a new distribution to Chile, to the headquarters in Latin America, the subject of another chapter.

Generally, the low production can come from situations outside the scope of the company and are limited only to the family or couples. These are issues that destroy the mind of the seller. For this reason, we always had a black box at the entrance of the office with some little papers on the side where they had to write and then put their personal problems inside the box and where, once a week, we burned them in a kind of small Viking pyre type fire. It was a symbolic way of keeping them out of the work environment.

We always repeated and emphasized very punctually that of "zero tolerance to attitude problems", in spite of all the good energy that circulated in the offices, because, as we know, negativity is contagious and so is positive energy.

Everything depends, in these cases, on knowing how to detect in time those people who do not understand this philosophy of work and expel them before the plague spreads and extinguishes the flame of fun and the good attitude of those who are true sales professionals, which are those who constantly laugh, applaud each closing of their own or their colleagues' sales, shout and get excited at each new award that the company has. Their eyes are the eyes of the company. The company breathes in them.

Your sales groups will not be a cost, but a very important added value to take into account. Invest in them and you will see good results. They are worth more than a thousand advertisements, more than a hundred beautiful aides; they will make a difference.

We must be different, our attitudes will say so, our sales forces are the front line, we are the generals who plan, but they are the face of the company in front of the customers, they have to mark the way that we will call "the way of the dragon".

Chapter 4: The Way of the Dragon and the Turtle

"No one can escape the magic and magnetism produced by an attentive listener who attaches importance to what we say.

CARNEGIE

I have named him this perhaps because in the Chinese horoscope the king is the dragon. The word "dragon" derives from the Greek word drákōn, from the family of the verb 'to stare', which is applied to the gaze of eagles and warriors, among others, referring to the fascinating and hypnotic power of the gaze.

That is the attitude we always aspire to for our salespeople, that the power   of their gaze gives the potential client the certainty of what he is buying, the fascination for what he is getting, that with his gestures, words and eyes he hypnotizes the future client until he takes him in that first interview to a closing of sales and the signing of a contract.

This is how we always work; this is how we always achieve our daily sales in the heat of the moment. A day without sales is a day thrown away.

A salesman without a closing sale on the day has been a buyer of excuses why no customer wanted to buy, was a compulsive loser that day and carries in his backpack a heavy burden of all the excuses and negatives he bought in a lost workday.

We search our UFVs (sales force units) for those mythical warriors who, brandishing the word, win battles, interview after interview, closing after closing.

Often, the dragon plays an important role as a god or guardian or as a monster and powerful enemy. That is the guardian that we look for behind every incorporation, the guardian of our words that we need in our leaders to develop and obtain in each one of them, we want to see that god that is found in each person, hidden inside them, we look for that monster of sales, that powerful enemy of the competition of the T shirt that you wear.

Positive qualities are attributed to the dragon, such as a great wisdom and knowledge; applying this quality to our UFV, we can say that the knowledge of the script of the sales success we provide it with and that we practice daily, where we film each sales theatre to later analyse it. The knowledge of all the training techniques that we develop, and their workshops are the ABC of closing more and better sales.

Wise must be the salesman before each objection raised by the customer, wise before each concern, wisdom of our leaders to lead our sales force units (UFV) to victory.

It is said that dragons also have insatiable defects, greed and greed that lead them to devastate entire populations in order to pile up gigantic treasures, where the symbolism around the dragon is essentially that of struggle.

Precisely in our UFV scheme it is the struggle that characterizes these combat units in sales, the insatiable greed guides them, where one or ten sales a day should not conform to anyone, we see this greed in the dragon's path as a healthy aspiration to fulfil the daily goals proposed in our oath signed daily with the coach, to reach the other side of the sea and raise the treasure of victory, of the task well accomplished, devastating with our words any opposition, because achieving our objectives is the goal. Taking away the negativities of our environment, sweeping away our dark thoughts of bad past experiences and that must be stepped on in that time and place, liquidating with the arguments of the competition the complaints and the bad elements in our UFV. Success is not built overnight, but in small steps hour after hour, and there we must concentrate all our energy on each step.

However, this role of the dragon is not far removed from that of a guardian, which involves waiting and maintaining order in the organisation of the company. It is precisely because they are guardians of something sacred that they symbolize the bridge to another world or the test of every hero.

Heroes are those we train in sales, the proof is precisely to achieve that desired place in history itself; we must see if each one is satisfied with being one more among his equals or a hero for his family, children, parents, partner, society.

In our company we will look for heroes who become those leaders who give their all every day to achieve the objectives of the company and who lead them unfailingly along this path of the dragon to achieve their own.

Finally, we know that, among the Romans, the dragon was considered a symbol of power and wisdom. In the East, the dragon has always been considered a beneficial creature and a symbol of good fortune. In Japan, where they are wise, kind and always willing to help, being the official emblem of the imperial family.

Chinese and Japanese dragons symbolize supreme spiritual power, earthly and heavenly power, knowledge, strength and health. According to ancient Chinese beliefs, they bring rain for the harvest. In the Himalayas they represent good luck.

Our path, without a doubt, is that of the "dragon in sales".
Which way is that? It is the one that produces that intense fire that is gestated inside and that later is reflected in the passion to close the sale and thus add up hour after hour more sales.
It is a path of no return; the one who reaches that level of ambition does not cease, it

will be perceived in each of our conversations, in each of our words, in each of our gestures, for it is these gestures and words that will be taken, indeed, by our clients; it will be those words that burn in the ears, it will be the fire that will spread in a powerful frequency that will arrive and invade the subconscious of the potential clients so that they close a contract.

Every business conversation should be a closing of a sale. And that can only be achieved with the right words, with knowing how to time those conversations, with knowing, presupposing and being sure that it will happen. That fire of the dragon is the passion that spreads and that we must have to reach our sales objectives, always daily, never in the short or medium term, or leave the results for the next day. Sales are hot or they are not. Today we see on the Internet that there are sales funnels designed to accompany the process until the purchase of a book or a product, very effective, by the way, and that are handled with robots programmed to close the sale hot.

The closures are for the same day, they can never happen by tomorrow. Tomorrow is a new day and it has to have its own results. The client must perceive the opportunity that is slipping through his fingers. Closure burns. The flame lasts an instant, the instant of the decision well made and supported by the right words to be pronounced in every sales speech.

Each professional sales conversation is a start of our play, where the main ac tor is us and the client will be our spectator who will get the message and close the deal, because when he receives us in his house or shop, he has already paid his entrance fee.

It will applaud our performance or not, it is not a matter of chance, it will be our full responsibility; excuses do not exist to these instances, excuses are for the losers, to justify their mediocrity, inefficiency and lack of gratitude before the opportunities that are present ed to them to have an excellent profession and a wonderful future in sales.

We weren't born to fail. We were born to succeed. We were born to give the most beautiful and different note we can in the context of the symphony that must cover the world with good attitudes, and thus be able to heal a society that disarms in perpetual discouragement without finding the way of the dragon.

We are in a sleepy society, without destination, without mission, without love. If we do not love ourselves, how can we then love our neighbour and our family, what can we give to others and what can we contribute to our society if we are like turtles?

We will not feed our children only with excuses that we always expose in the face of failure, we will only feed the turtle that we carry within us, that failure by our own decision that we wanted to be.

If we do not have that daily fire and results from the first day, we are on the path of the turtle and not the dragon. The dragon has wings, he is strong, he exhales fire from his mouth, he is the king in the East. The tortoise crawls, is slow, shy, always seems sad and is asleep.

There are many entrepreneurs who end up being turtles and time catches up with them and undoes them when they cannot move forward because they do not know how. Here we will break that chain that ties us to the past and that we do not know how to cut sometimes, that will drive us to be a new man, full of virtues, love and money in abundance to be able to help and sustain the world around us.

This is the philosophy that we must instil in our cadres of supervisors, coordinators and managers. We must form an army of dragons, not of turtles that come to hinder our dreams and desires and to cool our hearts, to infect us with their failures and to want everyone to accompany them in their mediocre vision of things.

Turtles are resentful of professionals; usually they are professionals too, but of job hunting. Therefore, let's know how to detect them in time and get them off our front lines.

Zero tolerance for those with attitude problems. One bad apple rots the rest. And if we see that the cancer is very advanced on one of the work fronts and we could not detect it in time, let us resort to taking out the whole group, for there will be no return. They are infected and will slow down the rest of those who are motivated. Without them, you'll see how easy everything will be again. Sales will magically resurrect, and tranquillity will return to the green pastures of our company. This method that we used always gave the expected results.

Chapter 5: Ending a stage. Searching for a new world

"The vast majority of people who are unable to accumulate enough money to meet their needs are usually easily influenced by the opinions of others.

NAPOLEON HILL, Think and Grow Rich

The climax of our history is yet to come, it runs through South America, Central America, Mexico and Europe. The same frenzy in the search for a better life leads him to ride wave after wave chasing dreams until he reaches the top.

The burning desire is the invisible force that will move him, the whisper of the wind that will tell him in the ear to go on, despite the storm, and at every step he takes without faltering until the final victory.

The journey begins in those Latin American societies which, in their early days, were the Mecca of fortune seekers, exiles and adventurers of all colours, race and religion in search of a new opportunity for their lives.

Those Spanish, German, Italian, Chinese, Japanese, Polish, Arab and Jewish grandparents, among many others, forged towns of strong, intelligent and hardworking people who, with only their dreams on their shoulders and with perseverance, were able to build all kinds of companies, factories, shops and even large corporations. How did they do it?

They did not know about positive thinking, were not professionals, did not have titles and, in some cases, did not know the language of the land where they landed. They burned their ships in order to conquer the heart of an empire: their own dreams. They had nothing to lose and the future smiled upon them, that future that could not be worse than the past from which they came.

That is the basic condition for undertaking, not to be tied to old schemes or thought patterns, to old debts that don't let us sleep. To be able to start over, not to be tied to our city, our friendships, family, profession, place of birth and customs. And the list goes on, even each human being has his own and it is very personal.

Let us remember that doubt has three brothers: failure, mediocrity and fear.

We must break those bonds and walk again as our ancestors did when they migrated in search of better living conditions that they could not find in their homeland.

But it is important not to be tied to the land of our birth for any reason. Nobody chooses where to be born, but they do choose where to develop.

Or, as St. Thomas Aquinas said: "Our country is not of this world". We are just passing through, like tourists, so it does not matter where we develop our happiness, the important thing will be to find it in the place that God has arranged.

If we go to a more mystical plane and give added value to our lives, we can say that we have two paths: to leave a trail of good works in this world and people who can affirm that it was a pleasure to have known us or to end our days like mediocre shadows that passed fleetingly, in trapped cobwebs, inert in a dark corner, full of problems, excuses and accumulated debts in pursuit of a life of fictitious tranquility that we never reached, because that world, as an employee with a minimum wage, does not exist; it is a bubble of miserable life that we make for ourselves and that we not only give to ourselves, but also give to our loved ones.

If that place, city or country doesn't give you what you deserve, leaving is the first step up the ladder to self fulfillment.

I see so much unemployment in many countries that I do not understand how they do not have the courage to change or emigrate to better directions or better business opportunities. Suddenly, fear paralyzes them or perhaps they think of that little security and com fort that the closest family environment provides. Those who have that support will think that it is better to keep getting a miserable salary than to take risks and, if I don't make ends meet, I suppose they will think, my family will help me.

Many, faced with any problem, imagine that their parents, friends, siblings will be there, without taking into account that, on many occasions, they too go through the same vicissitudes, transforming everything into a vicious intrafamily circle where no one can help anyone because you don't know who is worse off. Instead of providing a solution, we become a burden to those we claim to love. Selfishness prevails out of fear always and on every occasion.

Do not look back as you go forward; if you have to leave behind friends, family, customs, paralyzing fears, envy that debases and postpones, debts that cause severe depressions or those negative words that some people tell us, go ahead! Even more so if you are afraid, because you will break with the scheme that we impose on ourselves from the centre of our negativities.

If we intoxicate our days with phrases issued by the turtle chorus that always slow us down, we will end up like those who pronounce them.

78

It's those phrases such as: "It's not that business for you", "you're too old to start over", "you're crazy to leave the country", "it's impossible to reach a million dollars", "you don't have the guts to do it", "it takes a lot of money to invest", "you should go back to that old office job, which at least paid you a basic salary", and the phrases go on. Those are the tips we don't need to hear any more in our lives.

Hope is forged from positive thinking with positive phrases, a clear objective, with a lot of courage, passion and with the certainty of going to a new life of happiness.

In addition to the phrases of those who say they love us although their ignorance is so strong that it precedes and envelops them there are so many other situations that we will try to warn them so that we can remove these stones from our path.

Chapter 6: Our Profession Enslaves Us

"Your bitterness, your jealousy, your guilt, your resentment. Ask yourself, "What would happen if I left them behind?"

ANTHONY DE MELLO

Another issue that enslaves some human beings is their blessed profession. Our pride in being professionals in that career that we studied with so much love and that we believed was the basis of the fortune and happiness that it was not. It is the same one we dreamed of forging a future for ourselves, the one our ancestors prayed for us to project their frustrations without realizing that our DNA was different.

One of the main stumbling blocks I have noticed in all the societies and people I have come across is their lack of motivation to change.

And when I talk about change, I even talk about profession if we detect that the current one is sinking us economically and we cling to it like wood in the middle of the wreck instead of starting to swim towards the beach we see in the distance. People think that just because they have a university degree it gives them a guarantee too.

Statistics show that more and more graduates are joining the ranks of the unemployed. They are employees who are considered overvalued and where many of the companies flee before their important curricula. Nor do they adopt a humble position because they believe that their profession qualifies them to occupy a high position without going through places, they would never have imagined in the labour scale; steps necessary to reach higher positions.

They are eternally dissatisfied, and this clouds their vision to be able to start their own business, encouraged at all times by their fear of failure. We must move mental structures and reach the balm of our thoughts in order to make those changes.

They are those people who, in front of anyone, need to say that they are professionals, who studied a university career, who expose their degrees without anyone asking them for them; all this to make a difference that does not exist or to cover, in some way, the reality where they are: at the bottom of their shattered economies and, of course, not exercising in the least their profession successfully.

They will remain blind to the world, they sense that they have achieved nothing, but they do not want to admit it. They think they'll make a difference.

Once, Henry Ford was on trial in the middle of his golden years. He told the prosecutor that he was treating him as ignorant because of his lack of education, and before which he asserted that why did he need to have studied if the cheapest labour was the professional one and with the money, he had he could hire any professional he required. The inventor of the automobile had not even finished high school or college in his adolescence, like so many other successful people like Graham Bell, and the list would be endless.

Study, of course, helps to cultivate us, but it is not at all a determinant of success in life or in business; moreover, many are hindered and frustrated in their lives by being limited in their professions, which do not give them any joy; they hide behind a papyrus that, in practice, is of no use to them, only locks them up, numbs them and does not let them see beyond their noses.

Of course not everyone who follows a profession is unhappy with it, and there are even success stories in it, but the frustration and the global debt show us that most professionals are on this side of the field, and there are more and more who are swelling the ranks of the unemployed or semi occupied, who work at anything other than what they studied or who are desperately looking for a way out of debt with cards, mortgages, banks, vacations, cars, their life in instalments.

Their professions enslave them, they do not know another world, they are afraid to venture into the unknown and, even if they had the guts, they do not know where to start, they repeat old schemes, try to develop their careers or revalidate their titles in other lands and end up waiting forever for the fact that the claim is made in that new country. Many of them fail because they do not know how to sell their services. Selling is everything and we will need to implement it in everything.

Chapter 7: Vicious Turtle Circles

"A failure is only the spice that will spice up success."

TRUMAN CAPOTE

They are circles that depress us, overwhelm us and suffocate us. They are communities of people who repeat the same patterns of behaviour over and over again. They are held together by comfort or ignorance. We have found four, but I assure you there are many more.

We have, in principle, the circle of the eternal students, who are those who spend the years of their life studying. They do not understand that study should only focus on one stage of life: that of adolescence and not adulthood. In reality, that circle is used to cover up our disappointments and frustrations in the face of life's negative vicissitudes.

There are those who say they are studying after thirty years and who never finish their careers so as not to have to face the world of work or business, simply because of the panic they have printed on their foreheads. They prefer, then, to frequent that area of comfort that makes our mediocrity. Nobody will ask them what their average was in school or university, but if they know how to sell, if they know how to organize a company, if they know how to lead a human work group, if they are orderly and pay attention to the directives that emerge from the main management of a company.

They would like to be others; perhaps that successful businessman or woman, that successful scientist, that successful sportsman or journalist, that successful in their profession. From there, then, comes a resentful life, a life that has no air and drowns them out by itself. Their faces denote that tiredness, that continuous disillusionment, that negativity made flesh.

They are those who justify everything in not working or having a mediocre job, the lack of dedication in their work, of enthusiasm, which affects the taking of action in their lives, all because they are studying to obtain a university degree, and then what?

Sometimes, they delay the completion of their studies, as if they had run out of a comfortable way of life, where they have an answer for everything from the perspective of their careers, but starting a new competitive and unknown stage in their lives terrifies them, the present and future that will be for the rest of their lives paralyzes them, so they delay that moment as long as they can, because they know there will be no turning back. That is called immaturity.

Or have we not sometimes met people who are in their thirties and still studying, and even others still living in their parents' house? They say they work from their homes and in reality they do not leave their lair, they do not seek to improve themselves nor do they want to leave that vicious circle of the studious so as not to have to face the challenges of a society that is more and more competitive every day and that demands that we put everything we have into it to get out of our vicious circles of mediocrity that we create for ourselves mentally. In short, our turtle is comfortable eating lettuce.

I have also known those circles of the eternal job seekers. These are what I call job seekers, and I have known them for more than twenty years as an entrepreneur in the sales organization in eight countries. They are those who spend their whole life buying the newspaper or searching in the web portal of their preference on weekends or Mondays to appear interested in their economic future and systematically repeat that action of buying, writing down and sending their professional resume, which is summarized in a veneer, or they are those who worked in six jobs in one year and their resume is referred to a pile of obvious failures. They are enemies of perseverance. They do not understand the game of success in life, commitment to themselves and the place where they work.

Everything is completed by going to one or two interviews per week and the mission is already accomplished for themselves and their suffering family, who support the basics of their lives, food and a bed; these people can be called parents, siblings, wife and even good friends sometimes. Always, behind these, we will find a good Samaritan.

As a justification, they cling to the opinions of the news media, where every day there is a crisis and an economy in supposed free fall, whether in the world, in the country or in the government of the day, and thus they become judges and champions of justice and authorized to criticize the ways in which the political and economic life of the country is conducted. Another justification is based on the fact that there is no credit, much less employment.

There are more permissive economies that subsidize eternally and form another vicious circle: the circle of the unemployed, where they have become accustomed to not working and receiving a kind of subsidy for not doing so, where the government pays them for being unemployed while they work underhand in another undeclared job. What counts, in the end, is only the votes. It is a luxury held by those who pay their taxes.

I have seen that even immigrants in many countries of Europe receive unemployment benefit, including illegal ones. For example, a Latin American once came to our offices claiming that he was fed up with not working because he was only travelling around Eu rope thanks to the subsidy given to him by the government of that country Spain. It is incredible how a good political action or intention can become an abuse.

People take advantage, prostitute the good intention of a country and take away the true meaning of it. It is a culture of unemployment that can only be deactivated by reactivating the productive apparatus of small and medium sized enterprises, banishing subsidies ad eternum, but we leave that to the economists. It is up to governments to promote young and old entrepreneurs with cheap credit so that they can provide jobs and contribute to the growth of countries and societies with their taxes.

A fourth vicious circle from which we cannot escape, and which inevitably transforms us into turtles in this society as well is the circle of those who take the easiest path to develop their life plan. In this field, I must highlight two divisions: bad employees and bad employers.

In the first, we see how bad employees do not commit to their jobs and their companies. They go unnoticed in their jobs, making their day a waste of time. They don't bring any energy, much less imagination or motivation to their work. They are looking at what ritual their cell phone, their computer or their watch.

He is the first to wait for the call or WhatsApp of a friend or partner who will take them out of their glass or concrete prison for a considerable time, which they consider to be their monotonous work. Or we can also find those who use all the options that cyberspace offers them: chat, matchmaking or even the most upbeat pages to make their work time go by faster and more entertaining, and then they look at the clock to certify that it is aligned with the longed for and expected time, that of the departure. Not a minute more, no matter if the phone rings for a lastminute purchase or a customer needs our urgent advice. The only thing that matters is to run away as if it were a marathon start.

Bad entrepreneurs are those who constantly seek to implement unjustified policies of cutting staff, of delaying payments as far as possible, of skimping on increases for a good production achieved, of renegotiating commissions when these appear succulent for those who worked them.

They are those who evade taxes, steal sales items from other companies, those who do not pay their debts or declare bankruptcy in order not to pay them, or those who, with their products, swindle the consumer, providing a bad service and products that have expired in time.

The list is endless of the mismanagement that these provide to all of society, employees and consumers. There are all kinds of them, but they all have something in common: their selfishness, pride, bad intentions, their transmission of negativity to their environment, their domination of people through fear and not by example.

They are feared, hated, never appreciated. It is like a tsunami of rotting water that gathers along their path and, when it reaches the shores of their own existence, bursts into their faces, leaving them where they started. Those who have managed to escape from the blow by their cunning sooner or later get their due here or in eternity.

Chapter 8: Debts

"You are on the road to success when you understand that failures are mere detours."

GILBERT CHESTERTON

If we speak of paralysis, we can argue that one of the things that produces the greatest paralysis in our lives and does not allow us to move forward is that produced by debt.

These may have been innocently contracted in pursuit of family progress, with their respective interests or strange financial manoeuvres that make us not only lose our heads and deviate from our professional and private life purposes, but also bring about the typical family or health disorders due to the economic strangulation of money and other perspectives.

As long as he's a slave to debt, he can't pay it. Slaves generate nothing but anguish, hard work without pay or satisfaction, and never amount to anything more than a plate of second rate food and a bed on which to rest their battered bones.

Don't be a slave anymore. Abraham Lincoln abolished slavery more than a century ago. What are you waiting for to break that mental chain that squeezes your brain and jumps on your insides, twisting them at night in endless fatigue, and that generates, like Niagara Falls, endless arguments in the bosom of your home? Throw away those chains so that you can move forward and run again on the paths of a happy life.

When debts squeeze you, think that they can be paid off at the right time, but they should not be a priority in our lives if you are having a hard time and do not have the funds to pay them. We must generate the funds so that, when we are in good shape, we can refinance these debts and settle them from a better economic position, with a million dollars or euros in our account, for example.

If we concentrate on debt, more debt will accumulate; that is for sure, it is the law of life.

Don't be a slave to debt, for your chains are thick and heavy, the slippery ground that can drag you to a mighty river from which you cannot easily escape, and that will be your new home: the choppy waters of a rushing mountain river that rises and falls among stones that strike you even at night.

Perhaps the proposal is not very formal, but if you are not prepared to deal with this weight, better leave them aside, take care of generating money, do not worry about debts that already in time and form will pay. If you concentrate on them and postpone your projects, they will vanish like ice from the mountain tops in the summer.

If you decide to stay at home, in your city or country, good for you. But your change must be radical. You must set aside all the stones in your mind that we have been talking about. Renegotiate them and don't keep torturing yourself, concentrate on your projects, don't pay more attention to them, give them their fair share until you succeed in business and can finish paying for them. Focus all your attention on making your projects a reality.

Listen to your favourite music, read motivational books, go out to dinner, travel on the weekends, go to the movies, watch funny movies, comedies whenever possible Mr. Bean, Torrente, the Spanish, or Jim Carrey, the American, are my favorites go to the theatre or dance, do yoga, play a sport, golf, Ping-Pong, tennis, soccer, whatever.

Practice charity, which is one of the principles of total, material and spiritual wealth. And forget about debts, don't take them as a problem, let them melt away in your mind and make a comfortable payment plan in which you can get in tune with them by following the business plan I propose in this book, which will be your mentor of success in your life.

Chapter 9: Breaking every paradigm

"As soon as man abandons envy, he begins to prepare to enter the path of bliss."

WALLACE STEVENS

The problem in moving forward is the paradigms that we have in our beaten mind. Hit by bad experiences with partners, friends, family, acquaintances, competitors, girlfriend and even his wife.

Mediocrity abounds everywhere. The mediocrity of those around us is like a constant bombardment of our path where later the infantry of envy will unfailingly advance.

What are paradigms? Well, simply put, they are those thoughts that slow us down. They are those thoughts that we wrongly cling to. They are thoughts that we think are real, imposed by culture and society, that do not allow us to glimpse other life or thought options.

For example, to understand it more schematically, I'm going to tell you a little story. On a road I was crossing a pig. A car driven by a woman passes by, dodges it and continues. Once the bad moment is over, the woman sees a driver approaching at great speed. When he passes very close to her and at a considerably high speed, she manages to warn him and shouts: "Pig!" The man, indignant, thought that she was insulting him, so he turned around and, in the distance, began to insult her without realizing that, turning the curve that followed, there was the pig, against which she crashed.

The man had the paradigm that he was being insulted for the way he drove, but in reality, what the woman was doing was warning him about the pig crossing the street so that he would take the necessary precautions. How many pigs do we come across on the road of our lives? How many paradigms in our minds and do we end up crashing into them? We must clear our minds to start the change.

From those first immigrant grandparents came these children and grandchildren, who, not having the drive of their ancestors, did not have that courage to break life paradigms in many cases that did break their ancestors. But, thanks to the change in economic conditions brought by their grandparents, some children and other grandchildren squandered their fortunes and saw their estates become extinct like dinosaurs before the impact of the meteor, falling from a wealthy class to swell the lower and middle classes.

Those children or grandchildren of immigrants were ruled by fear at a crucial time. Fear of change, of taking risks, of going outside the comfort zone, of taking new paths like those of our grandparents, fear of life, which, on many occasions, leads to drugs and alcohol.

Living is unsafe, it's risky, and anyone who doesn't assume we're in that vortex of life isn't often in tune with the planet we live on.

No one is safe even with their jobs, and if not, look at the amount of unemployment being generated by the global crises throughout history that have wrecked lives and businesses. Nor are we totally sure about personal security. When we read the news, we see that no one is exempt from the fact that at some point they may be the object of a theft of a cell phone, of an intrusion into their home, of having their car taken away from them or, even worse, suffering some form of kidnapping, such as the attempt we suffered in Mexico in 2006.

Nor are we exempt from exposure to disease. According to books that seriously address these issues, we are told that most of them are generated by our own uncertainty, our own mind with its negative thoughts and frustrations.

I wonder what we call a sure thing. It sounds like we will have social security and, when we are sixty five, we will have a miserable retirement with much more deplorable health care in general in most countries of the world.

Or is security working eight hours a day, going on holiday when the company allows it, putting up with all kinds of bosses and sticking to the consequences, aiming for a pay rise when the cost of living is already sky high? Is security a minimum fixed salary of four hundred dollars or a thousand euros? Do we call this job security? I call it security for those who still see life from the perspective of fear.

Fear of breathing, of advancing, of throwing oneself into the unknown, preferring a security that does not exist in life. Nothing is safe. If not, ask all those who lost their homes in the Caribbean or Asian hurricane season or in a tsunami, in a tornado or in the face of the loss of a lifetime's savings when a financial institution goes bankrupt. The only safety I know of is that of cemeteries, where nothing happens.

I propose something different, to break with mediocrity once and for all, to move forward with our faces up to see the horizon of success that we must reach. Many are content to work with their parents or blindly follow the path they have laid out because they believe themselves powerless to develop their own life project. It is easier, more comfortable, to live with the parents, to work with the father and even to live off the father without working. They are part of the mediocrity that today abounds and creates social crises.

I'm not saying that if our father is a successful businessman we can't join the family business; in that case, it's always valid, and even more so if we do it responsibly, giving our best and, if we were lucky enough to be born into an economically well-off family, this book will also help you find explicit ways to grow the sales of the family business.

We must change the conformism for the awareness of our mediocre lifestyle, the fear for the courage to advance in a business life that will be full of stones that we will have to kick one by one with firmness to clear our progress.

If we are not willing to kick them all and only want to kick some, we will continue to stumble and slow down our walk. Let's not have compassion on the stones, the stones are just stones. These stones can be of different colours and specific weights.

There are blacker and heavier ones, there are also beautiful shades, but they also make us stumble. Friends, relatives, employees, confidants; in short, any one we have close to us can be a potential stone. I am not saying that everyone has bad intentions, but some say they want the best for you, they say they are positive and highly motivated, but everything remains in words, because their gestures, attitudes, energy that they radiate, their looks or gestures before our progress say the opposite to what they express in words and their results.

In order to identify them better, we can limit them to people to whom everything in life is going badly, great misfortunes happen to them or they have great depressions and negatives. They seem to shine at times, but it is just that, a fleeting moment, so much so that many times we appreciate and help them, we treat them like brothers, they can seem funny, intelligent, they can be professionals, lawyers, doctors, accountants or simple people who approach us.

There are plenty of examples in my life, so I warn you: we all have some around us. Just look around you and perceive them, be suspicious, analyse their attitudes and you will recognize them. Kick those stones far away.

Chapter 10: Analysing our environment. Banishing Envy

"When envy is strong, the person will feel hatred and animosity towards the one he envies. He will wish him harm and murmur against him. Such feelings of hate are very destructive. If a person has a tendency to feel envy, his whole existence will be plagued with anguish. He will be waiting for others to make mistakes so that he can rejoice when they do.

PELE YOATZ

The envious person does not want your belongings, but that you no longer possess them and that you remain in the same condition or worse; in short, he seeks our destruction, as strong as that. There is no such thing as healthy envy, like the crutch that is repeated to exhaustion, for example, in Spain.

We must isolate ourselves from the negative characters that always surround us like crows waiting for the death of their prey to absorb our last energies. The suck energy is like the suck goat, but in an earthly version, since the others do not know well where they come from.

They live immersed in their mediocrity and want us all to be immersed in their same condition. No one likes to sink alone; we must take into account that a part of the world's population suffers from this great defect which is the practice of selfishness. We should first analyse our environment before starting our project.

These individuals, close or not, let's know that their negative vibrations also affect at a distance, they carry different wrappings, but they are always the same, we know them with different names in each life story: bad friends, some relatives, brothers, cousins, bosses, coworkers, ex-girlfriend, ex-wife, all characters are potential suspects.

It is only a matter of time before one of them reveals his intentions and it may be too late when we find out. They often go unnoticed as being interested in our problems, but I would say, in fact, they are lurking; they carry such a negative charge that even electronic devices break down by their mere presence, and this is no joke, I have experienced it. It is very real, they will never let it progress so that it will always be there, in that same place, next to it, sunk with the anchor in the bottom of the sea.

As their life is synonymous with failure and their mental scheme is very strong, they are arrogant, selfish and stubborn, only taking the exit door is left to us and walking away as soon and as far as possible. Or if he were an employee, take him away from our company, no matter if he seems to be the most fun employee at times. Even if we believe that we could not continue our schemes in the company without his presence, let's do it without hesitation and see the miracle happen.

Our experience dictates that, believe me, there are these negative entities that negatively mark our businesses and lives. Therefore, if you detect or are at this moment thinking about someone that you suspect or realize you have close to you, get rid of it now, have a hunch, use your intuition; of course, subtly, so as not to offend your feelings, because the force of your dark desires or your uncontrollable envy will devastate your most beloved projects if you keep them close to you and do not do it subtly.

Eventually, if you don't take the first step toward independence, you'll wonder again and again why nothing you do works for you. Then you will drown in a beer or the liquor of your choice with that friend of yours who is always, coincidentally, in the bad moments, because you have not yet been able to know the good ones because you are always surrounded by the same thing.

One piece of advice: keep a close eye on your projects, your travels, your economic life. Never say where you will travel, or what your own company will have, do not even keep in touch by email or WhatsApp. That's how clear the steps are if you want to climb this path in your life.

My uncle Cuchi /Cuqui/ is pronounced in Spanish, whenever he was asked how he was doing, he would answer: "Tirado". We didn't know if he was pulling a heavy life or a cart full of money. By his expression, which generated nothing but compassion in whoever heard it, he seemed to be pulling the cart of a heavy life. But, in reality, he hid his enormous fortune behind that expressionless face; it grew day by day. It is a good practice I learned from this curious uncle Cuchi.

Shut up your economic life, hide it, it is a first tool to start walking in the beginning of the end of your old schemes and paradigms of life.

Break up old friendships that don't contribute anything and are suspicious of a life of frustration, burn those books that speak only of suffering, don't read about the end of the world, or Nostradamus, or the Mayan prophecies, better forget them; don't watch the news, don't listen to more crises, listen only to what is necessary to the politicians, make good use of your hours of the day, don't waste your valuable time in the Internet communities.

Focus on the goals we need to achieve. Read motivational books, successful life stories, look on the web for topics that will make you grow spiritually and economically, investigate what new businesses are in vogue in other countries, make your best version of them wherever you are.

The search for artificial love via the web is a reason not to leave behind a late adolescence full of frustrations, finding in those marginal actions a little adventure that will only bring misfortune to your life if you are already committed.

Know that the product of your frustrating economic situation also brings frustration in your partners, and then you look for a small crack where you can escape to drown your hardships in someone new who listens without problems, supposedly in sight.

We have to choose between the world of business or the world of the search for stealthy love. One world does not complement the other. Either we are hunters of pleasure and excess or we engage in agriculture to harvest money in abundance.

They are opposite schemes. Energies that we use in one direction or the other. Obviously, I'm not saying that you don't have sex with your lifelong partner, but I warn against adventures not out of moralistic, but out of realism, because they distort our times, they bring problems, they take away energies needed to concentrate on what really matters, they don't allow us to concentrate on our money and dream factory. We must live as much as possible in harmony in order to achieve our superlative economic goals.

If we channel our energy and time into stupid immature adventures, the result in business will be fatal. Something must always be given in exchange for changing our lives for the better. Dedicate yourself in your free time to your family, who will thank you, and you will see your economic life flourish.

In these lines we must also highlight the negative influence of some couples that we have at that moment by our side or we have arranged to spend the rest of our lives by mis take. Yes, it is true that there is a saying that says that behind a great man there is a great woman or vice versa, obviously, it is also true.

There are couples who, because of their culture, education, resentments, examples of life through which they have passed in their childhood or through various situations experienced during their existence, become a time bomb and another stone on the road to success for someone who wants to be an entrepreneur and generator of success.

I've seen it every chance I get. The examples of failure that go hand in hand with an interested or toxic couple are countless. Some women or men have always sought a place in the world, trying to conquer a wealthy or powerful couple. Some succeed, others do not. Many times, in the face of the insecurity of their lives, they join with a couple of occasion to which they see some economic potential and, therefore, a security umbrella for their existence. At the same time, it turns out that it was all a lie that they bought, and the deceptions appear, accompanied, sometimes, by furtive new loves, until that badly initiated relationship is cut off definitively.

Many people, unfortunately, tend to choose their partners badly, who in many cases turn out to be love phonies and compulsive mythomaniacs par excellence.

A person unable to project himself in business buys illusions that will never come true, sees capacities in the other that do not exist, everything ends in disillusionment. Some people manage to get out of the spider's web, others cannot; they wonder where they would go and then they endure and forgive supposedly all sorts of affronts, betrayals, and lies.

Those who suffer from mythomania also suffer from envy and invariably be tray. These practices only delay and harm those who practice them; sooner or later, these dark characters are discovered, and they will never reach the dreams they aspire to in their lives, they will only experience flashes like fireworks.

Other people want to dominate with their mediocrity and destroy the capacities of the couple to be able to reach their destiny. Both men and women who hold this harmful position against their partner are potential traitors and a stone in the road as well.

Let's remember that behind someone great there exists as a couple someone equally or even greater. Success will not be obtained from the hand of the wrong person, interested or negative, let us not deceive ourselves.

If we love our partner, then let's cure ourselves together by reading motivational books, let's do sports together, let's go out and have fun like the first day of the relationship and let's also start the company together. You will never regret the commitment you made. First the inner change, then the decision, the project and the accurate action of both of us as a family.

My stones have been many. I kicked them one by one. Some examples and stories begin with some employees or poorly selected couples who will never stop appearing in our lives, but it will be up to us to know how to identify them and have the courage to get them out of the way.

A particular case that serves as an example of what we are trying to explain was presented to us at the office we opened in Peru. Its name is worth forgetting. We will call it Fatalities. It all started in Buenos Aires, in our offices as distributors of the American brand. He was a boy, apparently, humble and punctual.

When I asked him, he was there? He accompanied us on the adventure in Peru. There he suffered a lot of detachment, especially from his girlfriend, a secretary of our company. He lived depressed, in spite of the luxurious apartment that we rented to him, a semi floor in Benavidez Avenue in Lima that we had arranged for employees and that he shared with

three other elements that also accompanied us. He drove one of the Mercedes vans that we were able to take to Lima, Peru. In those months, love resurfaced in Fatalities' life from the hand of another Peruvian secretary.

When we went to open the Mexico branch in the face of Peru's closure for reasons beyond our control, Fatalities was not very sure about joining us.

The sale in Peru, when it fell into his hands, precisely, fell and crashed, reaching the lowest levels ever seen in our history. It was a heavy stone. It arrived in Mexico City a month after we did. He was housed in a family's house that provided him with a room to rent. In that month, he used the phone line to talk secretly with his Peruvian girlfriend. He devastated her when a very large bill arrived that he did not pay, because he had run away before.

In the meantime, we were in the preliminary stages for the start of the operation in Mexico with the American security company. A month after we arrived, he told us he was going back to Peru. That he wanted to be there for his Peruvian girlfriend's birthday was the silly excuse; his world was an excuse for continued failure.

We had spent on airfare, housing and living expenses during this time. Before leaving, we warned him that if he returned to Lima, his girlfriend would not look at him with the same eyes, for he would return in defeat. He would no longer have the luxurious apartment or the truck we had already sold. Our advice was to wait for his girlfriend to be legally admitted to Mexico so that we could live together again without complications. He didn't listen to us. Impatience won out.

Last we heard; the romance was short lived. Back then, his girlfriend's mother put him in charge of her photography shop. Eventually, the stone melted him down and closed him down. The girl left him for someone else, probably without such a bad vibe, and, as a corollary, he had to return to Buenos Aires, as he told us some time later in an email, sitting on the steps of a bus whose drivers were friends of his father and who covered the Lima Buenos Aires route. Three days on those steps and not a penny in his pocket. That's really what we call stone people.

Conclusion: never move anyone, no matter how trustworthy you think they are. No one is indispensable, only you. We must stress that it is essential to keep gossips away from the company. Never move any friend, employee, family member, etc., if we have decided to take the path of relocating to other lands with our project.

Another piece of advice is not to relate easily. People are very nice everywhere, but everyone is looking for some benefit from you, unfortunately.

There are few people who work with their hearts and really believe in friendship. Most are in search of some advantage. Let's keep our eyes open. Every stone has a great component of envy. Jealousy slows down and is one of the worst feelings a human being can have. Envy is the antithesis of love of neigh bour. It is on the opposite side of the word "friendship". Envy delays, sinks and kills.

Therefore, when we detect any stone in the way, let us not have mercy, for they will not have mercy on us and our interests. He who can hear shall hear. Do not be blind and think that everyone means well to you. Don't be innocent. Stones exist, they are mental tortoises that abound, they are parasites that enter our lives to block them and destroy our progress. In short, they are great resentments.

Chapter 11: Opening Doors

"Man realizes himself to the same extent that he commits himself to the fulfilment of the meaning of his life.

VIKTOR FRANKL

By the end of 2001, Argentina was in chaos once again. This time, with the help of a bank corralito. People began to panic and started withdrawing all their savings from the banks. The banks, in turn, decided not to hand over a single penny, arguing that the customers' money was no longer in their coffers. Yes, it was that simple. This situation, I believe, was the high point of my hope in that country. It was a scenario I never expected to hear or see, it was the hell Dante described in his play. But there, in that country, he was presented by some unscrupulous bankers and politicians in all their splendour and brazenness.

By that time, we had a successful company, a distributor in Buenos Aires, with employees like the ones I described above, in a party atmosphere and achieving the million-dollar goals in one year easily. It was all heavenly, ideal; we lived in a bubble while outside our offices the magma of discord was soon to burst; it was overheating like the caldera of a volcano.

I decided to undertake a new adventure by continuing with the same line of business, as an associate company of the U.S. group. At that time, the rumour began that they were about to open operations in Peru, so I headed there without further thought. It was the prison of the corralito or the freedom to continue on the path of success that we had experienced in Argentina. Previously, I communicated my decision to our partner, with whom we made a settlement.

He tried to convince my partner to stay, but it was no use. The uncertainty, the marches, the changes of government followed one another, three or four in one year, the breaking of the windows of the banks by hooded men who confronted the police in the streets, the pots and pans of the neighbours sounded like a symphony at night and the meetings of the same on every corner of the city at sunset were already a classic; it was not a good sign that something was changing, but that it was getting worse. People were never able to recover their entire savings again.

I travelled to Chile first. There were the directors for Latin America of the U.S. corporation. I didn't know anyone of those levels, much less in Chile, I didn't even know who I had to address, and behind me there were nothing but pleasant memories with a taste of tango.

In Argentina it was my partners who had the relationship with the managers of the
Argentinean power station; therefore, my presence in Chile was not even a reference point.

With me I carried a portfolio presenting my achievements as one of the most successful offices and my UFV (sales force units) plan that had surprised the corporation's sales trainers so much.

I found out, through the Yellow Pages guide, the address of the corporation in Santiago de Chile, since I didn't even have it. I didn't call; instead, I decided to go directly to them with just my folder, my business plan and my suit.

It was a multistorey corporate building with a luxury door and reception, as befits such a New York style corporation. I went over to the counter where the receptionists were. One of them, without much of a smile on her face, greeted me. I presented my personal card and told her: "I was a distributor in Argentina, and I would like to talk to the general director of Chile to present a project about opening in Peru, which is the new region to be opened".

The lady's surprise was great when I also added that she didn't have an appointment and didn't know who to talk to about it. Immediately, her answer was that it was impossible for any director to attend me, because they never attend anyone, much less without an appointment, as she said, very sure of what she was saying.

Instead of settling for his answer, I insisted without knowing where I got the strength from and said: "I come from the other side of the mountain range especially for this, please help me to get this interview; if you don't get it, I'll leave by the same door I came in and you won't see me anymore".

To which he replied that he would try, but that it was certain, as he had already stated, that I would not be received. He picked up the phone and called the country manager, that is, the director of that big building, of the megacorporation from which the corporation managed all of Latin America. I could not believe how "good" the receptionist had been. I think she called because she was convinced that I would not be attended to and that she would prove me right, and so that, in the end, I would not bother her anymore.

His face transformed when he was told from the other side of the phone to come up, that it would be a pleasure to receive me. He told me later that this was the first case he had ever seen happen and that it was my lucky day.

I went upstairs to the offices of the country's director general, who was a Mexican. He received me very well. I told him about our experience and the achievements we had made in Argentina.

I showed him our photo album of the training trips, the diplomas obtained and our business plan. He was satisfied and surprised by our method.

I expressed our intention to invest in the new opening that the multinational was planning in Peru. After a long talk, he offered me to stay in Chile, but I told him that I considered Chile to be a very saturated market, since it was one of the first countries in Latin America where the multinational landed; Peru, on the other hand, was a virgin country.

He understood perfectly, so he asked me to get in touch with who we will call Carlos, who, at that time, was in charge of opening the offices in Lima. I left that meeting very happy, the doors were open.

The corollary of this story is that you never give up, even if you think it's im possible. As long as there is life, there will be hope and you never know when the opportunity will open the doors to success definitively. Let's say "no" to the fear of trying a thousand times until we reach the goal we set on our path. Perseverance is the key; action and the conviction of triumph are decisive.

Chapter 12: Pursuing a goal

"Follow the opposite path from the custom and you'll almost always do well."

JEAN JACQUES ROUSSEAU

I ran to the first phone I could find to communicate with my partner and wife even then. On the other side of the mountain range, it looked like fireworks full of joy that exploded through the phone. The first step was taken. She prepared everything for the departure. That Fatalities we talked about joined the adventure, a secretary, a supervisor and a sales supervisor, all of them Argentineans. I forgot about the two cats, a Siamese and a black cat that years later the much talked about Fatalities would leave lying somewhere in Mexico in our absence.

They left Buenos Aires with all kinds of luggage in one of the Mercedes Istana vans. They left Buenos Aires and cut the Argentine territory in half, travelling through several provinces. They crossed the Andes like San Martin and arrived in Santiago de Chile.

For my part, while those preparations were going on in Argentina, I travelled to Lima to make my first contact with Carlos. In Lima, not even the furniture was ready at the corporate headquarters. Everything was limited to a semifloor in a good area of Lima. I was the first one to show up asking for a distribution, but I was the last one to get it. Later I will tell you the details, I will talk to you about the envy and how bad a director this Carlos turned out to be. His end was also regrettable, since a month after starting the operation in Peru, he was thrown out of the offices without being able to take even a pen from the desk he occupied.

A few years later, in Mexico City, life sometimes shows you the face of God's justice or of the laws of the universe that God planted; to our surprise, this Carlos visited us, since we were number one in sales and, therefore, a potential client for what he was selling as a free promoter: cable for installations.

We've always seen the end of those who act with bad intentions in life. In this area, we have seen that many commercial managers are clouded by their arrogance. They think they are eternal and untouchable at the top of the corporations, and nothing could be further from the truth. They fall like hail from the sky when they least expect it.

As you can see, I have strayed from my first contact with the ineffable Carlos. Very nice, but it turned out to be very false. It all seemed unbelievable at first. I rented a whole flat in Miraflores, on Benavidez Avenue, for the travelling group in the first instance. Immediately, I returned to Santiago to wait for the contingent that came with my partner.

I was really excited at the time about the big changes we were adapting to. For the first time, we were touching uncharted territory. Countries never dreamt of, dream landscapes, different foods, incredible cultures.

I already knew Europe, Cancun, Brazil and Punta Cana as a tourist, but this was something totally different, because it was about settling down in a different country than usual and setting up a company for the first time in unknown terrain.

We stayed in Chile for a couple of days before starting the journey from Santiago to Lima. It was five days with its incredible nights of travel through deserts, seas and jungles, unique landscapes that mark those ancient territories of the Inca civilization.

Since nothing could be sold in Argentina, since the money was frozen in the banks and the trucks had cost quite a bit, we decided, in order not to lose part of our capital, to travel with it and try to sell the truck in Peru after nationalizing it, and in the meantime, to use it for the sales force units.

We started one morning in February 2002. We crossed the whole of Chile. Beautiful landscapes. Our first destination was the Atacama Desert, one of the hottest in the world. While we were shooting on the Pan Americana, I was behind the wheel of Fatalities. At one point, a police patrol stopped us for speeding. We knew these guys were tough, but we figured we could talk nicely like they did in Argentina. Nothing further than that assumption.

They took away Fatalities' driver's license, another example of the stone man, and asked us to wait three days to pay the fine. We asked, we begged, but it was all in vain. So, we drove to the village where the offence would be and where the driver's licence would be. It could not be otherwise, nor was luck in this case with Fatalities.

The court told him that it was impossible to bring the date forward so that he could pay the fine and get his licence back.

We decided to continue on the road and abandon the aforementioned driving license, which is very difficult to obtain in Argentina. In those countries you have to pass many exams, as if it were a university career; likewise, and in spite of so many procedures, traffic accidents do not stop happening, unfortunately. On the other hand, in countries like Mexico, where everything is easy and bureaucracy is conspicuous by its absence, you can quickly get a driving license on the same day you apply for it and, incredibly, accidents are not so many and people drive carefully, that's what happened to me back in 2003; today I don't know if it's still like that, but back then everything was easy in Mexico.

We were approaching the Atacama Desert and the heat was being felt. It was a snow white spot, but it was boiling sand. On that route, which seemed to be made of dust, a last post appeared to stop, eat something and carry water, as the next place was far from this last point.

We began to move forward through a lunar landscape dotted, at times, with incredible archaeological remains of the Inca culture. We stopped at one of them. It was unreal.

We never stopped to sleep. We drove in shifts. After a few days of traveling, we reached the Peruvian border.

Incredibly, in the rush to travel, once again, Fatalities and the other two girls had not been able to finish the passport process and believed that Peru bordered Argentina and would not need a passport. Nothing could be further from the truth, since Peru does not border Argentina and that is where they realized their miscalculation of geography. So, they went down to talk to the Peruvian authorities, who, always very kind, let them in, while their passports arrived in Lima.

We continue on roads never imagined. Bordering mountains where only one car could pass and where, in some stretches, the small route or rocky strait was inclined by forty five degrees due to the earthquakes that occurred in the area. At the sides of the road there were a number of small square improvised chapels with candles lit inside; I could not imagine who was doing this work, for no one could be seen wandering about in these places. We assumed that they were truckers who took these routes to carry their goods. Some altars were dedicated to the Blessed Virgin, and others, who knows what kind of idolatries they really feared to observe. Knives hung from these makeshift shrines framed a scene from a horror movie at times.

We seemed to be enveloped in an atmosphere brought from other times, the absolute solitude, the desert in all its extension and expression, the mountains hit by the constant earthquakes twisted the path of the road along its cliffs worthy of respect, which seemed to end in the underworld. One early night we reached a point of no return.

The little towns along the lonely road had no electric lights, only candlelight. The faces of their inhabitants in the darkness of the impenetrable night drew a landscape of diffuse, almost ghostly shadows that followed one another on the edge of the dark asphalt, among the dust, the dry earth and the stars. In this context, that night we passed by one of these places with its dark and strange inhabitants.

We then commented on how lucky we were that no one stopped us and assaulted us, for that was the impression the journey gave, when, suddenly, someone almost drowned in his choppy words, at the sight of the fright, shouted: "Waico forward! ».

Waico is the word they use in Peru to describe an overflow of a river that drags large stones and all sorts of things. We stopped. The first thing was to think about going back to the little town immersed in the darkness of the night, where people shone with machetes at their waists and where alcohol was the common currency among the shadows. Backwards,

101

nothingness and perhaps misfortune; we risked having a bad time. Ahead, just a chance to get through it alive, maybe. At last the courage to cross that overflowing river emerged. At that moment, I thought that, if all this was worthwhile and necessary to continue our successful enterprise in another country than the one, we left behind in ashes, after the moment of doubt, I said: "Go ahead!

For a moment, I came to miss the corralito, the nighttime demonstrations in Buenos Aires, the union marches and the roadblocks. To top it all off, we were three young men and three young women. If they saw my partner, a blonde and very beautiful, coming down in those moors, and the other two girls, also well presented, we were lost. But we decided to cross the waico without further ado.

We consulted it together, even the cats participated in the debate, because they looked at me disconcerted, with eyes as big as the full moon. They seemed to sense the danger.

We all made the sign of the cross and took courage. In front of us there was a river, whose depth we did not know. There were some big rocks crossed on the road that covered half the water coming from the right side, coming down the mountain, while on my left hand the river cascaded down, who knows where, in an endless precipice.

Every time I think about it, I wouldn't repeat it. All at once we decided to move forward and not stop shouting until we were on the other side. Dodging stones that kept falling, plus the ones that were already in the way, we reached the other side; there wasn't that much depth, even today I don't know how we crossed it.

The next day, we arrived at a small town already in the Peruvian highlands. We were very hungry after such a night. We entered the first place that looked like a typical food office. There was nothing else. We had gone through the whole town and the most decent thing seemed to be this place. When we entered, we asked for a menu or the menu of the day, but it didn't exist.

There was only one dish to taste. "Well," we said, "nothing could be worse, at least something was better than nothing. I asked what the delicacy was. They answered that the dish was cui. I had never heard that word. I asked him to show me what it was. In the back of the restaurant there were some people tasting this curious and tiny dish. When I saw on the plate a kind of field rat open in the middle, with a long tail and everything, we decided to run away and wait for the next town. Maybe we would have better luck and some ham and cheese sandwich would be waiting for us.

And to think that Peruvian gastronomy is among the best in the world, and that I certify it, but that town seemed not to have passed by.

The route began to deviate through landscapes that were both silent and beautiful, through seas and jungles, through the Nazca lines, lonely deserts with dunes that ended in a sea of incredible deep blue colours, whose contrast with the desert, combined, resulted in a unique image. We arrived in Lima after five days of uninterrupted travel. All to embrace a dream of success.

There are no limits, as you will see, when dreams are strongest. There are no waicos, no jungles, no deserts, no cliffs, no stones on the way that can hinder the progress towards the destination that we, with passion and certainty, trace. When we are aware of success, it reaches us irremediably.

Our first objective was fulfilled: to arrive at our new home and set up our company. Before I returned to Santiago, I left a lawyer to set up the business partnership. When we arrived, we rented our first office, an old house in Miraflores, and waited for the signature of the distribution contract. We had arrived first, but we would sign last thanks to the bad predisposition of the commercial director, the superb Carlos.

Chapter 13: Our Peruvian History, between Pisco and the Lima Cause

"If we intend to move forward, we must go back and rediscover the precious values, because all reality revolves around moral foundations and because all reality has a spiritual control".

MARTIN LUTHER KING

Nothing was structured yet in Lima. It was just Carlos and a couple of other employees. We got there too early. We started talking to other distributors in Argentina. But, once again, we fell into the trap of business friendship.

In business, there is no such thing as friendship; moreover, it is a bad word to keep in mind, we will always be disappointed.

In view of the situation in Argentina because of the corralito, many people took up our idea of opening a distribution in a virgin country like Peru. Everyone started to contact us to find out about the place and the conditions to enter the business. Some old acquaintances of ours also joined these instances. They travelled to Lima and we got them an appointment with Carlos.

We speak very highly of them. They didn't return the favour, they spoke ill of us for no reason, because we had never had more commercial dealings with them. Their strategy was to defend us before the multinational, saying that we had no experience, because in view of the lack of personnel to move to Peru, the idea of these businessmen was to associate with us, and so they proposed it to Carlos.

Over time, Carlos proposed us to make a partnership with them as the only way to obtain a distributor in Peru. We could not believe it. Since they had no one to send to organize everything there, they preferred 50% of something to 100% of nothing, and they knew about our expertise in sales organization; therefore, it was safe business to associate our forces for them, but not for us.

We didn't need investment, neither did their presence, because they were always below our numbers in Argentina; these people didn't contribute anything, so it was all a trap. We were outraged. Carlos told us that if it was not like that, it could not be. What a bad person we thought this was, who some time later would become that cable salesman on the streets of Mexico.

After so much effort, we had to share our company with two small vultures who had no more than one year of business experience in this field. We couldn't believe there was no one else in sight to jump on this mental midget of a sales director.

The operation began with some Peruvian companies. We had already been waiting for two weeks, plus the months of previous waiting from our arrival to that day.

We heard that we would be visited by the directors for Latin America, two Chileans who were very dear to us at the time. We asked for a meeting and Carlos refused. We stood guard at the offices until one of them showed up. Fortunately, he wanted to interview us. He knew about the recommendation that the director of Chile had made. He asked us why we hadn't started yet, since for him everything was in order.

We talked to him about Carlos. He promised us he'd talk to him. Our prayers came true. Then the new national commercial manager appears on the scene, which we will call Mayo.

A real motivator and an excellent sales manager. We met with him and the next day we signed the contract almost two months later than other companies. Carlos, as we mentioned, was fired after a month without any prior notice or time to explain the reason for his policies. Those two other acquaintances who wanted to set us up with Carlos sold out little over the months, bad deeds never pay well.

Immediately, we climbed to the first position in sales over all the distributors, more than twenty. We opened a new office in the luxurious San Isidro. We began to travel inland to set up other offices there. Sales were on the rise. We made a trip to Paracas for training. A truly magical place. We stayed in a top class hotel in the area with all the salespeople in the company.

We apply the same sales method. The results were visible during the months that the American company was present in Peru.

At that time, for being the first place in sales, the vice president of the corporation visited our offices worldwide. They had a great dinner in the best hotel in Lima at that time. They displayed good food and typical dances, speeches and drinks.

On the other hand, in those instances, Fatalities took over the total management of sales, since the two girls that we took over, inexplicably and to our astonishment, left the company for a supposedly better economic proposal that ended in total frustration for them, since soon after they returned to Buenos Aires after going through terrible experiences where they were taken to the Amazon jungle, suffering all kinds of humiliations until they were able to escape, as they told my partner before returning to Buenos Aires, in a kind of confession and repentance. They also told him that it was Fatalities' stone that encouraged them to leave our company, and that after doing this, he kept all the command of the operation, to our misfortune.

Knowing the character, and over the years, I've come to believe them. So, we went down to a third place immediately, as was to be expected with such a burden. It was also the last month of sales in Peru. Two offices, one structure, everything was paralyzed because the stock on Wall Street fell to its lowest level.

One day in September 2002, the directors of Latin America gathered all the distributors together again in the same hotel as the inauguration to inform us of the definitive closure of the offices in Peru.

All the distributors were outraged. We, after a few months of operation, many of them in the first place, had recovered the investment and earned a few dollars, but the rest were about to start operating or had committed to buy vans, fit out offices, among others.

All the distributors in the hotel room had been stunned by the news. They started planning to go through the courts. We, however, saw the opportunity and the bright side, so we chased the two corporate executives out of the elevators in a hurry.

I ran to catch up with them. I was able to intercept one of them. As the elevator de scended, I expressed our desire to continue in another country with the company. He asked me if we were crazy after what had happened. I answered that we were not, or maybe a little, but it was nothing serious. He told me that he would be sending me an email to answer me so that I could expand on the subject, but that it was feasible.

This is what I call perseverance. While the other companies were lamenting and de bating how to make a judgment for the damages allegedly caused, we did not hesitate. We knew that every trial entails an eternal wait with no guarantee, and to this, we must add the cost of the lawyers plus the headache. The courts of any country are crammed with unfinished business and bad lawyers abound and abuse them.

We were invited on several occasions to participate in long discussions with lawyers who would resolve everything in one fell swoop, that's what other distributors told us, because we never went there to waste our time. We were in a hurry to close two offices, liquidate the payroll we had and wait confidently for a future full of light was what we did.

In less than a week, the long awaited mail appeared. We were asked, in return, to sign a settlement and withdraw a check for the payment of commissions that had been withheld from us for possible future departures and that we had not generated due to good sales work. We agreed immediately, and that same afternoon we went to collect and sign.

On the same day of the settlement, we received a call from the director of Latin America, offering to meet to discuss a proposal for us. It was an afternoon at Larcomar, a shopping mall in Lima that is very well done in terms of architecture and charm. There, over coffee, he offered to move our company to one of five countries that we wanted and where they had corporate headquarters.

The options were Argentina, Chile, Brazil, Costa Rica or Mexico. The first two were discarded because of what I told you before. For example, in Argentina the situation remained the same, in Chile the market was saturated, and in Brazil, the Portuguese language was not our strong point. There were two options left: Costa Rica, which is a dream country with a lot of economic potential for investment, but we let ourselves be tempted by the enormity of the market offered by Mexico, one hundred million inhabitants, its good people, its dream landscapes and its rich gastronomy.

I had already been on vacation once in the Riviera Maya and I liked everything, not to mention the landscapes. Also, in Mexico, the number of distributors had been reduced. We had everything ahead of us.

He gave us the contact in Mexico City, and we headed there. I took the first plane in sight while my partner finished liquidating everything once again.

We loved Lima and Peru, the people are friendly, with a rich culture, open to foreign investment. It seems to me one of the ideal destinations to start over.

Lima is a beautiful, archaeological and cultural city, exquisite food, ceviche, octopus with olive tree, the Lima cause of chicken or shrimp are my favourites, along with pisco, a drink of incredible flavour; a sea that resembles a postcard brought from other times; the ravine is the bohemian of the night, while the pearl that goes into the sea is, without a doubt, the Nautical Rose, and if we add a walk through Miraflores, we will be captivated by the charm of Lima. If we want to fall in love even more, we can read a poem by Gustavo Adolfo Bécquer, my favourite poet, while we taste a pisco at Salto del Fraile, which is the ideal place, where the waves break with all their bravura until they splash us.

A few miles away, the beaches of Asia are a delight. To get there we must pass through a lunarlike landscape full of sea, desert and Inca pyramids. Something incredible.

To conclude, I'm going to bring up an anecdote that happened to us in Lima and that perfectly paints a picture of an important issue that we must take into account when we set up our sales organization in any country.

We experienced what it was like to pay a high or low commission, but with shortrange incentives, rewarding high production. We started, as always, by rewarding production with bonuses and prizes, plus a low commission for each account. At that time, we had two offices, one in San Isidro and the other in Miraflores.

We paid a salary plus a commission to the salesman of twenty dollars, while the other distributors paid one hundred for each new client recruited, which seemed like an exaggerated commission to us.

At that time, I commissioned each new contract at almost $800. It was a truly memorable business; with that amount, we had to buy the equipment and do the installation and service when it was due. It was a golden time for the American corporation and its stock on Wall Street was always up. Everything seemed to be out of a Disney story.

We had an interesting sales and installation structure that we were able to form immediately after arriving in Peru. When some businessmen began to contact some elements that we eliminated due to low production, it was that the panorama became a little complicated for us. They were paying a hundred dollars commission and we were paying twenty dol lars. We were worried.

A bad counsellor is to feel fear; the same at that moment penetrated our foundations. We were first in sales nationwide among about twenty distributors. Fearing that they might offer our salespeople better terms and thus disrupt our sales force, we also increased the salesperson's commission to one hundred dollars. Then everything collapsed. People were no longer motivated as they were before the increase.

It was like a lot at once, and why else, they wondered. Now there was no prize to be won. Everything looked small. The scheme didn't work, and it never worked for all those distributors we saw implement it in all the countries where we set up our organizations.

People move better with high profits to high productions. A high commission for a low production numbs, does not motivate, does not produce positive energy, kills ambition. This was our first lesson in sales organization. It was that way that we always, from that moment on, paid normal commissions and great prizes to the production, achieving the results, that the company needed a thousand new accounts per month, and so much so that our sales coordinators always surpassed the line of four thousand dollars per month in profits.

As a corollary, Peru is a wonderful place, with incredible people and a country worthy of any intelligent investment.

Chapter 14: Arriving on Aztec soil

"When you see the applause of triumph, let the laughter you have caused by your failures ring in your ears as well.

JOSÉ MARÍA ESCRIVÁ

I arrived in November 2002. It seemed like a giant city to me. It has thirty million inhabitants. Its volcanoes, the Popocatepetl and the "sleeping woman", crown the city. It's a beautiful sight on clear days. Around the city, its forests and mountains fill it with a unique greenness. Places like Ajusco, Cuernavaca, Valle de Bravo, the rock of Bernal, Tequesquitengo, the thermal waters in Tequisquiapan, Guanajuato, or many other destinations delight on weekends. It is a country of such a polychrome and diverse landscape that one will never get bored with discovering new tourist adventures. There are unique places, friendly people, unparalleled attention, unique delicacies to taste, and a history that will leave us speechless, where the Aztec and Mayan cultures mix with the Spanish and dazzle us at every turn.

When I spoke in a previous chapter about the lack of bureaucracy in Mexico and the great possibilities for foreign investors, I am not exaggerating in any way. To give you a concrete example. To gets the residency, called the FM3 document, we approached the Mexican consulate in Lima, Peru. There we said that we wanted to invest in Mexico and that we were distributors of that company. In forty eight hours, we obtained our residency as investors in Mexico and our FM3. Incredible Mexico, a great country, unlike other countries where everything is much more complicated, as happened to us in El Salvador, for example.

Peru and Panama are also very receptive countries and easy to obtain residency, they are very open to foreign investment and are very friendly people, like the Mexican.

The first thing we did was to attend the meeting to present our project to the new commercial director in Mexico, a very nice American from San Diego.

In the American corporation, I met many Americans in those years who were directors of the multinational; I must say, based on my personal experience, that I never came across an American with a bad attitude in the corporations, they always walk in good humour, they are very friendly and enterprising worthy of imitation.

On one occasion, unknown young Americans introduced themselves to me and my wife and helped us with a small altercation in a hotel in Cuzco when I visited the wonderful Machu Picchu. This is how they are always, given to help in every occasion and place these nice northern Americans. Perhaps it is not for nothing that they have reached the summit of success as a country, despite the crises and wars.

We, in particular, could be said to have learned a great deal from American sales methods and philosophy. They are great promoters of culture, which is reflected in their great thinkers, films, books, companies, and transmitters of an idiosyncrasy of life aimed at the culture of work and personal success like no other.

The director from Mexico was quite enthusiastic, we were already backed by a few years of experience in two countries in the same company, so he was amazed by our per severance. Immediately, I set out to build a business partnership, the first essential step in starting a business venture.

A month later we were ready to start. Company registered in the public registry, social security, foreign investment institute and tax department.

We went in search of the office we got in Colonia Roma, where an earthquake of significant magnitude made us dance like never before, and the desks also danced while, holding on to the little train, we tried to outline some broken prayer among the three of us who were in the office that day, late at night. In the distance, the fires from the electrical installations on the lampposts sparkled like fireworks on New Year's Eve. That's how Mexico received us, with a somewhat hectic party, only the mariachis were missing. Luckily, on that occasion, it didn't go over too well and there were no injuries or falls from buildings.

Immediately, the director told us that of the eighty distributors only three remained, since the rest had been thrown out because they accumulated many casualties and fraud. These three remaining distributors were completely disappointed, they hardly sold any more. He asked us to talk to them and try to motivate them based on our experiences in how they could reorganize. We set out to get the job done by the country's operation manager, so we did, we contacted them.

In a first meeting, we were asked what we were doing there if it was all over. We, on the other hand, began to talk about the virtues of the American company and the great prospects for growth, but even the almost eight hundred dollars they were paying did not excite them; it was eight hundred dollars for each new commercial or residential contract, which was a challenge for us and an excellent payment for our services from the corporation.

We focused on our growth when we saw the lack of motivation that these last distributors of the brand had. After seeing our beginnings in sales, everyone got excited and began to develop again. The corporation reached over forty distributors soon after, based a bit, I think, on the enthusiasm boost we gave them.

We initially set up the notice to recruit staff in all areas. As you may remember, the Argentinean we had brought with us, Fatalities, left us because of his supposed Peruvian love. We were alone, my partner and I, when we received a desperate email from a certain Javier, a real character we had met in Lima and who was the manager of those businessmen who wanted to associate with us, trying to harm us with Carlos in Peru. He was a nice guy, very happy, he had sold almost nothing in Lima, and we knew that he had only dedicated himself to wooing another Peruvian and was in love with her, without being paid much in love with her.

In the mail, he asked us to please take him to Mexico, since he had stayed in Lima without a dollar because those businessmen who were friends of Carlos had not paid him either and had returned to Argentina to escape from the situation.

He was practically on the street, as the former commercial director of Peru had him staying in the house for a few days, but his limit of stay was already running out for obvious reasons. Our first thought was negative. We had been burned by this Fatalities who had returned to Lima and we did not want to pay another ticket again. Such was the insistence that he ended up calling us Mayo, that commercial director from Peru, asking for this unfortunate man too.

We were touched by the situation, feelings in a company are bad advisors, we said; likewise, we decided to pay him a ticket and get him a location in the city. His stay in the company did not last more than eight months, since he also left us because of his Peruvian love and a series of adventures that we will relate.

At that time, sales could only be made to credit card users, which limited the market considerably. But we were waiting for better times. That's what it's all about, always waiting for the moment in these corporations when you're a distributor.

And here's an important lesson. When it comes to large companies using distributors and dictating their policies that agents must obey to the letter, there are going to be different contexts or moments. It is important to know that there is no evil that lasts a hundred years; therefore, let us know how to wait, be patient, accompany the different moments of the corporations without giving up.

We also intuit that the loving Fatalities returned to Lima for this reason, the topic of credit cards, along with the excuse of love, which did not last long. His paradigm dictated to his head that it was impossible to sell to customers who only had a credit card, there would be no market to his mind, everything would be a failure, he began to think with his small mind and the fear of failure paralyzed him. And since he believed that in Lima, he could develop some delirious business, he made the decision to leave.

Instead, this Javier had nothing to lose. He knew he was a good salesman. He was, and he proved it, too bad his emotional imbalance betrayed him.

We were not afraid to sell only to credit card users, and so we moved forward with blind faith in the project and the country we had chosen. Never back down is the watchword.

If we see that the corporation changes its policies for any reason, let's stand by it so that, when the winds pick up, we can gain momentum and sail towards the success that awaits us.

In this context, we sold and climbed to first place among the other remaining distributors. People started to join, the trainings were daily, and the motivation was also high. We applied the method learned, which we will explain later in the book, and it also gave the expected results. Quickly, we were in high five figure bills selling to customers with cards. So much progress was made, and we were crowned in this way, we were very happy.

Soon after, they released the credit. The expectation that we had accumulated in order to increase sales turned out to be a reality. I remembered then all the companies that were in conflict with the American corporation and that were still far from making their demands come true, while we continued to invoice the same amount of commissions that they were paying from the beginning, those eight hundred dollars per new account that were given only in Mexico, while in other countries the scheme had changed and the same had been cut.

Incredibly, and despite the drop in stock in New York and its main CEO out of the game in that 2002, the corporation in Mexico continued to move forward, wanting to grow and maintain a practically captive market that it had managed to obtain in three years of operation. In that year 2003, we managed to connect some two thousand new clients and surpassed the million dollar mark.

Then, as we will see after a small cut, we restarted in May 2004 with a new commission scheme in which, if the business partner reached a target set by contract, you would be around six hundred dollars of commission. Between that date and May 2006, we achieved the figure of three thousand five hundred new clients, and we were always in first place among more than forty new distributors.

They had restructured the corporation, and everything was on track. Year after year, we surpassed the million dollar turnover figure as distributors.

Returning to the situation of the beginning of our company in the Federal District of Mexico, while the issue of selling to card customers lasted, our sales manager, Javier, remained. Unbelievably, he was also stung by the topic of love by correspondence with his former love from Peru. Over time, we discovered that the girl was dedicated to the easy life and he made it even easier for her, sending her about a thousand dollars a month, a third of what she was earning in our company.

112

He called a friend to work with us, an alleged star salesman whom we will call Matich es the nickname used in Mexico to name the meddlers.

This ungainly character of Uruguayan origin was a real busybody. He showed up with his girlfriend on his back, like a backpack, for which he also applied for a job. The young woman said she had mastered the administrative arts to perfection, and Matiches, the art of selling, so she was left to lead a sales force in the area with our scheme. At first, she did quite well and understood the method.

Javier began to argue that he felt very lonely and that it was his intention to bring his Peruvian girlfriend.

We couldn't believe it. History repeated itself over and over again with the Peruvian girlfriends. To be able to bring her, special permits are needed, such as a visa, and to reside you need an FM3, an indispensable document for foreigners in Mexico.

From what we know, he got a lawyer who specializes in immigration. In less than a month, we were already counting on the presence of this nice girl with slightly strange habits.

The training trips followed one another without sparing costs for vendors and supervisors, where we performed various activities. We went on them in Acapulco or had meetings with juicy grills at Mount Ajusco, or even training sessions at Lake Tequesquitengo or at the Valle de Bravo and its Golf Club.

In places like Teques, where after sales training we would take the boats, in which we would sail the lake of the same name and tie up a banana boat or water skis for everyone's amusement, and at night we would get on a boat that would take us on a tour around the lake to the sound of the disco that was playing there.

Once we participated in an Aztec temascal, which is an oven sauna built of bricks where several people get in and occupy the figure of the circle with someone who is the di rector of the meeting in almost total darkness, and where, through a small door, hot stones are introduced that generate an irresistible steam at times, incense in between, and where one has to put his head on the ground to be able to breathe when the atmosphere becomes unbreathable. The duration is three hours for those who want to consider themselves warriors. We did it with our managers and some supervisors, I remember. They all came out quickly from the bottom of one whenever the little door was opened to put in more stones and incense.

Then, when they come out of that hell, they bathe you in herbs and give you an infusion. The next day, don't make any plans, you won't be able to do it, because you will sleep all day. Few of us graduate that day as Aztec warriors enduring the three endless hours.

Other meetings with managers are held in Cancun and in Valle de Bravo, a paradise worth discovering. We also conducted training on the beautiful beaches of Huatulco. With all this I want to tell you that, as you will see, with our sales methodology to implement it is possible to be in the best places and share them even with your employees or schedule courses and trainings for them. The money will flow like the rivers from the mountains to the bowels of the seas, this is for sure. Therefore, do not hesitate to invest part of what you earn in your greatest added value, your most precious assets, your leaders and employees of your company.

At that stage in Mexico, Javier ended up leaving after being abandoned by his Peruvian love. He couldn't stand it and followed her to Peru, where we lost track of him. He didn't do it without first, together with Matiches, selling part of our sales force to the competition.

We discovered them within a week of executing his plan and he made the right decision, which is incumbent upon every major company, to kick that distributor out. At that time, a new layer of supervisors was beginning to emerge who were distant from these two.

Whenever there are old structures in the middle it is difficult to form new ones, as the old sales elements will try to make you 100% dependent on them and the rewards or any compensation will go through your hands and not those of the new people.

It's very important to be in the detail when you recruit new staff. You must isolate them from the rest to train them separately. It is essential to encourage them from the outside until they are mature, until everyone has put on the shirt and is in such a degree of excitement of motivation that it is noticeable, that is to say, that they cannot resist one more day without going out to conquer sales.

We concluded that Javier, despite the support he received from us in all his whims, plus the three thousand dollars he took in monthly, engineered the whole process from the hand of his friend Matiches. They were discovered by my partner, who, when passing by an avenue in the city, saw with astonishment how groups of vendors dressed in our bought uniforms were leaving, and at his head, as their organizer, this sad and spoiled Matiches appeared.

Before leaving the country, Javier, the Argentinean, called us in tears. He apologized for stealing about thirty pieces of equipment from the winery and argued that keeping his girlfriend was too expensive. We laughed; the whole situation was funny. Eventually, we gave up on the complaint, it didn't make sense anymore.

We had paid Javier's fare from Lima and three thousand dollars a month, invited him to dinner at least once a week and gave him a company van to move around in. I had even lent him an apartment to live with his girlfriend without paying rent; besides, he went around with the company Cancun and Acapulco all paid up and I thought what a pity that this way he answered us, I felt really sorry for his attitude.

It was really to cry about as he cried. I consider him an idiot, a madman or a little of both. It's amazing, there are times when I think some people don't value what they have, abuse the trust and end up betraying. It's sadder when people from the same country as my partner, who is Argentinean, betray your trust after everything was given to them like brothers.

Maybe the end is always known, all of them end badly, because bad actions do not pay for the one who does them.

There are other employees who, imbued with envy, try to destroy what we build. Envy grows in neglected societies where failure, at every step, sets the pace of life and those negative minds find no other way out than to display those lowly feelings for those who reach out to them.

That is why we must find the right people to help us move forward on the road to business success, never giving more, even if you like an employee. You must never accept capricious positions. Never give a second chance.

Chapter 15: A New Stage in México Lindo

"Commitment is the courageous response of those who do not want to waste their lives but want to be protagonists of personal and social history".

JOHN PAUL II

It was the end of 2003. Everything had returned to its place. The names of the coordinators were different: Mauricio, Ariel and Flavio.

The corporation hired a new commercial director who was accompanied by a kind of Argentinean secretary or assistant. He revolutionized the lethargy into which the corporation had fallen in Mexico. It also changed the general director, one of the best corporate directors we have ever known.

This new director applied new ideas, all of them very good, among them the incorporation of this new high performance executive. The new director began by cleaning the house inside, sweeping up half the corporation's staff. It is unfortunate that this is a very common practice of bad managers, who, because of these issues of fate, land in the corporations. We experience it even in Panama and Costa Rica, in other companies that are completely different from each other. Perhaps it is due to their fear of relating to historical elements that are in the same. They also liquidate old distributors in the first months, even if they are successful.

I discovered that these directors generally have one common denominator: their big ego, a marked envy of the successes of some distributors, contempt for the employee and a dictatorial handling of situations.

The new commercial director put together a great presentation of the new commission scheme, in which those who produced the most were rewarded. The launch site was Acapulco, in a superior five star hotel.

It was something that captured all the senses of the whole company. Everything was lavish, very well done, with a high degree of motivation. It lasted three days' worth remembering. Already during the time of sale, I generated weekly breakfasts with all the distributors, in which the projection of each agent and his concrete results were evaluated. It moved the foundations from the bottom up. This earned him some enemies in the international arena, as he was gaining power within the corporation, or so he thought.

A few months later, before his first birthday, he was dismissed by the Latin American regional management. His project remained and was implemented by his successors, while he returned to his former position in mobile telephony in Mexico.

In that 2004, it was our turn in the flesh to be liquidated by this director in his maelstrom of finding victims to execute like a zombie from a horror movie. After several presentations and taking advantage of the absence of the Mexican CEO of the company, he asked us to sign a settlement without any excuse. When the CEO returned, I wrote him an email to find out when we would sign the same.

In view of the surprise and confusion, he invited us to a working lunch that the commercial director frustrated, so I insisted, and he received us in the offices on Insurgentes Avenue, in Mexico City.

He asked us not to leave, since we were number one in sales and he really didn't know for sure why the new commercial director made this decision in his absence. Without a minute's thought, we said yes. In truth, we were very comfortable with the company. For years, until our kidnapping attempt, we were number one in sales every month and that sales director was soon fired.

Right on the day of his farewell, we were at headquarters looking at some client accounts with my partner. It was when one of those Chilean Latin American directors who helped us so much in Peru came in and then invited us to participate in Mexico, to perform an almost surgical operation to fire the commercial director, with a check in hand and a cardboard box to dispose of the few belongings. He and his Argentinean secretary were on the street in less than half an hour, literally speaking, crying on our shoulders; incredible the turns of life.

At that time, we were contacted by a new element who had fled from the Argentine economic scene and who had met us in Lima, a certain Francisco, manager of another distributor who had been very well connected with my partner.

When he arrived in Mexico City, we picked him up at the airport as a courtesy. We had scheduled a trip to Cancun the next day. It is an anecdote that encompasses and draws the profile of certain characters that we are sure to encounter in the field of sales. They are the ones we met who sell themselves as the great geniuses of sales.

In some cases, you have to get them off your back; in others, grab the right words and start hitting hard, metaphorically speaking, on every comment or stance of arrogance that you insinuate.

This was the case with Francis, who was forty years old; the more adults and the more failures, the more arrogant they became. On the way from the airport to his place of accommodation, where Flavio and his family already lived, he tells us about his company in Argentina. He had even left a factory in the hands of his brother. Generally, another

117

characteristic is that they act as compulsive mythomaniacs. Given the overwhelming success he was exhibiting, we assumed that he would be touring Mexico and that he was not really coming to work. At least this one had paid his way, we thought.

Upon arrival at the location, we introduced him to the team of people he would join the next day. The proposal had been made to him via the Internet and he had gladly accepted it. At that moment of saying goodbye, he asked me to speak for a moment, at the side and alone.

Incredibly, he asked me for an advance, since he didn't have a penny, even if it was fifty dollars, that he could manage all week. He didn't know the place, he didn't know the food prices, he didn't know anyone, and in his desperation, he asked me for only fifty dollars. We gave him a hundred and told him that on our return we would talk about his place as coordinator within the scheme.

In spite of his arrogance, he proved to be a good element together with Flavio, the other coordinator; they both had three very good campaigns with us, such as 2004, 2005 and 2006. Mauricio, that 2004, decided to return to Argentina, because his wife was pregnant and wanted the child to be born in his country. We saw him again at the beginning of 2006 and he joined the new stage in mobile telephony.

They were three wonderful years of absolute stability, more than a million dollars a year, always projecting the same scheme. In January 2006, the corporate leadership changes again at the highest level. During that time of boom, the three CEOs were good helms men in difficult times for the company. However, the fourth director was a failure. The sunset was in sight.

One of their first measures and objectives was to liquidate the old existing structures, cut commissions in half and declare ourselves "commercial promoters" instead of commercial allies, which we had become since 2004. Between 2000 and 2003 we were dealers, then they called us allies and now we were only promoters and we charged less than half the commission. We didn't like that, we thought it was an abuse and, above all, the bad way this new director was treating us. In November of that year 2006, we signed a settlement after almost seven full years of accompanying the American corporation's project, in which we had a blind faith that even made us cross mountains, deserts, rivers and jungles; in short, strange lands to accompany our dreams and strengthen that commitment with the multinational that always responded so well.

Our settlement recorded an excellent performance in this last period. This was stated in the document that was given to us as a final settlement. We considered it to be a success and did not really understand why this radical change in the commission policy and the selection of the new CEO, who had no idea where he stood. Seeing the picture, we decided to implement a change of course to quickly jump, if necessary, to other business options.

We investigate all possibilities, cable TV, fixed telephony, GPS car technology and mobile telephony. We opted for the latter. With our background, it was easy to negotiate our incorporation into this type of company.

In this case, it was only necessary to find the right moment when new distributors were needed to increase the sales of any corporation. And the time was right. My partner, who has intuition for everything, mentioned a Cuban administrative officer we had in our offices, who contacted one of these cell phone companies and asked for an interview. He did so and got the meeting easily. Never believe that you will not be received with open arms, someone will always be waiting for your professional business services in sales organization and administration, your experience and investment in the project.

The meeting didn't take long, neither did the firm. At that time, I was living in a golf course in the city of Leon, Guanajuato, because the insecurity in Mexico City was already to be feared. I went there once a week and stayed at a hotel near the offices, which were on Reforma Avenue, right in front of the Angel of Independence and in front of the Sheraton Hotel. Then we moved them two blocks away, to London Street, always in the banking area, known as the Pink Zone of Mexico. This is a very touristic area of the city. There we rented two complete floors of office space, which we kept during our incorporation to the cell phone industry.

Later on, we arranged two more floors in our old building in Colonia Roma because of the large size that the commercial operation had become.

The first month on the cell phone we sold four hundred and four new customers with contract values exceeding fifty dollars, so we received a commission of approximately three times the plan sold for each new customer who purchased a postpaid term plan plus prizes awarded by the brand.

This amount was only with one sales force unit consisting of a coordinator, two super visors and about eight salespeople arranged in the area. In the second month we doubled to eight hundred and eleven activations when two more coordinators moved to the telephone structure, moving them from the American corporation, which was already starting to implement its new scheme of commercial promoters with low commission.

Imagine that for an alarm, in this new scheme, they paid the same as they paid for a fifty dollar postpaid contract in cell phones, and let's agree that it's not the same to sell one product as another. The important thing is to know how to adapt to the business circumstances of the moment we are living, without despair and knowing that there will always be a new opportunity that will lead us to success if we do not stop focusing on our economic goals.

For example, an electronic security system is much more complicated to sell because it involves an installation that takes about three hours and people are not desperate to get a piece of equipment; therefore, the production that is achieved is lower compared to that of cellular telephony.

The third month he crowned us with 1,296 accounts. In only three months we were playing the two thousand five hundred contracts with our method of selection, organization, training and motivation. Also, in that same time, we were climbing to a turnover of almost half a million dollars. This scheme is also perfectly applicable in mobile telephony in the area of prepaid airtime with recharge or in any product presented to us for sale.

As knocking door sales force units, we were among the pioneers in Latin America in that early 2006 in Mexico; we were already doing it in Argentina with another company in the years 199798, applying the same method that we perfected, based on our experience, precisely in those years in Mexico. Today, many companies carry out, or try to implement, this successful sales system. But we know that the distribution company that implements it must have lived, felt and breathed the success experienced with this type of sales. We have seen many fails because they could not organize it properly. Examples have been left over from acquaintances in cellular telephony who could not control this scheme, much less achieve successful results in the long term.

This is the proposal. The cards are dealt. The moves to implement are below. Let nothing and nobody stop you, then you can take care of those debts, of your friends, of your unfinished studies, of your hobbies, of your daughter in law, mother in law, of your parents, of your brothers, of your community or country.

First things first, to achieve economic stability, to share and generate jobs to activate depressed economies in the countries where they feel their roots or in their own land, taking care of the stones, of which we already spoke, and isolating themselves, even if only for a while, from their closest environment.

The energies are very subtle when they act for both good and bad, the latter being driven by negative feelings from those we encounter or sometimes from those around us.

In these periods of economic stability, once the sales apparatus we will talk about next was put in place, it has allowed my family and me to travel the world from one end to the other. Europe as a whole, from the Côte d'Azur to the Amalfi Coast, Venice, Portofino, Genoa and Rome. Amsterdam, the Picos de Europa, Switzerland, Austria, Germany, Portugal, Andorra, Greece, Croatia, Rhodes, Istanbul, Antwerp, London or Paris were some of the destinations. It is endless to describe all the places, there are more than thirty five countries we visited, and lived in eight. Canada everything, including Quebec, Toronto and Montreal up to Whistler or Lake Louis, in the Canadian Rockies, always stopping in some hotels that are taken out of a fairy tale, stand like castles in the middle of the mountains, surrounded by snow or at the edge of frozen lakes that are used as a skating rink and where they have fires too.

In the Caribbean, the British Virgin Islands are my favourite, next to St. Maarten or Riviera Maya, from Tulum to Cancun, from Punta Cana to San Andres Island, Aruba or Curaçao. Cruises of the Italian or American brand by all the seas, the Greek islands or the Caribbean, Roatan, Jamaica, Cayman or Cartagena have been some of the periplus, we know all Central and South America. We even drive our own sailboat on a voyage from St. Martens to the British Virgin Islands with Italian friends.

When do we work? you may ask, but always. There is time to enjoy and work at the same time, it is only a matter of planning well, freeing the mind and knowing how to refer those we intuit deserve it, because no one is perfect. We always find employees and managers to take over the operation. I wanted to bring them into this situation not to tell them about my tours around the globe, but to make them realize that all this is within their reach if they apply a good sales organization, and to let them know that it is not a slave job, like so many others, where you cannot look away from the cash register or have weekends or nights off, as it happens in a restaurant, for example.

In our companies, work was rarely done on Saturdays and Sundays. It's not necessary, the production will always be there. When the machinery is started, nothing stops it, it will be like a tornado of passion that generates new customer accounts always, every day, I assure you. And your investment will be minimal, as we will see too.

What killed the project in Mexico was the insecurity, which was already a daily issue, unlike when we arrived, that the situation was not as dangerous as it had been since 20056. In those years, I lived in a PH in Colonia del Valle, around the corner from my favourite restaurant, where every other night we would enjoy the culinary delights of the place.

Then I moved, fearing for safety, to La Herradura, a beautiful colony near Polanco and Chapultepec. It had a heated pool, a security checkpoint for the residents, of whom there were no more than ten, and to top it all off, it was close to the office.

One noon, on Revolution Avenue, in the middle of a busy traffic light, a blond man in a jacket, very well dressed, approached me while I was in my 4x4 truck with the window down smoking a cigar.

I assumed that he came to me to ask for some reference, since the traffic was not moving. Well, no, he did it to ask for my wallet, and he exhibited a large calibre gun. My partner, who was in the seat next to me, was stunned at the moment. I asked her to put the gun away. The guy seemed pretty polite. I was lucky to get an exemplary thief and on top of that, a suit, what more could I ask for. I gave him my wallet, which had about five hundred dollars in cash in it, and told him not to take the cards, which he agreed to do, and he reasonably returned them. Then he asked for my TAG H watch, worth about a thousand dollars. I think the day had been made. In the meantime, he had already put his gun away. I

121

begged him to leave the watch with me, but he threatened to draw his gun again and shoot, so with a smile I agreed to his not very nice request.

Then he disappeared among the cars, crossed Revolution Avenue and got lost crossing the street. Immediately, people got out of the cars, some insulted him even when he was already far away, of course. That was the day I decided to go and live in the interior of the country and to step as little as possible in Mexico City.

The place chosen was León, Guanajuato, the last Spanish bastion in the Mexican independence, and there the beautiful city lost in time stayed. The sky of León is so clear that it seems as if reflectors at sunset illuminate it, just like the one in Madrid. There I lived the 2006 World Cup, obviously my team was the Italian one, and we were also going to the Argentinean one; there, in Leon, strangely enough, they were going to France, the country that invaded them at the time. I never really understood their particular preference. Every time France played, they would rouse the French cocks, but when the Azzurri team killed Zidane and his teammates with their historic goals, my screams drove them out of my house, in the middle of the golf course, a little bit in revenge because most of them wanted Italy to lose.

In short, it was a place of charm in the region of Guanajuato, without a stain; it seemed like one of those cities lost among the alleys of time, but with some modern touches. There we opened a branch where we managed to get about three hundred more postpaid accounts every month. The trip to the city was done once a week or every two weeks to control the situation and shore up what was worthwhile.

Perhaps you have discovered, from the real stories we have lived through and that I am telling you, how simple it will be to maintain this organization once you start it up; it begins to walk on its own. By exercising normal, intelligent control over situations, everything will take its course to achieve the expected success.

The secret is in giving, in investing in internal marketing towards our employees, while to keep up with the times it is necessary to provide aftersales service to customers to avoid customer complaints. These are two vital organizations in this business that we propose. One is administrative, to follow up on the customer, and the second is a well selected, permanently trained and motivated sales structure.

After years of beautiful living and rich eating in Mexican lands, the first robbery I had suffered was not enough, the worst was yet to come. The unthinkable happened. The golf course was heavily guarded. It was impossible to get in. No one had ever been told where he lived. No one knew at what point he might show up at the office. My clothes were very informal, I felt protected in a way. I had taken all the necessary precautions against the criminal wave that was hovering like a black cloud over the dreamy and mariachi Mexico that had so captivated all our senses.

Mauricio had a very bad temper. We had about ten administrative employees and a permanent accountant in the offices. The whole administrative area was in charge of two sisters who turned out to be sinister, they looked like the girlfriends of the Chucky horror movie doll, the cursed doll.

They started working in 2004. In 2005 they had retired because of a heated discussion we had with one of them, the youngest and most disastrous. Very far from what a flower is that was her name, this employee, on that occasion, urged her sister to retire as well; nothing important was the case being discussed, but it transformed it into something personal and terrible, it also dragged her sister's boyfriend, who was a sales supervisor. They had the same name, unusually. They were both Flor, but one had her name in the indigenous language and her older sister in Spanish; in short, they were Flor and Flor, for us they turned out to be a bouquet, but not precisely of flowers, but of problems.

We never allow in our company the formation of couples, it is a time bomb within the same, just have to wait for the moment of detonation, neither brothers, friends and girlfriends, because we have tried them in all these formats. Brothers fight, friends' envy, girlfriend's jealousy with other employees, and so we could continue and expand, but it is not worth it.

Sometime later, in the face of the very bad experiences the young sisters went through, low pay and abuse from their employers, they began to call desperately and intermittently. We were making about $1,500 a month. Where were they going to get that money? Impossible for two girls under twenty one and twenty four, where the base salary in Mexico was less than two hundred dollars.

It was because of their insistence, the bad time the administration was going through and for not finding the right staff to face the rapid growth of the company that, by mistake, we decided to take one of them, the biggest one, which was not the one with the previous problem, but had participated in some way.

In her work she was serious and efficient, she was the one who never generated the problems, but who was unfailingly dragged by her envious sister to do things that limited with stupidity and nonsense.

A few months had passed when a new administrative vacancy arose. The older sister begged us to reinstate her younger sister day after day. Once again, our stupidity was playing tricks on us. Due to the great growth we were experiencing and the lack of suitable personnel, we agreed. We didn't take care of the detail, we thought we could control the situation if it came up again. The lesson is that second times are not good, much less when they quit with such a deployment.

As I mentioned in a previous paragraph, Mauritius had a bad temper. He was fighting with the administration in the daily sales rush because they were not able to process such a large number of daily requests properly, despite having about ten clerks.

One day in September 2006, Mauricio insulted them and chose the youngest for his rampant attack. Not only did they run insults, but also requests through the air, aiming at the girl's head like missiles. All this was done in our absence. Mauricio, tactlessly, in the style of the brave football bar, destroyed the harmony we had managed to achieve for so long. We were on a business trip.

On our return, we gathered the people involved, we had scheduled a trip to Madrid to set up a branch office and we wanted to leave everything very much in order and cut off that hostility. We all agreed, but their stubbornness and pride were stronger; they are people who seem to carry a stone around their neck, they never change, they will be recognized by their stupid pride, clinging to their world of selfish habits, at times they invent an economic world that is not real to demand profits that not even in their dreams they imagined to collect, they have a high dose of envy; therefore, they have very bad luck in everything they undertake.

I remember that it was at night, while walking through the Royal Palace in Madrid, when I received the call. It was Flavio commenting that everything had exploded again, but worse. The younger sister, who was in her third month of pregnancy, reported Mauricio for attempted rape and called the police. Mauricio was all of the above, but never a rapist.

Because of the pregnant woman's accusation, he had to hide in the building's door man's apartment. The police looked for him for an hour, the office was in chaos. Everyone was stunned. My Madrid night was thrown overboard. The mistake we made was our own, that of rehiring people who once let you down; these types of individuals will be the ones who seal your misfortune.

We return immediately to Mexico. Both sisters were thrown out; in fact, we asked them to calm down and take some time to decide what to do. We also thought of compensating them for the services rendered and terminating the employment relationship. We had to restructure the administrative area, but we had all the sales force material intact. That was a good thing. But the worst thing happened.

Mauricio was a casualty too, we suspended him. He was hiding at home with his family, wife and young son to avoid the police officers, who turned out to be friends of the two "flowers", one of them a cousin of the little coven sisters. We were trying to put a cold shoulder to the situation. One of the Mexican sales chiefs had disappeared for a few days without explanation. Someone saw him plotting with the sisters in a night bar, along with a group of people of dubious reputation, which caught the attention of whoever came to us with the comment.

During those days, one of our Argentinean coordinators, Francisco, the superb, was kidnapped by judicial police. He was held at gunpoint for six hours in the middle of the day, and all the cell phones he had in his truck were stolen to give out to the clients they had hired in previous days; all this before the astonishment of an entire sales group of the company that was left shaking. The telephone extortion of the sisters and her boyfriend was now intolerable. They wanted a large payment in exchange for leaving us alone. While we were negotiating the conditions, like a film with Denzel Washington, the one you will surely remember, the one about the kidnapping of the blonde American girl in Mexico, they hit us in the office, expecting to find a warehouse full of cell phones; luckily, there was none.

Flavio and other employees were left tied up on the floor. To top it all off, they drove three cars to pick up my partner's sister from the house where she lived in Guanajuato, with her partner and her two year old son Luciano.

At that moment, it was fortunate that it was not as if an angel had passed by in a prudent lapse of time before taking them out of their house with their wings and out of the clutches of the policemen who had become thugs and kidnappers in their free time. Poor my dear Mexico, what suffering they are going through, I have lived it in my own flesh.

The Mexican coordinator seemed to be in the mix, despite earning over two thousand dollars a month. We didn't want to negotiate anymore. We had a very prestigious lawyer at our side that I will not forget. With a strong personality, he was one of a kind. He contacted us with the highest authorities in the city. They treated us excellently, attending to our problem immediately and referring us to the heads of the judicial police, now gone, as I understand it. Francisco made a photographic recognition and was able to recognize those who had held him against his will at gunpoint, while others recognized those who had robbed the office, names and participants in the events came to light, all of them were from the Judicial Police. Mauricio was still being sought by the patrols, already dressed in uniforms by the friends of the little flower sisters.

We, my partner and I, deduced that, in view of the complaints filed by Francisco, plus ours, everything would become more dangerous if they knew where my partner's family lived; it was just a matter of time before we found out about the golf course in Guanajuato.

It was then that we decided to get tickets for the whole family and to move towards the security that Europe was offering us. Being Italian citizens, it was easy for us to return home, far from so much injustice and impunity.

It was the best decision, why risk more, it wasn't worth it. We tried everything. It was useless. The complaints were lost in the courts, the judges were removed for a moment from their posts, then reinstated. We left behind beautiful years, full of good stories. I think I left a little bit of myself in Mexico.

The summons to testify came a year later, the lawyer told me I had to return. Imagine the welcome that could await us, not for a million dollars would we touch Aztec soil once again. In that year that it took justice to summon us, we could have become just another statistic, but justice has its times, they say. It's impossible to go back and testify about events that took place a year ago in a context of insecurity, as was the case in the country.

My scattered investment. Hastily sold furniture, house, cars, everything in a lifetime.

My whole life was behind me. Luckily, my savings were safe in Europe; it was all we had left, along with my motivational books, my philatelic collection, my guitar and thousands of pictures accumulated from so much walking.

Chapter 16: The Spanish Dream

"Some people get into the bad habit of being unhappy."

GEORGE ELIOT

I visited Spain several times as a tourist. I was very attracted to its culture, its food, its customs and its people. Unfortunately, once our project in Mexico was finished, we had to start again in distant lands. In the early days there were daily calls to our staff of coordinators in Mexico, who were still liquidating all the loose ends that had been left; the liquidation of so many employees, of whom, in many cases, we kept fond memories; all in a gruesome context, everything had to be done while avoiding threats of all kinds from the Flor sisters and their police partners, who were summoned by the authorities, as well as other employees. No one came to testify, they preferred to hide, and justice was conspicuous by its absence.

The family of my partner in full, father, mother, sister and nephew, moved to Spain to avoid the kidnapping promised by the sisters and their accomplices in emails that I still keep in the company's mailbox. It was all in the movies. To avoid leaving Guanajuato, we decided to take them to Cancun in a rented car, and from there to board the plane that would take them to Madrid. Previously, a few days, we lodged them at the home of a Catholic priest, a true icon and friend in the city of Guanajuato. Once in Cancun, they boarded the plane safely. The sisters had sworn to my partner that her family would not escape without us paying a large sum of money, so difficult was the situation.

We met with the people of the American multinational again in Madrid in 2007. They paid very well, four hundred euros a bill, and gave us the equipment they approved separately. This was a big difference from the nonsense that was implemented in Mexico, when we gave up in 2006.

Our successes in sales had crossed borders and had reached Spain, where they were opening a new commission program called Alliance Program; it was the much talked about commercial ally that was invented in Mexico at the time, with excellent results, and that the new leadership of 2006 had transformed from a commercial ally to a commercial promoter, lowering the commission by half. While Spain went up, Mexico went down, even though it was the same corporation, that's how incredible things are in international corporations sometimes.

Keep in mind that there will always be a new opportunity in sight; when one door closes, another opens for an entrepreneur who is clear about a sales organization. It is a question of always looking for and finding an open door where you can develop your project.

127

We must know that the project must always be presented to large corporations that need to sell their services or products. They are the ones that will be able to settle in time and form the important sums of money that their structure will produce, and they are the only ones that can and that have contemplated significant amounts in their budgets for the payment of commissions to their distributors or that can get to pay a million or more a year for the production that is generated.

I remember that distribution companies received more than a million dollars a month for delivering electronic security systems without charge to customers for a monthly fee that did not exceed forty dollars. What was the business then? Simple, Wall Street and your stock price in that context.

At first, in Spain we were going through a bad psychological time. The blow was strong. So strong was it that poor Flavio, in the first six months, suffered a heart attack with his young thirty nine years. They did a catheterization and he had to return to Argentina to recover. It was a major loss, for we were very fond of him.

Mauricio tried to reach Spain and was rejected by the authorities for being declared illegal when he stepped on Spanish soil, so he was sent back to Argentina.

The famous Fatalities, who became a brother in law in Mexico, after making a series of mistakes again, ended the relationship with my partner's sister. It was the right moment to get rid of this heavy stone from that distant Peru. Yes, you read correctly, the famous Fatalities reappeared on the scene a month before the disaster. By email, he applied for a job, and since we were so well off financially, we decided to give him a second chance. See what happens with second chances? It wasn't a month after his arrival that everything happened on Aztec soil, very strange indeed; there are times when I think if such negative people can really trigger such great misfortunes. In the meantime, the aforementioned Fatalities had joined the Guanajuato branch as manager. He also got engaged to my partner's sister. So now he had become a kind of brother in law, to top it all off.

When we moved to Spain, we left the sale of our personal belongings in their hands. He was in charge of the transfer of my partner's family to Cancun, and from there he took the flight to Spain. We didn't want to do it from Mexico City or from Leon, Guanajuato, because we didn't know for sure if the kidnappers would be able to control those airports; being police, it could well be like that, we imagined.

Nothing was left from the sale of everything, as it was used to live for Fatalities. Then he rented a van to take him to Cancun, which cost a fortune. Once at the Cancun airport, he said he did not have enough money for his ticket.

My partner asked me to reconsider for her sister's child. Conclusion: I ended up sending him an extra thousand dollars for his ticket and, after a few days, I had to meet him at Barajas airport.

128

In Spain we did not take advantage of the opportunity that the multinational gave us once again. We were a little saturated after so many years in the ranks of the corporation and still a little destabilized by so much bad experience with the theft and attempted kidnapping. We also had an interview with the corporate director of a major cell phone company. This director was enthusiastic about our proposal. The commission scheme he presented to us was very complex, so we preferred to take another proposal.

Amongst all the options, we have chosen the German company and a marketing consultancy project in its incipient electronic security project. We also signed a distribution agreement with this great German company.

He was a very slow working team at the time, let's agree that these were his beginnings in this business in Spain. Everything moved at a pace unknown to us, a security system took fifteen days to be delivered and installed; impossible to project large production figures.

Remember that we must look for high demand products that we can deliver to the customer within forty eight hours, at the latest seventy two, in order to keep the need for the purchase in the customer's mind.

When we saw the slowness of the scheme and other inconveniences, crisis in the middle in 200708, we decided not to continue wasting our time and decided, after a year, to slowly project to return to Latin America; added to that, Fatalities thrown out, Flavio infarcted and Mauricio rejected at the airport; only Francisco was still standing, it seemed a defeat in the worst of battles and in retreat. Others in this circumstance would have crumbled, we were on the verge, but we understood that this situation was part of the zigzag path that we talk about going down at some point in all business life. The mistakes made were our fault and we were paying for them; we were very permissive with some situations that led us to these instances.

Meanwhile, our reality was passing by and we prioritized having a period of relaxation and doing some tourism to get rid of the stress, for which we travelled and enjoyed all of Spain, what a beautiful country! History at every step plus its delicious meals.

We must always validate or rather test the ground when we arrive at a new location and try to help and influence the policies of the corporations to improve their operations. In our experience we have encountered white elephants as companies, where any change to improve a preestablished scheme was long overdue.

In spite of everything, we sold security systems and GPS for fleet control very well. We sold very well for a short time, because the crisis hit us like a giant wave. The transport companies contracted in their expenses and the sale was stopped drastically. Everyone wanted to wait for the situation to pass. Beautiful Madrid, Spain too. We are located in Las Rozas, a luxurious neighbourhood on the outskirts of Madrid. The banks drastically reduced credit, construction came to a standstill and we suddenly found ourselves with the highest unemployment rate in Europe.

The value of the mortgages had skyrocketed, so all over Spain, families who reserved money for recreation, leisure or tourism were affected. The crisis was on the inside and this was felt by the population.

In that context, for each employee without papers, the fines started from six thousand euros; therefore, that option was ruled out. The operating costs became unsustainable, the continuous inspections took place in a restaurant and a cafeteria in which we invested.

In the middle of the crisis we managed to sell them. It was very interesting how we did it and it showed, once again, that perseverance and decision are key in any business we try to carry out. I think this is the lesson of this chapter, the rest is an anecdote of our Spanish experience.

The cafeteria with Argentine style and products was sold for a while before leaving Madrid. There were attempts to buy the restaurant, but none were successful.

We left it in the hands of my partner's sister. Months passed and nothing happened, while we, in Central America, planned our return to the Latin American sales scenario.

It was when we got tired of waiting and decided to return to Spain to liquidate the business in a week at the latest, we said in those days. It was like that; we took out the ticket and planned the return only for a week. The crisis was then more intense in Spain, but that did not matter to us. We had the firm conviction to achieve it, to sell the transfer of a business closed six months ago seemed impossible, much less to do it in just one week that we had given ourselves.

We arrived in Madrid in silence, no one would know of our presence, all in order to avoid the negativity of our friendly neighbours, who were watching. We published a small notice in the newspaper. Two interested parties called. One of them bought. We signed the papers one day before the departure of our flight before a notary, met with the owner of the premises and settled an outstanding debt, which he was quite grateful for.

I myself was in awe of the power of an absolute decision that one projects, where no turning back is conceivable, and which had borne fruit in the times we had imposed on ourselves and in the midst of a crisis never before seen.

This is a clear example of the power of the mind, of focused thoughts with millimetric precision that we can all implement and irreversible decision making. We had no doubt that something was going to happen when we made the decision to sell the restaurant back in a week. We just have to believe in it and take action, we just have to ask the universe and our wishes will be granted.

Those who do not have clear objectives will not be able to advance in the jungle of negativity that exists around us. Even if the fears we may have appear for a moment, let's do it anyway, let's move forward until we achieve the desired result. The subconscious gives everything that is desired and that it believes is possible. In this sentence there are two important statements. To understand well what desire is, imagine that you have walked in the desert ten hours without water, what would be your desire? Drink! Your desire for money must be this imperious if you want your subconscious to attract for you the prosperity you seek. The deep nature of the universe is abundance and prosperity.

The second important statement is "everything you think is possible". This notion is very subtle, and you must understand it in order to make the most of your subconscious. If your desire was to win the first prize in the lottery, your conscious spirit would reject that idea because your reason would be telling you that it is impossible. You must be realistic and consider a desire for money that corresponds to your value system.

Taking action is the key, it is what destroys fear, it is what cancels out the mental paralysis, to which we are often exposed. We are governed by paradigmatic paralysis, sometimes the result of fear of making a decision that involves us in a whole and that we must advance into unknown territory. It seems that we want to move forward, but excuses are beginning to surface at every moment or, worse still, we think about what our environment will say about us in the face of our actions.

We want to, but the impotence we experience, mother of the bad experiences before us, gives us the main reasons not to move, we do not risk, we prefer to stay in our mediocre world or that things are solved by inertia and alone with out our interference. Sometimes we think that it is easier for us to convince ourselves that what happened was due to some strange reason of destiny, we do not want to make ourselves responsible or get involved in our failures, or that our environment judges us as such failures; that is why we prefer not to move forward, not to move.

We must take action in our lives, set our sights and shoot at the target we project and where we need to concentrate; only planned action will bring us closer and closer to the goal. Projecting and executing, that is, moving into action with unwavering faith in the positive outcome of what we are about to undertake becomes indispensable.

In Central America, we are returning to our sales profession in all its expression. Spain was very tormented by all this situation that was happening during those years. Unlike Latin America, which are countries where crises are the bread and butter of every day and where people see crises as something normal, but they do not paralyze them. Negativity always drags us to the bottom of the situation and does not let us come out of it, it chokes us irremediably.

Chapter 17: Between Two Seas

"He who corrects you for the defects you have loves you more than he who praises you for qualities you don't have."

Bible, Proverbs 9

One of the impressive economies of the Central American region was, without a doubt, Panama City in 2009. It was a small Miami. A lot of foreign investment was concentrated in those years. The dollar is the official currency. It has a stable government, economic balance, affordable taxes with a 7% VAT, a bay to fall in love with, modern buildings, a coastal strip that looks directly at the sea, a strip that embraces the entrance to the canal, which is of unparalleled beauty, called Amador.

After our trip through Central America and after a brief step to know El Salvador, which took us there a commercial advice for the company of radiotelephony Red, owned by a nice Colombian, we settled down in Panama definitively.

El Salvador and its exaggerated bureaucracy to be able to legally reside in the country or install a company became unsustainable in those years, despite the good offer from that company. There is even a prison for illegal immigrants, believe it or not, and with the rise to power in those years of a former guerrilla group, added to the latent insecurity that existed, was not a very desirable destination for business at that time.

We were still able to discover a new country, the people are very friendly; in that short time, we made a significant number of relationships and friends. It has dreamy tourist spots and its beaches invite to surf, which is a sport very much practiced there. It is highly recommended to take an exotic vacation, not to reside, at least in those years.

Panama was our next destination for almost eight years; when we arrived, everything was easy, from obtaining residency to a bank account and they welcomed the foreigner with open arms.

The corollary of our experience in selecting a good destination for investment is that we must look meticulously at who governs, their future economic measures, whether they are pro entrepreneur or against foreign investment, are very important guidelines to know what to do. It all has to do with the capacity of those who govern, beyond their political tints. It is a question of capacities, guarantees, justice and state vision that can harm the installation of our foreign investment.

At that time, back in 2009, we decided to land our ships in Panama City. The name Panama means 'abundance of fish'. Modern city, incomparable landscapes with the entrance to the interisland canal in the middle of a calm water bay, heat all year round, complete infrastructure for investment. They said it was a small territory, but where money flows easily, and I was able to confirm this version in those years.

The only problem I see with Panama City is the lack of control of a hellish traffic. Car crashes are a permanent feature of the city. The traffic lights are like fruit trees on the corners.

However, the Panamanian employee is very efficient at work and knows how to work with goals and objectives when trained. In summary, the evaluation is very positive in terms of the human factor. Well, one of my children was born there, so I was left with some of the commitment to this welcoming land between the seas.

Moving on to the issue that concerns us in Panama, at first there were two cell phone companies. At the end of 2008, two more were added. They came in with a great publicity campaign. What is interesting about this cell phone business is that it is virgin. In view of this comment they will say that I went crazy, but no.

I can assure you that even in the most saturated countries in the world in the mobile phone market you can make a super production of sales.

Why do I especially defend this position? It's very simple. In more than 90% of the users, the clients use the prepaid system, that is to say, the famous electronic recharge; it is the system known by all where you add credit as it runs out, with the consequent headache that brings at night to get credit or the high cost of the calls, and what to say of the Internet.

Those who distribute this product receive miserable commissions, the business is aimed at quantity, but a very important number of clients is needed to obtain interesting profits and to get an important distribution network that, generally, is already taken by the competition.

The solution to premises in a shopping centre is undoubtedly the organisation of a door to door sales force, UFV (sales force unit), of postpaid plans, currently adding TV, Internet and landline services for the home, which many companies in many countries have developed as another important source of income.

What I also propose is to become a distributor of products that have a contract.

The contract or tie up of a certain number of clients is what large corporations look for, and there we always find our business opportunity, our niche in all types of products and places.

The example of the cellular telephony is easier, the need is created, what we must encourage is to change the old cellular or prepaid plan for another of postpaid contract where the client pays a monthly fee for the subsidy of the equipment or the purchase of the same one and the service of communication plus Internet for a derisory price, saving, this way, an important amount of money, in the end.

Imagine that there is 90% of the market to be conquered around the world in this modality. There is, within this modality, the possibility of selling hybrid plans, that is to say, those that when the contracted plan is finished the user can charge airtime.

The commissions that these companies pay, of two or even three times the plan sold,

other companies in the sector add incentives to reach certain sales productions.

We must change the culture of noncommitment to a term contract. We must change that view of things first us as entrepreneurs, then change our employees and inject a new sales culture.

Culture implies ways of behaving. The judgment or evaluation the client makes of us is the feeling that will govern his or her psyche. We are constantly evaluated on a daily basis in every sales conversation.

After the purchase, the first three months are of vital importance, since the conviction of the benefits of our product will be a consequence of our good service or attention to the concerns that the customer may have. After these first months of evaluation by the client, the loyalty is a fact. If there is not an optimal aftersales support device, a part of our sales will be diluted.

Here we must have confidence in our brand, that it will do things right. It is also import ant to have a structure that follows the new customer.

A client always wants to test us once he hires. There will always be something he didn't understand correctly or forgot to explain. They come to the service centres and there the organization must have qualified and trained personnel to explain plans and promotions.

In Panama we achieved what no one else had achieved up to that point by implement ing our scheme. One of the cell phone companies was desperate at the time when two major competitions were entering the market in 2009 but was able to stabilize with our momentum. There were 6174 new postpaid customers in a first year, although it sold twice as many, but they could not process it due to the lack of suitable personnel for the task and despite the effort of the general management, which even opened on Sundays for us.

When we arrived in Panama, no one was selling a single contract. The distribution structures were prepaid and totally depressed by the threat of new competition.

134

If you approached a store, they didn't know how to offer you a contract, much less how to complete a contract. In that year 2009, out of a total of 41,905 new subscribers according to the newspaper La Prensa de Panama, 12/1/10 in the whole country, in this type of postpaid contract, we had 15% of the total market, having established only one office of one hundred meters and an average commission per account that was around two hundred dollars with the prizes.

When we arrived at the Panamanian coast, we had a meeting at one of these companies that had also just set foot on land. They didn't give us much thought. The second meeting was suspended. We never really knew why. They are those commercial directors with very limited vision.

So much so that, in less than a year, those directors who had treated us so badly and dismissed us were no longer occupying their comfortable seats. When they're in those leadership positions, some think they're gods of Olympus on earth. Then, in 2013, we contacted our company again and were accepted as distributors immediately, after the thorough investigation that partners always do in order to join one of these corporations.

At that time, a former deputy director of Telefónica asked us to join the team, which we did. In view of the important offer that arose in Costa Rica, which we will relate later, we decided to give the company to our friend and to set off alone to Costa Rica. Today, he is still the most important distributor of that brand in Panama, although he was never able to form a postpaid sales force as we explain in this book, as he confessed to us at a pleasant dinner, we held years later.

Going back to our beginnings in Panama, the day our plane was taking off to return to El Salvador, we thought of calling our old Mexican cell phone currency, which we had not visited yet, because we believed that the first option was safe based on a first meeting that we had held on the recommendation of some close acquaintances of the general management of this international corporation that we had discussed in El Salvador.

A voice from the other side full of enthusiasm was heard, telling us that this was precisely what they were looking for, new distributors, and we fell like a ring to the finger. Our plane was leaving in a few hours, so he proposed that we come to the corporate headquarters in an area called the East Coast to meet; at that time, he hooked us up with another equally enthusiastic director who attended the meeting. Everything went smoothly when we were just a few minutes away from giving up because of a bad experience with the other cell phone operator.

The doors were already open. They didn't have a project like ours. The first one to attend us was a newcomer to the corporate structures; that is why he was so fresh; meanwhile, the second one did not last another month, because after meeting us they dispensed with their services. This began to delay our incorporation a bit.

At our insistence, the deputy commercial director, a Peruvian, rushed the issue and everything went in perfect order. He was another one of those intelligent directors who, fortunately, exist in corporations as well.

We achieved figures never before seen. So much so that the company changed the whole scheme of things and stripped the entire distributor organization of the premises they had been assigned for care and put them to work copying our scheme of just selling contracts. Previously, we were called to a meeting with the CEO of Central America to present our project and have it a little clearer to clone it in the whole region, at least those were his words. There we also presented a network marketing scheme that we called NECXUS for cellular telephony that, over the years, they implemented without our presence.

The results of those distributors were not surprising, since they were bad copies; they never consulted us to put the system into practice, we were only infiltrated by personnel of these distributors and systematically copied, but it was never easy for them, since the secrets that this scheme and this profession keep are very vast and you will be able to find them in these pages, in the next chapters in Part III.

All this was a bit annoying for us, because in all these years and countries we were adding the attention of other distributors, they were even copying our ads in the newspapers, taking out identical ones.

We were selling about two thousand accounts a month and half of them went into the garbage by mistake and lack of training of the corporation's staff. They were always careful to congratulate us, except for the CEOs, who were almost always on our side and who recognized our work and supported us, while in middle management circles we were only jealous of our results and the money we earned, I guess. This was always the flip side of our success.

In Mexico we were bothered, like few others, with the excuse of the casualties, but when we finished and it is signed in a settlement that we made before a notary, only counted two hundred and eighty five casualties out of three thousand five hundred sales in our last period of operation, which covered a year and a half. Another number or justification could not be found. But the ordeal we had gone through nobody took it away from us; the grey hair I comb today did not either.

Your greatest competition will not be on the street, but in the very bowels of the corporations, in your fellow travellers, the other distributors of the same brand; there will be the fiercest competitors when they see your sales results.

Finally, the CEO of Panama decided to undertake a campaign to harass our company in order to negotiate a decrease in commissions. Terms not accepted by us.

He said that we were making more money than he was and that this was not possible.

What moved him was his mediocrity and evident envy. He forgot that one takes a risk in these cases and invests his money and time knowing that he can lose everything and gain nothing, since he only receives commissions on sales.

Risk taken with faith and determination in the short term pays off, and very well, in a sales organization. The CEO developed a whole fictitious web of infusions that, in the end, proved to be nonexistent. So much so that his righthand man, an Ecuadorian, who was the one to implement such a strategy for the reduction of commissions in Panama, later already as commercial director in Costa Rica, asked us as distributors, a letter that I keep as a souvenir, and soon after assuming his new position, the corporation took him out of its ranks forever.

Chapter 18: Pure Life

"What a pity to stop being happy in the now by crying and sighing over a past we can no longer remedy and suffering for the future

JOHN LENNON

Costa Rica is a country whose activity is focused on its capital, San José. It is rich in nature, with friendly and extremely curious people. They ask you everything about your life at every moment, in any circumstance and place, in an elevator of a hotel, at the airport, buying the newspaper or in the taxi.

We arrived there at the invitation of one of the mobile phone companies in 2011. It was an opportunity they gave their best international elements. This country was about to open its doors to mobile telephony, which until then was only in state hands.

As it was a new international operation, the company that invited us was in chaos in all its departments. We were summoned twice, took a plane, paid for a hotel and everything turned out to be very informal. During the third trip, I decided to go knock on the door of the competition, literally, already tired of so much inefficiency.

The newspapers were alarmed that the state-owned company would lose 50 % of the market. I saw in it our opportunity. We arrived requesting a meeting with the head of sup plier procurement, who welcomed us with open arms. Our proposal was simple, to stop the entry of all mobile phone companies with our scheme of sales force units. The project had a strong impact on its main directors, who soon received us, and we were able to present our plans in a PowerPoint presentation.

They soon agreed to sign a one-of-a-kind contract at that time. We would be the only postpaid partner among some two hundred companies in the country that had been working with them, some for more than ten years. This raised concerns later on in time.

The sale was a success. The plan was to sell only to historical customers with higher minute consumption and to make them a contract to retain them for a period of time of about eighteen months so that they would not opt for the new competitors. In exchange we requested three months of the purchased plan as commission for our services. Everything seemed to smile at us over time. Sales were flowing like water from a mighty river. The sales groups were very good. We had taken two Panamanian managers with us from Pana ma who had all the experience to take the initial steps. My first daughter was born there; the professionals in Costa Rica are excellent, the doctors, lawyers, among other professionals.

I don't know if it will be a very good country to invest in, but I must admit that it is very fertile, because I had my two children there after fifteen years of marriage. But the time has come for the intrigues of a sector. They were unionized employees because they were from the government. The two hundred companies began to lobby to give our succulent contract to them as well.

A department manager, a character to forget, in truth I tell you, of an out of the ordinary evil and xenophobia, took the reins of the issue in favour of the latter. She even told us that she preferred to kill her aunt, in reference to us, then to kill her family, which were supposedly the two hundred prepaid companies, which she defended and which she had championed.

At the other end was the country's commercial director, another foreigner like us, a Salvadoran who was the mentor of our contract. We managed to stop the entry that year 2012 of those two big cell phone companies. They only managed to get 5% of the market between them. The state owned company retained all of its customers thanks to our presence on the streets with more than one hundred salespeople willing to work in this scheme that we mentioned of motivated door to door sales force units.

At one point, the CEO of the telephony part wanted to hand over the entire telephony package to us, even prepaid, when he saw and checked our results. But the pressure was so great from that misguided lady that she had to give in to her two hundred distributors and a large part of the hierarchical employees, who saw in us a foreign invasion of their domains and who risked their comfortable life of inoperative lethargy very well paid by the government. We ended up being very well compensated for the termination of the contract with half a million dollars plus commissions, which were always paid.

The saddest thing was how the other foreigner who was acting as commercial director and who signed the contract with us ended up being removed from his position. Our hiring was a success, but they did not want to continue paying three times the plan in commissions and neither did they want to give their two hundred prepaid distributors that commission, so they decided to cut at least conflicting, which was us, and that's how it was.

Shortly afterwards, the company that invited us to participate in its new operation and its CEO requested our incorporation. Unfortunately, because he failed that year and collect ed less than 3% of the market, he was removed from his position a few days before signing a contract with us. Faced with this unexpected change, we decided to end our Costa Rican adventure and return to Panama.

There I conceived two very famous restaurants in those years, one of Argentinean style meat cuts and another of historical cuisine, the first of its kind, I think, worldwide, based on the favourite dishes of the famous people of history, from Cesar or Da Vinci, through Napoleon and up to Marilyn or J. F. K. But that's another story. Panama in 2016 entered a deep economic crisis that devastated it.

My tour continued in Medellin in response to the proposal to obtain a cell phone distribution with the number one company in that country. Medellín, a city that has won international awards for its modernity, among other things, incomparably beautiful mountainous landscapes, but it still has two problems to solve: pollution, which kills more people than drug trafficking, and insecurity, which is latent; otherwise, I think it is an excellent destination to propose an investment.

Chapter 19: Is there an ideal country to invest in?

"Before you're diagnosed with depression or low self-esteem, make sure you're not surrounded by idiots."

JOSÉ MARÍA ESCRIVÁ

"The smaller a person's character is, the smaller the problems that make him sad and angry.

PASCAL

In Panama I dedicated my days to writing this book that I present to you today. It was the year 2013. I only visited two of the most important publishing houses in 2014, and the CEO of one of them accepted it immediately, but I had to travel to another country and my children were very young and I still wanted to add other details to it, which I put into practice at that time.

At the same time, I had my second child, conceived in the "tica" mountain, but born by the sea in Panama. In those years I also studied all the details of the sales scheme through network marketing, network marketing, which I wanted to incorporate into these pages as another important form of marketing, and selling through robots in social networks, the ecommerce that I expose in final chapters.

One was a steakhouse style and the other was the first historical restaurant in the world, a different concept, where all the favourite dishes of the famous people in history were dis played with their original recipes, which took me months of research. Between these two and a wine club, between the three of them I had fifty thousand followers, which is not bad at all in a country like Panama. Both lasted until the crisis in Panama was extreme in 2017, and the rents, impossible to sustain; in one we paid twelve thousand dollars and in the other six thousand. We must always take into account that a restaurant will be profitable as long as the rent does not exceed ten percent of its turnover.

In those projects too, we had to build the work of both of them from scratch without being architects or anything like that, but we managed to do it and we did it with a lot of effort and determination.

First and foremost, we must have the firm conviction and passion to achieve results at any time and in any place. To choose the ideal site, we must feel comfortable, at ease; it will be like love at first sight that enters through the eyes. It must fascinate us from the very first moment.

Every country must guarantee us financial and legal security for our physical investment, and for our family with a wide range of study houses for our children.

Easy to be able to rent a house and an office with economic rents without greater proceedings of guarantors and all that history that exists in some countries.

Speed and ease of residence procedures are also essential, and where you see that there is no xenophobia towards foreigners. It happened to me once in Medellín that the head of immigration sentenced me that if my six year old daughter's birth certificate did not arrive in twenty four hours, and she only had to renew her application, she would have to be de ported, when I had residency for three years as an investor, the mother for two and the little brother for another year; therefore, all in order. She was telling us to leave and not invest in her country, obviously, that was the message. I thought, "What a crazy thing to do with this person. The next day, the much talked about departure arrived and his visa, which by law was renewed, was granted. It was a fact that really touched me, and I determined soon after to end that investment in that country. Therefore, you have to be very careful with this type of situation that can complicate everything.

The country of choice must have bank accounts opened without further formalities, which are opened within the day and can be obtained at least a debit card and a printed check book at the time for a foreigner. For example, Mexico or Colombia do not take more than fifteen days to issue a resident's ID.

We must take into account that its inhabitants are friendly and receptive to foreigners, that they breathe in their streets the good energy of a population with good service, where their infrastructure is modern and friendly to nature and modern means of transport. A place where communications, gasoline and the family basket are accessible. Public safety is a fact and the crime rate are low, the sun shines all year round and there are opportunities beyond imagination. It is essential that commercial activity is constantly on the move and that people consume, buy and restaurants are full, a fact that tells us a lot.

Where nature beautifies all its streets with splendour, the employees are friendly and understand what it means to provide good service. Taxes should not stifle investment, employee social charges should be bearable, and salaries should also allow for profit maximization from prizes, abundant commissions and incentives. It is important to aim for superior quality, organic and locally produced food, with a variety of high quality international products at a very good price.

Where there is a strong currency, which can be dollarized, and its economy is thriving. Where there is freedom of expression and where justice is serious in its decisions and guarantees legal security for individuals and companies. Where buying a high standing property is easy and economical, without having to spend a lifetime paying a mortgage. Where the banks help their population with credit. Where services are all of a high standard. Where luxury is commonplace in their shops, stores, cities, in their shopping centres, in their rich cuisine and in their neighbourhoods.

If your choice of life meets all or some of these qualities, don't hesitate, but it should beat in your heart. It is better to develop in cities with millions of inhabitants rather than in small towns. There are countries that end up being executioners of our interests and investments. In others you will feel the xenophobia that is unfortunately present and that is based on a culture of ignorance of some people. Foreign investment is the engine of the economies in many regions of the planet and one that no government should ignore.

Obviously, many countries in the world have some of these positive characteristics, but their economies do not get off the ground and so people become negative, depressed or insecure, as in Mexico, which, in my opinion, is a country that has all the positive conditions for investment, but only the latter is missing to comply 100% with the announced characteristics.

Peru, Argentina or Colombia are also excellent places to start the journey as an entrepreneur. Europe is incredible for its beauty, food, culture and its people; therefore, it is not to be discarded to initiate there, in the Euro zone. The United States or Canada are always among the best, without a doubt.

In short, the important thing will be where your heart beats, there you will sow with passion and obtain the projected and imagined fruits.

Part III

The road to success: how to achieve it step by step

Chapter 1: The Secrecy of the commercial project

"You get so much more in a month by taking an interest in others than you do in two years by trying to get others take an interest in us."

CARNEGIE

First of all, it is very important to propose a commercial project to the corporations or companies that provide a service or product that we are interested in representing. We will contact them, since they are always looking for distributors that make good sales productions with a good customer profile that commit themselves to a purchase of a product or a term contract in exchange for a service. You should always make a previous study of the market in which you intend to develop your distribution company. There are many doors to touch of great brands, but they will have to choose the most convenient for their interests. Go looking for one company at a time until you see if you like the economic proposal or not, it is the most convenient.

It is my recommendation to look for a company that has these characteristics: a very good international or local trajectory; that is going through a moment of change or has destroyed its commercial apparatus, recently incorporating a new management team; that has before its doors an important competition proposed and it is at a "mental" disadvantage with respect to these, or that, perhaps, is in its commercial beginnings in that country or region.

Examples I draw on from my own experience were almost all of them.

At the beginning of the century, the American company was looking for distributors of its electronic security product all over the world, where for each electronic security equipment installed free of charge and delivered to its customers it paid approximately eight hundred dollars; there were distributors with productions of one thousand new customers per month.

There will always be an opportunity, for example, in our case it happened in Peru when he first started operations in that country, or in Mexico when he withdrew all his distributors to reorganize and gave us the opportunity to accompany him in 2003, or in Spain, inaugu rating the Alliance program, where both companies paid four hundred euros per sale in the same period of 2007.

Another example was Panama, where, faced with the arrival of two major communications in 2009, the company we signed up with was without major sales, with distributors depressed until our arrival. In a way, we boosted the company thanks to the

145

enthusiasm we put into countering those two companies, achieving the first year in postpaid contracts with our organization technique, 15% of the postpaid market of new contracts at country level among the four existing operators.

Our corporation paid three to four times the plan sold, and we sold plans of fifty dollars and up; therefore, our commissions ranged from one hundred and fifty to two hundred dollars per account.

Another example: that of Costa Rica, where in 2011, more precisely in November, and in view of the imminent arrival of two other large companies due to the opening of the mobile telephony market, which was no longer exclusive to the state, hired our services to curb this income, a goal achieved, since these two large companies only reached 5% of the market in that distant and 2012, its first year, which cost their main directors their heads.

And so, we could go on from story to story, knowing that this is a reality. Large multinational companies will always need distribution services, so this is an excellent niche for us to enter.

I recognize that the important thing in this type of multinational communications is to sell airtime and not a cell phone, but we must know that it is better to have a captive market by contract than another ephemeral one and prostituted by the prepaid that does not carry any contract.

Creating only a prepaid structure in telecommunications, neglecting the possibility of building a winning strategy in the area of postpaid with a term contract, is like having an incomplete strategy, at 50%, in a corporation that offers this type of airtime sales products; they should not rule out any option for the sale of airtime.

From my point of view, it is easy to develop two sales forces door to door, well separated in space and time, one prepaid and one postpaid, even in parallel, using a network marketing concept. In addition, we can add with the same strategy a third option for SMEs with postpaid contracts.

We will always be successful in contract accounts if we put in place a sales force like the one we propose in these pages; they will convince customers of what we want, because the market, is my personal appreciation, does 80% a professional and motivated sales force and 20% the preferences of customers, because they move to the rhythm of their emotions that the professional salesman sowed.

The customer, in general, does not buy; the seller sells with professional technique what the company wants to offer as a product and the market, in general, accepts it and imposes itself against all odds. Like that film, The Wolf of Wall Street, where nobody bought, but only their sales professionals sold them what they wanted, even if it was rubbish, as shown in the film.

146

We have to focus our offer on a few products, two or three, and always on a specific contract period, twelve or eighteen months, because that is where the most commission is paid, and you will see that for customers it makes no difference what sales arguments we put forward. We must note that our product is unique and covers a need always, a need that we must capture based on knowing how to listen to the potential customer in front of us.

In addition, it is very profitable for any corporation to retain an individual client or SME for a period of time and then try to renew it with some added value to the original proposal. It is to have a captive market if you offer a good service after the hiring.

In Argentina, Peru or Mexico, the alarms we sold were only of one type and brand, without any additional to avoid complicating the installation and to make it go faster to cover more installations daily. If the customer wanted an additional, it was at another time and had to combine their installation by a new visit.

In cellular telephony, in Mexico, we sold three models of cell phones at a single rate of over fifty dollars. In just the first three months of opening the operation, we achieved more than two thousand five hundred activations in 2006 and a turnover in dollars at the then rate of approximately five hundred.

Those who followed us in accounts counted on 50% of this production, but with thirty premises to the public and where their costs shot up compared to us, with only one office, but full of training and daily motivation.

We know that, worldwide, almost 100% of people have a cell phone, but most of them have cell phones that work only by charging prepaid airtime. Figures are calculated that about 90% of the world's population has chosen this mode. This means that there is a huge potential market without an open or hybrid postpaid cell phone contract or plan.

Imagine the development we can have in this virgin market niche all over the world. That is why the biggest promotions are in this type of hiring.

Telecommunications companies have an arsenal of promotions to commit their customers to a contract and, to achieve this, sales organizations are paid very well. This is a very good business option.

However, not knowing how to market these products based on a structure of distribution companies without motivation, due to lack of training and knowhow, all companies and their managers choose to go with the flow and fight for a highly competitive market, such as the prepaid minute and where the fight is fierce.

It is the managers of the corporations who must know that it is possible to set up a significant and qualified distribution structure of entrepreneurs who row in the same direction as the brand, with a sales force, even for the development of prepaid mentoring.

We can also implement it with other business options, such as cable television, electronic security, credit cards and a long list of products and services. One example of this I knew and lived inside as one more distributor and I want to put it as an example.

In Argentina, in the period of one fiscal year 20002001, forty distributors of the alarm company sold to 66,564 new clients with a zero investment in advertising by the corporation, the largest in the world in electronic security.

All this with an electronic security system in instalments of approximately thirty five dollars a month. He never advertised in any media at that time, but the company based its entire strategy on the sales force through distributors whom he continually motivated and paid very good commissions, as we have already described.

The following year, in the first three months, their sales increased by 50 % and they sold 25 877 new customers in the first three months of the year. That is how far I got with the arrival of the bank corralito in Argentina, which plundered everyone's savings and made it impossible to continue with the company, so we decided to move our operation to another country.

There were distributors with 14,510 accounts in that period and the one that followed was around 7,183 in the same time, where a distribution company in the middle of the table was positioned with 4,500 contracts in those fifteen months and the average among the forty companies was around 2,311 accounts.

Imagine that I was paying eight hundred dollars on account, imagine also how many new millionaires were born that year; they were entrepreneurs who knew how to take advantage of the opportunity that presented itself and were not afraid of anything.

The degree of fear in an entrepreneur is measured by his production.

The distributor ranking measures the level of fear of selling experienced by its members. In conclusion, it was the number one company in the security market in Argentina and the world in those first years of the current century and in only its first year of operations. This was achieved with sales techniques based on sales force, organizational strategy and a lot of motivation.

The proofs are conclusive, it is possible to achieve sales super productions with this distribution scheme, and you, my friend, can be one of the protagonists.

Let's take into account something important, and that is that the alarm market is very difficult to penetrate, because people think they do not need an electronic protection system. These results were those of a great American corporation, intelligent in its strategy, that only with a sales force and without any publicity achieved the conquest of a market like the Argentinean, Chilean and Mexican ones, and that repeated the same experience in several countries of the world; imagine how much easier it will be to incorporate this system in a field like communications, Internet services, cable television services, card banking or insurance services, to mention some.

Between 1999 and 2000, distributors in Mexico had also generated more than 250 000 customers for the company with revenues of around USD 10 million per month. It did not have to invest in infrastructure or advertising campaigns, because all these expenses were absorbed by each of the distribution companies.

Thanks to this type of operation, which was extended to more than fifty countries, the international American company achieved a capitalization value on Wall Street of close to one hundred billion dollars for 2001.

In the postpaid market, there is that percentage of the population we already talked about that does not know the great benefits that this modality entails. It is a potential market worldwide in which the entrepreneur does not risk entering because of fear, since he does not know it, just as some managers of multinationals look at it with distrust, since it is a market where we must know how to organize a professionally trained sales force, and most of them improvise in this area.

In addition, a very important administrative apparatus of containment must be in place to provide a service based on excellence; without the latter, it would be to navigate adrift.

This book responds to the specific needs of any company that aspires to success, emphasizing, as we have seen, internal marketing and business human resource management, a fundamental step prior to client acquisition.

If we concentrate the seller's mind on few products and few plans, one, two or maximum three, it will be very easy for the customer to understand the offer and make a quick decision, and much easier for the seller to explain the ben efits in a short time.

Then we can change the offer according to the needs of the corporation, month by month, to encourage the sale of other products in the same modality, selecting two or three at a time.

Another advantage is to provide the seller with the possibility of training properly and quickly to be able to achieve also high sales productions that in other companies would be difficult to achieve. It will be easy for the entrepreneurs to train and be able to develop the weekly selection of more and more sales structures until they saturate the market with their presence.

We should not be afraid to see on the streets an endless number of units of sales forces offering the same product, because we have lived many times that a sales team that happens first that we do not buy, and then another group appeared and this does buy the promotion.

It will depend, to a great extent, on the development of a professional sales conversation, based on a sales script that we will detail later, in front of the potential client and the positive attitude that emanates from the group to easily capture their attention.

With the energy with which our sales force units converse with potential customers, with that first energy they transmit to you, they will energize the customer in the same frequency during your presentation and you will see that, without much thought and in the heat of the moment, the customer will take the product or service offered to him. It is all a question of energy and security in the gestures, voice and professional words with which our sales units move.

Once we have selected the product and the plan in which we will set its commercialization, we will be ready to implement the technique that we expose and that will sweep with the market.

The fee must be one that allows us to receive a minimum commission starting from one hundred dollars or euros, and more depending on the product or service. This will also depend on the country and the corporation with which we have signed. Never accept commissions of less than one hundred dollars or euros for products in very high demand, and never less than three hundred in those products with low rotation, such as home alarms, because the numbers will not close.

In every country, a normal rate that we have to apply in our offer and that people can add to their monthly expenses without having to adjust their pockets too much in exchange for a good service will always be around thirty five to fifty dollars or euros.

Once the offer has been assembled and selected from all those that the corporation will surely present for your benefit, the technique is to go and find the client and not wait for him to show up. That is for people who are looking for a small income that is easy to manage behind a counter, without taking too much trouble and where the schedule is met without delay; they are the dinosaur salesmen who expect to be fed in their mouths like a baby and without much sales effort in exchange for a basic salary, holidays and benefits.

We propose just the opposite, a totally motivated group that goes out to conquer the market like dragons, with a very concrete technique and sales script, that does not have preestablished schedules for the daily work in its head, but that has daily goals and objectives to fulfil and that are very clear in its minds.

We will form a hardworking unit, where our intention will be to conquer part of the market and we will not stop until we achieve our goals, this has to be the idea that mobilizes us.

Part of the strategy is that the client is taken by surprise in his home between four and eight o'clock in the afternoon; that is to say, at times when the competition disappears, with an understandable, short and forceful offer that makes him vibrate with emotion, where that emotion must be transmitted by our sales man in every conversation. We propose four intense hours, since it has been proven that the level of excitement of a salesperson is those four hours.

Let's forget about achieving high production in sales by waiting behind a counter, placing ads in newspapers or on the Internet, or making small appearances on radio or television. First, all that is very expensive, and second, it does not achieve the results we are looking for. Everything complements the institutional image of the brand and helps in part, but in our trajectory, we have tried all possible sales techniques, telephone marketing, office meetings, sending offers via Internet, client portfolio list, fixed points with sales stands, advertising in the media.

As far as Internet sales are concerned, we must take into account that we must make a great investment in Facebook Ads, Instagram Business, Google Ads, among other options, in order to obtain results that can be complementary to this modality that we propose.

The most effective method among all those mentioned has been the knocking door, coupling the network of sales networks in a version of network marketing that we designed and supported by digital marketing funnels for the recruitment of potential sellers that we will have in a network scheme.

We have tried it, as is clear, in eight countries with similar successes in each of them, with intense rain or cold in Argentina or Spain in winter, extreme humidity in Lima, suffocating heat at times in Panama or a temperate climate all year round, with its large dose of smog, as in Mexico City or Medellin.

We did it with different types of sellers that we have dealt with Argentineans, Spaniards, Mexicans, Salvadorans, Peruvians, Colombians, Panamanians, with their pros and cons, more difficult or more docile, with character or without it, sentimental or indifferent others.

We achieved our goals with this method that we are presenting to you and you will also
be able to do it, without a doubt.

In Panama we have sold products such as fixed line phone or wireless internet with tremendous success and also cell phones under the sun and heat. Do not close in selling only what the market supposedly asks for.

If your corporation asks for a percentage or a quota of some other product, do not be afraid, always say that you can, take it as true that statement, do not hesitate and you will see the results.

The first person who has to be convinced and have blind faith in the project and the offer made, regardless of the competition, is the entrepreneur.

How can you expect your managers, coordinators and even salespeople to follow you with blind faith if you are the first to defect and do not believe in anything, much less yourself and your power to change situations? If a salesperson comes to tell you that the competition has a lower or higher rate than you, don't listen to him, don't be distracted, that doesn't matter nor does it influence the results that we will find month after month, focus only on your results, on your daily, weekly and monthly objectives; in short, on your numbers projected in principle mentally.

There's a lot of business. We can count on a distribution of cell phones, alarms, credit cards, memberships, appliances, language courses, cable or satellite TV, Internet, fashion, prepaid medicine, fixed telephony, advertising and all kinds of products.

Or we can also try to go it alone without the support of a multinational, through mini bank loans that finance our customers in their purchase.

One area to take into account, where it is feasible to apply this scheme, is that of electronic security. One way to start up your own company is by making a contract with a bank or financial institution and where your clients can acquire a credit card through that entity, from which part of their balance is debited in monthly instalments to pay for the service we offer.

The bank would finance, say, about six hundred dollars, which is the total we need to make a profit of about three hundred dollars per piece of equipment, and the client pays an eighteen month monitoring fee financed by the bank. That six hundred dollars includes our total costs, sales force, equipment to be installed, installation, our profit and bank interest. It's a beautiful project. Imagine multiplying those three hundred dollars by two hundred sales per month; we would get $60,000 per month selling only ten pieces of equipment per day with one sales force unit. In less than two years we would exceed one million, being the architects of our own destiny without a multinational in between. It is riskier, but very feasible.

Other options are the creation of a web application that has zero cost for our customers and that, through it, we encourage the purchase of certain products, in short, ecommerce; this is how Amazon or Alibaba, its Asian version, began. Today there are applications such as Shopify, Oberlo, which facilitate this type of commerce and, as I commented, in this case, we must invest in advertising on Facebook, among the others mentioned.

While the other option, without so much risk, is to go hand in hand with an already known brand, as we have proposed. Let us always remember that knowing how to take advantage of the opportunities that are presented to us in business life is of vital importance to achieve success.

The easiest and most economical thing to find is the professional hand in the different areas, which will help shape your ideas, plans and projects; surrounding yourself with the best is key. The main thing is to escape from the fear that gives us to explore areas that we do not know, such as web business or sales, try it and see. It will be very simple to find suitable personnel who will want to accompany your dreams.

Chapter 2: The first step, selecting the location

"What threw Goliath was not the stone, it was faith.

DANIEL HABIF

Entering fully into the subject that concerns us, the first thing we must look for is a place, a city that provides us with the conditions to start our new economic life.

If it is in the land where we were born, even better, although, as we said in previous chapters, it is not necessary; there are no borders to success, our border is ourselves and our mind.

I think that many times it is better for some people to be in another country, as they can be more concentrated and clearer of family, friends, curious people and a lot of negativity and envy. No one is a prophet in his own land, as the saying goes.

In general, choosing a country outside the usual one can be an interesting and enriching adventure, as it was for us. It can be in another region, province or department, in the same country, but we must always bear in mind that it is a place that is growing and accepts foreign investment to a great extent.

When one undertakes a project, it generates more jobs, better living conditions for many families, stability, enthusiasm and more wealth for the country, contributing with its taxes to the growth of the GDP. Generally, the immigrant ends up feeling a strong sense of belonging, much more so than some of its native inhabitants.

All countries are fertile ground for economic development. It is very important to look, above all, at tax policies, facilities for foreign investment, labour policies and that governments are particularly open to attracting investment and new ideas.

The immigration process is always feasible when one undertakes; we are never left without our legal residence. Nor do they usually object if you use the mandatory exit every three months to reenter and make up the time until your situation is regularized.

The problem in choosing a particular country is still insecurity as an Achilles' heel, although the situation is generally bearable at all times, although we must walk with our eyes wide open, taking care in the selection of friends, employees or domestic staff.

As far as foreign investment is concerned, we can say that it is a good option to choose some destination in Latin America for them to retouch their projects. In many you will find that the human material is very well developed, they are very nice people to deal with,

154

although you have to be in control of the situation. You will see that they like to work for foreign capital, to which they offer themselves very kindly.

Taxes in Latin America are affordable for any sales project. In addition, it has several large cities, in which it is very feasible to develop your new life project. They are modern cities, full of life, restaurants, shows, entertainment, etc. Canada is another attractive option, a really beautiful and modern country. If you can stand the winters and speak English or French well, it is not at all a problem.

Europe is a beautiful possibility. The European Union contains countries where the rules of the game are clear. Everything is a luxury and a pleasure to invest in some project in those latitudes while enjoying their culture, gastronomy and unique landscapes sprinkled with history. My preference is set on Italy and then Spain, mainly, because they have a very Latin soul and a culture very similar to that of Latin America, with people very willing to always give good advice and help, the bureaucracy is almost nonexistent outside their capitals, even though there are comments to the contrary, but I know well what I am talking about and, if I compare with other member countries, here you will feel at home.

The economic crises that sometimes arise in some countries and for periods lead to a significant degree of frustration for sectors of the population, which will affect our investment and which unfortunately feeds discrimination in some people towards the foreigner and becomes a way of seeing things wrong against the foreign worker or investor. We should not pay attention to any such behaviour.

What is different enriches, never harms a country's economy. Latin America was nourished by European immigration on several occasions, and that was the takeoff of development in the societies they are today. All that Spanish, Italian, Chinese, Japanese, Polish, Jewish, German, English, Irish, French immigration and more enriched, without a doubt, the Latin American countries.

In the end, the choice is yours. Whatever your sense of smell tells you. But you must take into account those aspects that we wanted to bring to you. Conclusion: let us look for countries where coherent people govern, where there is a free market, support for investors and clear play.

Chapter 3: Building the Commercial Society

"The secret of happiness is not in always doing what you want, but in always wanting what you do.

LEON TOLSTOY

The first thing is first, we must build a society, that is, the social reason for which you will be able to give life to the project. In this regard, I remember, on one occasion, when I arrived in Mexico City, summoned by the American company, I dedicated myself to looking for a lawyer to form the corporation that they required of me in order to sign the contract. For any beginning, it is essential to have the corporate name and the registration in the taxes.

I started by taking the phone book and the newspaper Universal, where some lawyers advertise their services, a common practice in any country that we should take into account; nowadays, the best thing is the web as well.

This is the most recommendable thing for when you begin to implement your society: to visit a minimum of three lawyers or notaries who advise you and to stay with the one that less adverse or negative commentaries have suggested to you; to verify whenever they have worthy offices where they take care of to them, can be small, it does not matter if their services and treatment are optimal, and, mainly, to verify and to compare the prices, that will vary incredibly from one to another by our condition of foreigners sometimes.

Once in Spain, the law firm I attended insisted that it was not possible to set up a company only for foreigners. In El Salvador, the lawyer we consulted in the first instance sent a messenger to sign before starting the management of the society, practically a will where he was the only heir of everything we did; of course, I sent him back and changed professionals.

Always go for the simple, for the humblest professional, the least negative or whoever puts the least objections before you; there is no point in these large law firms setting up a commercial company for you. In Panama, for example, they charged us about two thousand dollars; however, later on we found out that we could get it for up to five hundred. So, don't be fooled, be careful and watch out. These procedures take no more than a week, and make sure that no one imposes anything on you, not even your name.

In Spain, the first accountant I contacted insisted that there were almost no names available for companies, and so he added a few words to the name we had chosen and it looked awful, and I had to deal with it all the time; our company name was unpronounceable.

Knowing that names carry personalities and positive or negative aspects, it is always advisable to choose a good name. I once read that the number resulting from the sum of the letters in the company's name had to do with its further development. So much so that those companies that added up to one, four or eight were the most successful; Coca Cola, Microsoft, among others.

I spent some time doing this exercise with different successful companies and it turned out that way in most cases. Their numerology, the sum of their letters, coincided with one of these three numbers. Perhaps this is something to keep in mind when thinking of a good name. Nothing is lost by trying either, although I have developed companies that did not carry any of these numbers and it worked out very well for me too.

Then I found another lawyer with whom I set up another company in Spain and there was no problem with the names of the company; for this professional there were plenty of names, unlike the first one. Everything depends on the degree of negativity of the so called professionals that one comes across.

Therefore, I repeat, do not allow yourself to be manipulated by bad lawyers, who unfortunately exist, who will want to take you only on the side of their petty interests and, in some cases, with a dose of xenophobia injected with envy.

When I arrived in Mexico, I began my task of finding a good lawyer and accountant. Returning to the subject of incorporation, I encountered the same problem that occurs in almost every country.

The first thing they will tell you is that a company cannot be formed only by foreigners, since it must have a national incorporated in it. Let me tell you that this is not the case, of course. But this is the first thing you will hear until you find some coherent lawyer who will seriously advise you.

Companies take between one week and fifteen days to have the registration in the public registry. The market value, in general, is six hundred dollars or euros if you chose Europe as a base for your business venture or, for example, in Colombia it is practically free to carry out a SAS and they are done in the day before a notary's office.

In other countries we can find it for up to two hundred dollars, as is the case in Costa Rica, or between five hundred and a thousand dollars, as in Panama. Always be careful in whose hands you fall, because not all lawyers are reliable and, in some cases, they take advantage of the foreigner, since they put you in the category of supposed idiot.

The idea is to make them as broadly focused as possible, especially in the aspect of marketing and selling products and services. The first thing they will ask you to start the process, for sure, will be half of the money and three probable names.

Hire an accountant, as it will be necessary not to spend money on unnecessary expenses at first; to register the staff in the social security or to obtain the registration number in the Treasury and to take note of the taxes to be earned or the work contract to be implemented with your future employees. Once the act is obtained and registered in the public registry, the search for the ideal office to develop the project begins.

Chapter 4: The Business Plan

"To answer before you've heard what the other one just said is unwise."

Bible, Proverbs 18, 13

The first thing we have to do after the composition of our business partnership is to assemble our business plan to present to the corporations where we can be interested in our project.

In it, we must put all our faith and also the innovative ideas that we want to bring to the operation as agents or distributors and that will be reflected through our business plan.

Our plan opened doors for us in every country we went to and from major corporations. You will be able to modify your plan according to the circumstances, according to the product and according to the place or country where you are.

It has to be simple, but denotes strength and conviction, as well as projecting the results month by month and how we will achieve them.

It also has to show our work philosophy and perspective of seeing things in the business world. The strength of an organization lies precisely in its working philosophy.

It can be composed of photographs of training, personnel selection model, classifications and historical sales achievements if any, diplomas obtained, among others. The business is much more than a plan that will be only a projection and a map of the path to follow; they will be the actions that in the day to day will mark the difference.

It will even give you arguments to use in your negotiation conversations with the corporation and with the internal marketing you will have to implement. It will be a compendium that you can take as a guide and to obtain the expected and announced results. We must not forget that for the presentation we must have, first of all, the title of the project and a brief history of the company or a brief and schematic commentary of your experience in the business or sales world.

If you don't have an important record, don't worry; the important thing is to show that you will deliver, show confidence, show unwavering faith in the results. You will have an advantage over the rest, you will have read this book and you will be several steps ahead of any competitor, because if you follow the scheme to the letter, success is assured. Show vehemence in the statements you make to those who will have to ask for the first meeting over the phone.

It is always advisable to request a meeting with the distribution or sales director, distributor coordinator... Let's bear in mind that the highest commissions are obtained in the business of incorporating clients by contract.

At that first meeting, you will introduce yourself with the presentation folder containing your business plan attached. Show blind confidence in achieving important sales results, as this will be the key you will need to open the door to the international corporation.

Describe in detail, noting the year of each venture, the achievements and the sales numbers achieved, if any. Let's highlight the professional team that will accompany us or how they will select it.

Describe the skills in leadership, quality management, operations control, marketing, training and commercialization that will be implemented. Relate the administrative, operational, stock control, training and commercialization scheme and the projected results that we will obtain month by month.

Plan Outline

We must start from our "mission and vision". Then develop our objectives by establishing a twelvemonth sales projection. Clearly specify the mode of operation.

The inventory of equipment must be under strict electronic security measures of surveillance with monitored cameras. In terms of adding more security, we must add that each transport unit, whether staff or product delivery, must have a GPS system in place to know the exact location of them at all times and to check the sales work areas to avoid overlap ping groups and have better control of the routes to cover.

In addition, we must have a training room for daily training of the staff conditioned with all kinds of implements that will make learning easier.

Another topic to be developed is the type of "organization chart and its functions" to be fulfilled by each of the members.

Highlight in the plan the motivational incentives, such as diplomas, promotions by stars, winners' podiums, success club, training trips, sales floorboard and daily and weekly objectives, and preparation of the notebook of dreams to be realized of each element of the organization.

To set out in the organization chart the sales force unit and its composition, coordinator, two supervisors and eight account executives.

Arranging the daily and weekly floors and objectives of new customers to be met is vital for sales staff to set their minds to it. The whole structure must be very clear with the

160

daily training of the sales script.

Every good organization must have an administrative head and a control desk, which is the operations entry desk for the authorization of new clients that we will present to the corporate headquarters. It welcomes the new user by means of a phone call where the data provided in the signed contract are supervised and corroborated, verifying signatures and attached documentation and everything that implies the contracting of the service.

A customer service department will follow up by calling the client portfolio once a month to detect possible concerns

A head of inventory will be in permanent contact with the warehouse and will control the products to be delivered to the home, supervising the daily assignment, organizing the delivery routes. Having someone who works with social networks complements any strategy.

As for the "commercial strategy" of our plan, we will have a sales force like the one described, which will travel to different areas in company vans, with the knocking door sales technique.

The offices should have a space of about fifty meters for training workshops that we carry out through videos and PowerPoint presentations that will contain topics such as closing sales and their different ways of carrying it out, objections, difficult clients, sales attitude and life philosophy.

Our groups will work from Monday to Friday who meet their quotas, and who will not use Saturdays to recover production. Once a month or every two, a super training will be implemented in a weekend location.

In our plan, we cannot miss the philosophy of our company, which we will develop below for your knowledge and which is of vital importance to understand how we can achieve our objectives and economic goals with this type of organization.

We must apply an internal marketing as a priority that will decide the company policy, increasing the competitive capacity of the company; that is, we talk about the interaction between the parts that compose the team, the human group of the company, we talk about a marketing based on the people that day by day makes possible a result according to our expectations.

The strength of a company emerges from what the human group that makes it up does for it. Everything is based on our attitude towards our employees, who, added to their qualities, will generate the market space we want to conquer.

The competitive development model must be based on essential points of a scheme that I called PAMPA. To know that the feeling of belonging is to feel the company and its objectives as our own with love; in short, that the employees feel identified with the cause, getting to obtain the emergence of the mysticism in them to then be able to project our goals and achieve them through concrete action.

To make the sense of belonging felt, we must transform someone without any motivation into a locking machine; in short, from a turtle into a sales dragon. We must mobilize him from his lethargy, which began in a space of comfort coming from his different work experiences, and mutate him, that is, take him to a space where he can project his dreams and where his interests converge with those of the company and the human group that integrates it. The employee must be able to love the company's shirt as a fan of his soccer team in a world cup, because this will be the world cup that we will make him play, not on the bench, but as a starter.

Let's commit our executives to a sales surplus figure and try to convince them that it is possible and that everything is easily achieved. This will mean that the policies we implement in our internal marketing will make a difference. They will mark whoever joins this scheme with the stamp of loyalty. We must succeed in generating an addiction in the feeling of belonging. Motivating the positioning of a person within the organization is one of our trump cards to implement.

We must show that loving and intensely embracing what we do is the key to success. Without love there is a desert in our lives and in our work too.

Where this love for what we do is not felt, there is a negative feeling of not being fulfilled and an anguish where negativity invades us, and we do not give the expected result. To love our work is to embrace our dreams with intensity.

We must know how to transform each frustrated individual into a new individual, who is permanently looking for the daily result in his work and who does not allow that in each door that he knocks in the search of a new client he finds a new excuse for which the service or product cannot be sold.

In every sales conversation there must be a closure. One of two: either we close a new contract in every conversation, or every customer shuts the door in our face, where he convinces us with excuses why he couldn't buy from us.

From that position of love for what we do, we will reach the mystique, which is to have group consciousness and common destiny. It is the vision that we project into their consciousness so that it becomes an absolute reality in their lives. Mysticism is blind faith in the project in which we are immersed. Mysticism is understanding the sales goals we are aiming at.

Mysticism is the will that moves us to achieve in life, in all its aspects, results that otherwise we could not achieve without that spice, heights that we would see impossible to reach, seas that we would feel impossible to sail. It is the essential word that differentiates us from the rest and is the unconditional sister of faith.

We will know how to get it, how to maintain it, apply it and put it into practice on the sales pitch.

Another important aspect is to project the results on a daily basis, which is the key to developing the action.

To project is to materialize that which was first planned, like a big bang that flashes in our thought, in the interior of our conscious mind.

If we do not have a mental map that we can illuminate in our subconscious and write it down on paper and then bring it to reality, it is impossible to obtain the dreams that each member of the organization pursues to achieve happiness and commitment. That is what we must achieve in each member, along with the goals of the company, which converge in the same direction with their dreams.

When we plan, we also set a set of priorities as a course of action to follow. To project is to imagine, and that is the most powerful force in the universe. If we manage to hold it in our minds as true, that is ultimately what we will get.

Acting is the next step; it is to know that without action all the above has no chance of being realized. Taking the whole organization to action is what will give life to the project. From the first week, the first day, the results will be in sight and can be imagined in all its extension in the short and medium term. Taking action includes selecting, training and motivating the company's employees. These instances of the business must be assumed as indivisible parts of the action of the sales organization that we propose.

This scheme of internal marketing that we propose implies priorities, since first there must be our work group, which is the most important value that we have and that should never be considered as a liability, but as those that will alleviate the burden of business costs.

The reason for this firm statement is simple; if our work team does not feel that mystique, that belonging to the entrails of the company that we must instil in them and transfer to them, how can we make them feel anything when it comes to customer service?

You must understand that aftersales service and follow up, which includes resolving the customer's concerns, must be our obligatory goal, but that it will only be successful if we are imbued with the PAMPA scheme, which consists of the following words: to belong, to love, to mystique, to project and to act.

We need to demand better skills to select, train, motivate, compensate and evaluate the results of the employees, who will always be considered as an asset in the company and never as a liability.

Our business scheme proposes a set of studied and tested programs that we must take to the daily action, scheme with clear ideas previously elaborated in our mind, where we sift them until we get the clearest images of our objectives. Based on this, we will discover possible inconsistencies that we must correct during the daily progress, which will allow us to establish priorities and assign to those responsible for each sector the goals we want to achieve by correcting them with details.

Internal marketing is about valuing each member of the team. The priority in sales is placed in two places: the member of our work team and the customer. If our people do not buy the product first, it will be impossible for them to sell it. It sounds very elementary, but it is a reality that we must take into account.

We must maintain an open door position at the management level to our staff. Knowing how to listen to the concerns of each member is a fundamental part of a solid, well focused and motivated organization.

Example is contagious, and just as we instil the ability to listen, we must set the example. People are eager to be heard. This is an unusual practice in human beings, since we do not know how to listen; we live from monologues in daily conversations or, in other cases, we turn a deaf ear to criticism for fear of being judged and having our vanity hurt. We resent hearing a different point of view, as is usually the case in politics.

When a good sense of belonging is developed, it is more difficult for them to seek to leave the company. Strengthening the team, which is the line of contact with the customer, is vital. Investing in talent by enhancing their skills and giving them spaces where they can develop so that they feel an integral part of the company is a priority.

People need to feel supported, valued and rewarded on a daily basis; this generates a close bond of trust that is difficult to break.

We must banish all negative comments, for it weakens the groups like a virus. The leaders of the teams that we will prepare must have a high capacity of coordination, besides a good handling of the interpersonal communication.

Being a successful company is our main goal and it involves constant improvement in many ways.

The company must be perceived as an example of commitment to the customer and to its employees.

164

Practical ways to implement successful teamwork

The change is to know that there are old, perished patterns of organization and sales methods. Our exponential growth will be the product of the philosophy that moves us. Change must be present as a culture of our organization.

Changing the mindset of those who enter and injecting each team member with a dose of optimism and positive attitude will be our priority.

We know that most come to their new jobs with a series of disappointments that become difficult to remove when they take root in their minds.

We must be flexible and permeable to the proposed changes in order to be able to beat their negative work schemes that they bring from their old experiences. All this is achieved through continuous training and motivation.

The method is based on creating a positive and relaxed learning environment, team work, reading printed materials, videos of positive thinking and sales techniques, filmed dramatization, telling experiences in the field to get the nectar of why a sale has not been closed. All these things will form an important part of our daily training scheme.

New Ideas Program: It's vital to have a detailed program of overcoming constant

where the protagonist is each member of the company. Overcoming The daily routine

must be part of the idiosyncrasy that marks the members.

We will encourage creativity in each new element, promoting meetings where new ideas flourish. We will dedicate time to this creative activity, where we will also discover new talents with the professional profile of leadership that the organization requires; thus, once discovered, we will model them through constant training, empowering them as leaders of work groups.

Coach or training:

It will be a permanent training, daily, face to face, that we will perform with each member. There, the person is known in all his dimension. Their mental schemes, the family processes that can determine a behaviour and the degree of motivation and integration to their group of belonging. It is a kind of confessional alone with the management where you can capture the issues that are moving you and in what direction. This coach should be daily and one to one every morning.

Training modules:

Today's markets are very competitive and therefore mark the need to be prepared in every way, technically and mentally. We can't afford to have a depressed organization without an attitude. With the project that we will put in place, we will be one step ahead of any competition. The knowledge incorporated will be of vital importance to add to the daily practice. We have detected, on many occasions, that the seller is tied to his old sales mentality and does not assimilate new concepts well.

This results in a deterioration in the capacity to generate individual sales overproductions.

Others mix a little from here, a little from there and add up to what we have, but it doesn't work out either and you get poor daily productions. When that same member applies the "script of success" that we have prepared to professionally face a sales conversation he will not need anything else, he will be a machine to execute closings of contracts to new clients.

Applying what you have learned becomes vital. The training modules determine a continuous program of acquiring knowledge that enriches the seller's vocabulary and charts a path to closure and, therefore, to personal success.

That is why our foundation stone is teamwork. The learned theory

every morning will bear fruit during the same day of work, sometimes it will take a few days to catch on in their minds, but never go beyond the week to verify that the whole theory turns into more sales quickly.

The company must make available to its members a school of knowledge where, by steps, its members will be able to go up, and where each step achieved in each stage will be qualified and rewarded by means of a series of tangible and intangible incentives.

The company will be doing not very extensive training modules, but very punctual ones, directed like missiles to the centre of the sales talk; to hit the target is to close the contract.

Our system tries, with this technique, not only to change the old schemes or sales patterns and inculcate others, but also to underpin the internal change that the company transmits and that the person must experience fully.

Teamwork requires constant recognition of the good performance of its members. A true leader rewards teamwork and the high productivity of a group of people he has helped to form and with whom he works. A person praised by his boss remembers the fact much more than we can imagine.

166

We must select individuals who possess certain qualities, such as leadership, analytical skills, and courage to make decisions to solve problems and conflicts, in depth knowledge of the technique outlined in the success scenario, relationship management skills, and self motivation.

Chapter 5: The Recommended Office

"You are not more because you are praised or less because you are criticized. You are what you are before God, and nothing more or less.

KEMPIS

Look for the office in an area that is easily accessible by public transportation. Choosing a good location is critical to the success of the plan and to attracting the large number of vendors who, we must remember, are our most important asset.

It can't be less than a hundred meters away. The costs vary by country, but on average we can say that it can be around five hundred to a thousand dollars/euros.

The office must be fitted out so that we can have a training room, which will be the heart of our business. Always seek to make it bright and well ventilated. When you rent, go with the people who are less complicated. It is essential to detect the good vibration that the place has before renting it, there are places with very bad energy and, although you do not believe it, this prevents the normal development.

An anecdote about this happened in an office on Berna Street in Mexico City, in the middle of the Zona Rosa of that city. We rented a two hundred and fifty meter floor right overlooking Reforma Avenue and the famous Angel of Independence. After six months of operation, we saw that sales were not up to our expectations. Everything was calculated as always and we did not know well why if we were all the same, but the expected results were not obtained. One day, my partner saw a shadow of a child pass by, according to her. We all began to laugh, although she was not amused. Another day we stayed up late at night working and felt a child crying. Things were getting a little thicker and we felt something strange was happening.

We then consulted with the night security staff and they told us that this was the case, that it felt like a child crying at night on that fifth floor. The next day, the first thing we did was call the real estate company that had rented to us and asked them to at least change the apartment. It turned out that we were offered the 13th floor, which we accepted. After the move, everything began to work out as it should, and we achieved incredible bills of money. And so, we had a few similar stories that we were able to save quickly. It seems like a fantasy, but real or not, depending on who judges it, it would seem that some offices have a particular energy or other, and we must be vigilant.

The office must have a training room that will be the vital centre of daily training, meeting place and breakfast. We must also complement it with some games, such as a table football for the halftime.

To have numerous chairs for those attending the trainings, a white video screen and a projector, a sound system for the videos, a coffee maker with unlimited coffee, some snacks, such as empanadas or croissants, a large table per coordinator to arrange the groups there while training or motivating, a white board and coloured markers.

Another vital space is the sales management office, which will be a room dotted with diplomas obtained by salespeople and supervisors, statistics posted, and awards held by the organization. It will be an open door place where the concerns of each member of the company will be addressed one by one and a daily individual and group coach will be provided.

We will also have a directory room for more discreet meetings with senior staff. An inventory room that may be small but must have a lot of security and access by only one person, apart from the company's partners, plus an administration area.

With all these spaces we are 100% prepared; more is a waste at first. We can also rent a smaller office, of about forty meters, in the same building to arrange the administration, since it must be in a much more private and isolated area, since it must concentrate in every detail to achieve a good management of support to the sale.

I remember a company that we visited with my partner in Buenos Aires; it had a separate administration and control table so that you could only enter with a magnetic card. It will be essential to install monitored cameras that record 24 hours a day, which you can access through the Internet and from your cell phone.

As for the administrative staff, we must both ensure that, above all, they are very tidy, meticulous, patient and with negotiating power. We must bear in mind that this area serves as the support for the entire sales structure. If we have messy staff, everything will be com plicated. If possible, take young people to the sales area because of the intense physical wear they will be exposed to, while in other positions you can have older personnel.

Chapter 6: Recruitment

"The best medicine is to have a joyful spirit that makes us live happily every day."

SOLOMON

"He who can master himself is worth more than he who can master a city."

Bible, Proverbs 16, 32

The notice

In principle, we will post our announcement on the job search web portals. Still, in some countries, the newspaper is also used. There were two advertising variables that we implemented in our career.

The first one, more cumbersome and less effective nowadays, is the one that is proposed by making a call to a certain place on certain dates. For example, we place it on a Sunday so that they can show up on the following Monday and Tuesday in a hotel where we rent a room for such purposes, in a coworking or in our offices. This was a method where endless lines were formed, not recommended.

The second way is less complicated and more detailed. In the notice, we have an email address where you can send your curriculum vitae. In this selection, we avoid crowds and disorder in our offices. Therefore, my recommendation is to put an email address where the applications arrive and we, in the comfort of our office, can select the profiles that interest us.

With this type of notice we usually receive about five hundred to a thousand applicants at a time with their references. These figures are characteristic of Latin America. It is essential to always repeat them every week and never be satisfied with the structure we already have.

Moving the structure constantly is important. This generates in those who already work in the company a feeling that no one is assured a place in the company without sales production.

It creates movement. It generates positive energy to see new applicants being inter viewed each week on different days and times. Those who are already working will feel pressure to continue generating high productions, since they know that human material is not lacking, and the evidence will be before their eyes.

No one works with the same enthusiasm as when he joined on the first day and we'll see what new broom sweeps better.

We want to say that most of the sellers, with the incentives we give, it is difficult for them to leave or to lower the production a lot, but you will see that many new members will quickly look for the first places in the sales ranking, and that pushes everyone up, to look for better results.

Similarly, it is important to separate new employees from old ones, because the old elements try to take care of their position and monopolize the prizes and incentives and see in the new blood a strong competition; instead, among old ones they know each other and know how far they are able to go.

Therefore, it is important to form new groups with new leaders every time you arrange a new recruitment announcement. If you start filling teams where one or two elements are missing, it will not be the solution, try to incorporate only one element at a time in an old group; maybe your colleagues will accept it and we will be lucky.

You have to smell the mood and interests of each group very well and be expectant of their concerns.

Never in your call talk about soliciting door to door salespeople, as few people want to work under this modality; neither ask for sales experience nor call for several weeks in a given date.

People who seem not to transmit much during the selection and training period then turn out to be sales dragons on the streets; many are not considered the best talent and therefore we should be the ones to train them and get them to believe it.

We must bring out that hidden talent that most people possess and are eager to show once they gain confidence in their new job.

Don't ask for an excellent level of communication, which very few possess on their own initiative, and don't realize that we will be subject to a lot of stress; don't use negative words in our ads.

We should always mention the corporation's brand as a hook, our distributor's brand is not necessary. Describe that we are calling for a new opening of offices in that city incorporating a photo of a very young working group with smiles and without a jacket or tie will be an option. We can say that it is a product of high demand. We will call in our call for personnel for different areas and both sexes, executives, supervisors and sales coordinators, promoters, administrative, each identified by references if preferred.

First, we must form the group of leaders in all areas of the company and train them for a week. Then, the following week, we call for the other second and third line positions. The offer has to talk about an excellent salary according to aptitude, including the highest commissions and bonuses in the market for accomplishment of goals together with offering permanent training.

We must guarantee professional development with international projection if it is the case, along with a career plan and the opportunity for short term promotions, always high lighting the very good work environment, plus a monthly training trip with stability and work continuity, along with the biweekly payment of commissions and awards, promising a significant monthly income depending on the country in which we are.

We must also ask for some requirements, such as good presence, immediate availability, having full or part time, without time restrictions, that are proactive, dynamic, with initiative, ambitious, with ease of speech, 100% positive attitude and constancy, sales attitude and commitment to work, used to meeting goals and obtaining results and, very importantly, emphasize that it is with or without experience. We will train them; therefore, the experience will be of little value to us.

We rely on finding people with a positive attitude. We need people who are hungry and thirsty for victory, for wanting to move forward, to eat the world, and not well-educated individuals who have no ambition. We have seen in thousands of resumes that we have analysed in our business career that many professionals who have graduated from universities first put their profession before their skills or the story of the supposed compendium of solutions that they will provide so that we, as a company, will be tempted to hire them.

We need to know if he's still studying and at what times. We have had excellent salesmen who studied in the mornings and joined in at noon until night and developed a high average of sales.

Here it is essential to determine your work experience. If you come from the sales field or from the competition and are imbued with the same product, do not take it into account in the selection, because what you will bring will only be bad practices or, failing that, you will not be able to take the chip out of your previous experience with the same product and will constantly compare.

We also have those characters who promise to bring their contacts or client list, do not take them into account; usually the client portfolio has been stolen from other companies, and whoever did it once will do it twice, and their next target will be you.

Many times, he will have to endure the spies of the competition; we must be very attentive to these characters, who often reveal their true intentions during the trainings. They are the ones who will be desperate to write down in detail every word you say, every slide you show from your projector.

One important thing is to know the reason for the departure from your last job and the remuneration received and now intended. It is essential to take this information into account, especially in order to know why, since people repeat their practices, both good and bad, at work.

The remuneration of his last job, added to that which is claimed by the applicant, will give us the mental rank in which he would be happy. In this item, there are many who will seem delirious to you, who will claim derisory sums, two thousand dollars for a position; do not be afraid, if they meet the required profile, hire them, because they are those who see the forest and not the tree. Inside, these people want a lot of money and they know that in a serious sales organization they can get it, and here you can also give it to them.

Knowing what your goal in life is in the short and medium term is important. We will know whether or not you are depressed and, if you are, how committed you are to your dreams.

Many reach their short-term goals and there die, get stuck, disappear from production. That is why we must be very attentive to those moments in order to shore up the element with a lot of motivation and follow up. They are recoverable with daily training and incentives. If you see that it does not start again, do not hesitate to take it out of your staff, because it will spread its negativity to others.

Another important item is to detect the applicant's most immediate current need, which will show us the degree of desperation he is in at the moment or what his priorities are. Knowing what their job expectation is in our call, in this way we will measure the degree of commitment they intend to bring to our organization.

Intelligent selection

Here I will set out some of the keys in the selection of personnel that are decisive when taking such an important step. Before the arrival of the resumes to our email, we must, first of all, look at the picture they send us.

It is important that the photo stands out clearly on the resumes. If you smile, that's the attitude you're looking for. We must analyse if he shows a lot of seriousness in his gaze, inexpressive eyes or a lost look; we must always take note and evaluate a little more thoroughly in that sense. Remember that the first impression is what counts and the photo is like a first impression before the first interview.

The second stage is the phone call to make the first appointment. It should be made by a person who has a firm tone of voice, not a low tone, with no motivation for the listener and who, in addition, denotes a high degree of confidence in what he or she is saying.

We will also have a first evaluation of the interested party by telephone. It will be to observe his empathy before the call, his tone of voice, if he begins to question us about the employment, remuneration, and it is transformed into a reverse interview. In that case, we must desist from that resume; at first sight, it is a complicated or desperate character that will question everything, and we need relaxed and fun people, with a positive mental attitude and easy to handle, docile to the policies of the company, that come to give us solutions and not problems, for that we are hiring staff, and we must have very clear.

If you object to the time of the appointment, it may be a sign of a bad element, but it is not definitive, check it.

Know something very important, don't get frustrated. This game is like that. Out of a total of about five hundred resumes that can be sent to you, you will be able to contact three hundred, of which 50% will go to the personal interview, where you will only have fifteen to twenty items left per week and per notice. Before the end of the month, they will be reduced by half. Each person who calls will be able to reliably contact about thirty people a day who confirm their attendance, which we have already said will only be 50%; this has always happened to us in all the countries of the world.

In more than fifteen years of doing the same practice of selecting and training vendors, most of whom are not very experienced, and transforming them into professionals is what we have seen as a pattern to follow.

In that first interview, we must know how to listen to the potential employee, especially his or her previous work experiences, because that is where the details that will guide us in an accurate analysis of the interviewee reside. Man is, in general, a being of habits. He repeats schemes, with rare exceptions.

Therefore, if one of the interviewees tells us that he resigned from his last job because he did not follow the company's sales method or did not agree with his boss on the policies developed, or complained that he had to work very late, or that he reported the company to some state agency and even filed a labour lawsuit against it, we will know that this is a conflictive element and is not the type of profile we are looking for; he will not row with us to reach the company's goals. Most of the time they don't want the entrepreneur to make money, they have ingrained in their minds preconceptions that do nothing right for successful companies.

What is a preconception, specifically speaking? We can summarize it with an example that I once took note of in a course and that I found very curious. It says the following:

A group of scientists placed five monkeys in a cage, in the centre of which they placed a ladder and, on top of it, a bunch of bananas. When a monkey climbed the ladder in search of such precious food, the scientists squirted cold water on those left on the ground. After some time, when a monkey was going to climb the ladder, the others would beat him up. After some time, no monkey would climb the ladder, despite the temptation of bananas. So, the scientists replaced one of the monkeys. The first thing he did was to climb the ladder, being quickly beaten down by the others. After some beatings, the new member of the group did not climb the ladder anymore. A second monkey was replaced, and the same thing happened. The first substitute enthusiastically participated in the rookie's beating. A third was changed and the same thing happened again. The fourth and finally the last of the veterans was replaced.

The scientists were then left with a group of five monkeys who, although they never received a cold water bath, continued to beat anyone who tried to reach the bananas.

If it were possible to ask any of them why they beat anyone who tried to climb the stairs, the answer would certainly be: "I don't know, things have always been done this way here". Sound familiar? "It's easier to disintegrate an atom than a preconception."

There are questions that can give us some guidance in selecting the best sales element, such as the following: why do you want to change jobs, why do you want to work in our company, if you have been looking for a job for a long time, if you are involved in any other selection process, if you like to work in a team or lead and what experience you had in this regard, if you have ever been fired from a job, tell you about any problems you had in a previous job, find out what your strengths and weaknesses are and what your financial expectations are or how many times a day you communicate with your partner are some of the many guidelines that will lead us to a better selection of sales personnel.

As we can see, we focus on knowing not only the work aspect, but also the personal aspect in a synthetic way. It is very important to watch the positive attitude and gestures in every interview. The arrogant or proud will be positive to discard.

Let's take a good look in that first meeting at those who criticize everything or who give only excuses for not getting the requested job, excuses such as schedules, studies, that of those training days they can only go to two of them and that they can only go in the after noon, because in the morning they must finish something they are doing. These are always excusing for not making the commitment.

Also, when selecting, rule out the person who asks questions such as whether we will give him or her Social Security, what time you finish work, whether you work on holidays, what days you have off in the week, whether the holidays are paid and when they will be; All this makes up a conglomerate of excuses that the conflictive individual possesses, the one who comes to work and not to work or is only looking for a basic salary, that is, to change his time for a minimum amount of money that is only enough to pay debts and his life in instalments, without freedom, without being able to fly like eagles.

Of course, you will have plenty of backing, and on Sundays, out of business strategy and social sense, you should not work. You will also have a holiday period and a long etcetera, but what we have to evaluate in a first interview is whether the potential element is conflictive or not.

If you are raising these issues instead of selling yourself as someone who is going to provide solutions to our company, you are planting in our business mind a series of negative doubts that are part of your negative personality and, therefore, it is clear that it will not be an added value to our structure; if we are going to hire someone, it is only on the condition that they help us to achieve our objectives, we do not intend to be a charity company, nor can we waste our time with conflicting people who delay our plans.

That is why in this book I give you all the details so that you take note and do not stumble over these stones that will put your organization in check if you decide to incorporate them or will delay your time, delaying the goals to be achieved. This is where all companies fail, that is why it is so important to read these paragraphs several times.

All the individuals who make comments like the ones above are losers; moreover, they are the ones who will not sell anything and will only bring conflict into your organization. They are people who live from failure as a way of life.

From negativism they make their north, from envy their feeling, from destructive criticism their action against the interests of the businessman and his col leagues as well. Their eyes and glances will also tell us a lot. His questions, expressions, gestures, tone of voice, clothes, general appearance. If he sells his qualities with pride, he will not be of any use to us either, we must evaluate humility as positive and detect intelligence and skills.

Our profile is that of humble people, open to learning, young, smiling, with a good look. The one who enters demanding a high salary, let's discard it, forget it, is the one who only sells coloured mirrors and does not work to achieve results. Now, the one who asks and is interested in the commissions and bonuses he can earn by making a greater production is the person who will push our company to success. We were born to sell.

The successful man is a salesman in every respect. Those who have tasted the honeys of success in this profession know this well. It is a profession that re quires a lot of perseverance and immunity from the feeling of failure, because throughout the working day we will receive countless rejections of our sales offers.

There will also be the "yes" votes waiting for us after a "no" vote or an objection from a client, but they will have to put up with everything: heat, rain, cold, talking nonstop for five hours or more, feeling the rejection at every step and seeking daily success after those rejections; the result measured hour after hour generates that adrenaline that brings us clos er to achieving our goals a little more each day.

176

That's why we put so much emphasis on and apply so many motivational techniques on a daily basis, because we know that it will take them to achieve top selling productions. On the way we know that there will be many left who will not be strong enough to endure the epic, but we also know that we will reach victory with the bravest and most daring, with those whose north are the stars of success.

Once we have selected the resumes we liked, let's print only the first sheet with the main data, name, address, telephone numbers, personal data, profession, to avoid unnecessary expenses and waste of prints.

Important condition is that you and your partner make that first intelligent cybernetic ad selection. Do not leave it to chance or to third parties, and much less in the hands of companies that are dedicated to the recruitment and selection of personnel, because they are expensive and do not serve our business scheme. There is no one better than your own eye to watch over the profile of the closest collaborators you wish to have at your side in your company.

The basis of the business is based on a very good selection. If its bases are made of mud and not concrete, everything will fall down like a house of cards. The selection of personnel is a constant in companies that suffer from the same basic problem, the poor selection of their executives, the lack of motivation and, consequently, the high rotation due to not having constant training.

Some large corporations suffer because of naivety, an employee who does not have his shirt on, that is, the brand engraved in his heart and mind is a potential enemy within the organization; consciously or unconsciously, he will boycott the excellence that every corporation seeks to have in the attention of its customers or in its organization and to obtain good profits based on super sales productions and optimal management.

For these first interviews, we have always used a coworking or virtual office, which are so fashionable today, in order to sift through the selection without contaminating our peaceful environment which should be our usual workplace. There, in that coworking, unwanted personnel will be discarded. It will even be possible to implement it on the first day of induction, where the bad elements are still detected that we must remove without contemplation, because, as the saying goes, "a rotten apple rots the rest".

Ask yourself what an eighteen year old boy looking for a salesperson position has in common with a forty year old man looking for a sales manager or coordinator or administrative manager position. The answer is nothing. Therefore, implement different trainings for each target.

The eternal job seekers, professionals in this area, can also be found in that line; they will recognize them because nothing is good for them, they are nonconformists, they justify their inefficiency and frustrations by means of excuses to their families.

Something to note is that once you use an ad and it works, always repeat the same one, because every week you will get the same result, it is a fact.

Remember that you have to do two interviews before moving on to group induction.

In the first interview you will only have to test your profiles so that, in a second phase that will take place the next day, you can dedicate a little more time to those who showed the best attitude for the job and that we evaluate as positive.

Don't be afraid if you get an important line because you have been interested in spending some extra time with some individuals. If possible, have them come to an airconditioned room where they can listen to good music or, better yet, watch a motivational or institutional video of the company while they wait for their interview. This makes them more motivated for the interview and they are not thinking negatively or increasing their nerves with every minute that passes.

Don't throw away the ugly ones, because we have had incredible experiences of sale, what they don't have of pretty they have of nice and talkative. Don't get rid of those who aim to be inexperienced, they are a raw gem that you will polish. Be sure to call those who say it's their first job, they'll be the best you'll get. Don't exempt the quiet ones, because in the sales area they may be talking parrots, they may show some shyness at first, but when they let go, it doesn't stop them. Do not discard them because of social class, religion, race, sex or nationality; they will all enrich your company, I assure you.

Most people, when they are unemployed, are hungry for an opportunity, and what you have is much more than that to offer them. It will be a unique business model where they will feel contained, valued and earn a lot of money, which they would not get in any other job.

In just five minutes it will be sold or not. That is the time of all or nothing that always entails the first impression in an interview; if it happens, it will go on to the second call, which will be longer. In this first meeting, we must ask little and listen much.

People like to feel selected, so the more we go around the subject and the more time they spend in long lines or coming to each interview and training day after day, strangely enough, the more enthusiastic the applicant becomes.

I don't know why it turns out that way, but we have always noticed it in different countries. If they see that few people come to the interviews, they feel like that company has no perspective or the proposal has not been very attractive based on a superfluous evaluation that people make at that time and, therefore, they give up, even without listening to the proposal, because they think inside that they feel a little silly if they were the only ones who took the job proposal. I suppose it is part of our nature, it is the mass man that Ortega y Gasset described well in his book The Rebellion of the Masses.

If, however, the applicant sees a room full of people waiting in different areas of the office, with good music so that no one hears what we say in the interviews and avoid dialogue between them, the story changes, because he sees the company as burning in motivation and job offer. Besides, seeing so many people applying, it means that it is difficult to get in and that the company must pay very well, due to the amount of people, so the enthusiasm is contagious and the desire to belong to the work team increases.

At the end of the day, these applicants are our first clients to capture; they will see and feel the movement of your office, and it generates positive energy. Therefore, quote many people per hour to generate this effect.

It is advisable that the wait takes place in the same training room so that you can read the positive phrases on the walls, see the balloons with the company's colours hanging, the blackboards full of numbers that reflect objectives, the diplomas hanging obtained by the best, the winners' podium, the photos of the sales groups in the area smiling and others showing the sales training trips, and do not forget a coffee dispenser that can be served while you wait.

All this will create an atmosphere of wanting to be part of that organization, of wanting to belong.

The second interview is when we probe the candidate a little better, ask more questions and let him/her loose in the conversation. That day they complete the application and we ask them for a photocopy of their ID before moving on to the second meeting.

At that second meeting, already individual, for those who are selected, they will be called for an induction or first day of training. It is the day they are so looking forward to, as we will pass on to them the projection of the economic proposal, the organization chart, why and how to get the money we promise and that we assure they will get. In the tele phone call we will inform them that they have been selected for the expected induction, in which they will be presented with the employment proposal and the company.

On that occasion, we must give a strong and motivating speech that will make them tremble with emotion, which we must complete with some short videos, either an institutional one and other motivational ones that we can get from YouTube, where they talk about the law of attraction, among other topics.

Likewise, during this induction, we must tell them that they are still in the selection process and that they have not yet definitively joined the company and must go through a training session that will last two days.

This plan is mostly for salesmen. You are supposed to have already set up the sales coordinator and supervisor scheme in advance.

The more time you spend on training your sales staff, especially those in the hierarchy
supervisors and coordinators the better the results will be, because you will be building commitment and trust in the core of the structure. Invite them to lunch on pizzas if you feel it is necessary.

Make them feel part of a common destiny. Don't push them, engage them. Make them shout out the goals to be achieved day after day so that they nestle in their minds. Don't have breaks in the day. Let them withdraw separately. This is achieved by talking one by one about the proposal, the project, the objectives, what their contribution will be to the company and what we expect from it; every day we must go through this mental itinerary before each one goes home at the end of the day. This, at least, in the early days. Always be on the lookout for negative comments and cut them off.

Let us always prepare a greater number than we need in each position, for some will surely fall by the wayside. The watchword is zero tolerance for attitude problems.

Don't worry, next week there will be another selection, and so on every week, until we are satisfied with the number of members in the groups.

At that first induction the numbers will be given. If you decided to have a better base salary, recruitment and retention will be easier. People tend to stay in a job if they have a better base salary than just working for commissions; a salesman may have a base salary, a supervisor the same or with a small differential increase of more than 10%, because his main earnings will come from his bonuses and commissions.

It is a small initial investment that, together with the office, you will have to arrange by borrowing, applying for a credit, using some savings, selling your car; you will recover it in two months and, if you wait one more month, you will buy a better one.

Find an investment partner to whom you can propose the business and who will provide the total investment; in short, see how you do it, but I advise you that, if you accompany yourself with blind faith, the project will find its way easily. The money appears, is the least of it. Nor are we talking about impossible figures. You will see that a minimum investment is needed. I guarantee that, if you follow the map drawn in this book, it will be a matter of a short time before you get your hands on a million dollars, as happened to us on several occasions in different countries. Banish fear, your worst enemy, and you will see.

Base all additions only on the ads. Do not select friends, siblings, cousins or brother in law, among others; they boycott the position within the company of whoever approached them. Couples are not recommended, nor are relationships within the company, they should always be avoided.

Those administrative employees who insinuate in a job interview that they prefer an administrative position to a sale one is useless, because we must have a different administration than the rest of the companies focused on sales.

The ideal is to train sales managers, who are not common managers who meet a schedule and run, but must be intense, detailed, highly organized, mentally coordinated with the goals of the company, feel integrated into the project and do not spare efforts to achieve daily, weekly and monthly objectives.

Those who seek employment in sales sometimes do not discard them as administrative if the profile beats, because they are the same ones who will be able to carry out successfully an administration of this type, because their spirit is connected with them, they love the sale, they feel like salesmen too and they will be rewarded as such; they will be, thus, concentrated in the achievement of results and not in fulfilling a strict schedule together with a bureaucratic scheme that hinders everything. In addition, they will be able to understand from another perspective, that of the sale, the administration. We don't need bureaucrats, but action people in this area as well.

They must complement their experience with computer knowledge and have a lot of ability to work under pressure, along with the ability to know how to do things intelligently, without predetermined schedules. The important thing is to always find the desired result.

Whoever leads this sector must have an impeccable sense of organization of the detail and be a born leader to know how to refer other subordinates' part of the work, must establish priorities and maintain a fluid dialogue with clear guidelines and codes to be taken into account in the daily relationship with his or her leaders. He must even be an excellent motivator.

Take note, in the administrative field we need sales dragons as well, where they have to achieve results and accompany the fighting spirit of the vendors who are deployed in the streets. They have objectives, not schedules to meet, with a positive attitude as the first requirement.

In the interview you should sell yourself for the job by goal and under pressure to get results. We must assess the reasons for leaving your last job to detect possible patterns of behaviour.

We will be able to know if a salesperson, supervisor or coordinator was well chosen in the first instance during the interviews, then during the training days, and finally in the practice that will be done during two days in the area, in which the capacity of these people for the sale will be evaluated.

An applicant who in his first three days does not develop a positive attitude and therefore sales must be considered unsuitable to join our company. The results have to be from the first day, and we have to let the interested parties know it.

The maximum trial period for the definitive incorporation, after an exhaustive selection and training, is between forty eight hours and one week maximum.

If the character in question obtained zero sales in the first forty eight hours, a yellow light is lit, we can give him, if he has a good attitude, forty eight more hours to achieve a concrete result.

The profile we are looking for in a supervisor, coordinator or sales manager should be that of a leader. The basic qualities that we must evaluate in this selection, in addition to those described above, are the following:

Leadership. This means that you must get everyone to admire you and follow you blindly. Provide a positive attitude; you must motivate your team through overflowing enthusiasm. Humility, always the proud is rejected by your team sooner or later. Self-motivation; the company cannot continuously motivate a person who does not have the slightest self-motivation. Creativity, an essential quality to solve difficult situations in the area with customers or with your team. Proactivity; the supervisor cannot stand still in a corner and watch events unfold without his intervention. Perseverance, it is very necessary to achieve the proposed objectives daily. Dexterity, fundamental to organize the groups in the area and to accompany their development. Smile, every candidate must always smile. Ability to close sales supported by the script of the sales success. Knowledge; it is necessary that you know the sales techniques, how to apply them and teach them. Knowing how to provide goals, having to expose the daily objectives and monitor the results. Know how to recognize and take advantage of all opportunities and teach them to your environment. Support your people, seeing their evolution and recognizing their successes with tangible and intangible motivations.

We're talking about a whole character. A coordinator is a kind of small-scale sales manager, in that dimension we call a sales force unit, made up of two supervisors with four salespeople each, who are assigned to a rapidly deployable team. We've called him a coordinator, not a manager, because titles paralyze, debase and fatten.

We need to set up a mobilized and nonbureaucratic structure that will gain ground every day, deploying the best sales tools and strategies for motivating and containing human groups, where competition will be an essential ingredient.

What we will implement is to put in the uniform the position that identifies them, account executive, supervisor, coordinator, sales force coach, and also, we will add through metal pins the stars or dragons that correspond to the courses or skills developed or achievements made. They can be placed on the cap, shirt, polo shirt or jackets they wear for cold or rainy days.

The supervisor is the quintessential assistant to the coordinator. He's one step behind. He's getting ready to take over as coordinator. He's a born closer. He's a motivator, too. He has in his head the same mentalized daily goals that his team must achieve, and he doesn't let anyone down until he achieves them. Success is measured in centimetres and detail is everything. Poorly selected personnel can create a negative revolution in the company that is sometimes very difficult to contain.

Let's agree that we request employees to provide solutions and help us to develop the company's potential. Let's be clear that we do not pay for them to bring us conflicts. In or der to do so, it is better to avoid the bad elements. These can be smelled by certain attitudes, presence, questions, looks, energy that they denote in interviews.

The ultimate idea is to recruit people who have career aspirations and not just salary, who have short and long-term dreams, not that their minds are focused on meeting the most pressing minimum daily needs, as if they were going to put out a fire every day.

We have seen that the selection process comprises a multitude of schemes and guidelines that we must comply with in order to obtain a concrete result based on a unique, prepared and motivated sales force. It is up to us to banish fears and apply all our potential in discovering the detail in each interview to obtain an elite that will accompany us on our path in the path of our desires; fulfilling goals daily, step by step, you will go far.

Chapter 7: Business Induction

It's our light, not our darkness, that scares us. We ask ourselves, "Who am I to be brilliant, beautiful, talented, extraordinary? ». Rather, the question to ask is, "Who are you not to be? ». Your smallness does not serve the world. There's nothing enlightened about diminishing yourself so that other people don't feel insecure around you. You were born to manifest the divine glory that exists within us. That glory is not only in some of us; it is in each of us. And when we allow our light to shine, we give another people permission to do the same. When we are freed from our fear, our presence automatically frees others.

NELSON MANDELA

It is very important that you concentrate on these first two days of induction that we must carry out to strengthen the selection that we have made in the interviews. Here we develop the philosophy that we want to transmit in the training to be your most powerful sales force.

If you want to be successful in recruiting sales staff and consolidating a team, your speech must be compact and highly motivating. You have to sell to that audience which are your sales teams. It will be your most important sale. Selling the idea to a group of future collaborators is a real goal.

They must buy, be 100% convinced of what they have bought; that is to say, the company, the proposal, the brand, the product or service offered and their offer. There should be no margin of doubt in any of them, much less in you.

They, when withdrawing from their first day induction, must be convinced to continue with the training and introduction into the two day business ahead of them. They must begin to trust the project. They must leave enthusiastically.

On that day you will have to take care of the detail, nuance the meeting with coffee and some snacks. You can help yourself with PowerPoint slides. A festive atmosphere should be created, not a cemetery atmosphere, with good music to brighten up the day. This awakens and creates a good atmosphere of positive vibes.

I know that first day is the hardest, it will take a day or two to integrate. You'll probably find yourself fearful, insecure, distrustful, dazed and expectant. It is not unreasonable to have a couple of assistants from the same sales staff who can give positive feedback, when requested, about their work experience in our company.

184

I remember that, at the time of the coffee break, the applicants would secretly approach the employees who already belonged to the company to ask them about the work climate, the salary or the commissions and incentives.

We allowed this interaction because, in our company, money, a good work climate and high motivation always abounded. So, it was a very positive sequence.

At other times, I was the one who randomly called those arriving at the office to talk about their experience in our company.

Many commented that, thanks to their work, they had been able to build one more floor in their house, others said that they had won televisions, state-of-the-art cell phones, trips to an all-inclusive beach and we even gave a prize of a 4x4 in very good condition to the best coordinator.

Others told of the countless cash prizes they earned each week or that their monthly earnings reached two thousand dollars some months when they were only account executives in countries where the base salary was only about two hundred. This created a certain confidence and joy on the part of the applicants and, above all, an important desire to start in this new job that was presented to them as a real opportunity.

It is important that you study every sentence you will say very well and rehearse a few days before. Repeat, listen to your tone of voice and, if necessary, record yourself to notice the cadence of the words and to emphasize some point to which you want to give more importance so that on that day of the presentation everything comes out 100% and you manage to capture not only the momentary attention of those you have selected, but also their mind and heart, just like Di Caprio in the film The Wolf of Wall Street.

Each step must be unique, a set of words, as if it were a script that we must pronounce in order to convince those who will be present that day.

The presentation is based on saying who we are. A good institutional video helps a lot. Exposing the schedule and objectives of the course along with the immediate eco nomic future and growth perspective within the company. It continues with the story of the company's history at the international level, if any, and the local, numbers, number of customers, staff and philosophy.

We will then describe the potential of the market today, based on market studies that we must achieve. Expose to the audience that we have made an exclusive sales script that represents how to get daily results in every conversation.

The script is like a movie script, where we are the main actors, the client is our audience and who should applaud our presentation. That applause is the same as buying our arguments. That applause means a closure, that is, the main objective of each conversation.

The more days the initial course lasts, the greater the commitment of those who participate. During the induction of the first day, we must expose the example of the bonus scheme that we will implement.

When you make the exposure of how much you are going to earn, don't forget to have a big blackboard where the numbers are written down in order and the final number is highlighted in coloured circles; if necessary, erase everything and repeat, but always draw large numbers and explain until there is no doubt.

It is important to dress very well for this occasion, have a good watch on your wrist and always gesture and speak in a loud and confident voice. If you don't have any of this, borrow it. Some investment we have to make, minimum in our appearance.

We must know how to explain what a paradigm is with these examples. Did you ever think about this strange word? Perhaps not, but it is a word that often conditions us in our lives. In short, they are limits that we impose on ourselves. One acts according to the culture and education and one sets oneself limits.

Did you know that the inventor of the quartz clock was a Swiss and not a Japanese? The problem was that, in Switzerland, in his own watch company, he was told that this invention would not work. He took it to Japan and today this industry has overtaken Switzerland as the largest watch producer in the world. We call this that the Swiss company experienced paradigmatic paralysis. We all have some of it to a greater or lesser extent, and it is the result of some of our negativity, of our preconceptions.

We have an idea of everything beforehand; many times, we judge without even informing ourselves, investigating or just listening to our surroundings. We believe that we are being attacked all the time. That we are always victims; therefore, we must react and attack.

The paralysis that paradigms bring are the fears we have of failure, of prejudging our new work, of mumbling and saying "this is not for me" without even trying, of believing that all sales jobs are the same, that they never pay, that it is difficult, what my parents, my girlfriend or my friends will say.

We spend our time thinking of concerns that come from our negative minds and our previous experiences, which anchor us in the past and tend to repeat them.

To combat these paradigms, we must go to the heart of the matter and attack our sub conscious with statements such as "everything I want" and that "I believe that, with passion, it is possible to happen".

This formula contains two important statements. Desire is a concept that few people understand. Your desire for money must be so compelling if you want your subconscious to attract for you the prosperity you seek.

The second important point is a very subtle notion. The very nature of the universe is abundance and prosperity and you are part of the universe; then, in your deeper nature, you are receiving abundance and prosperity as well.

Always imagine the best of every situation that is about to happen, because that is what you will get.

Once, in Mexico, due to the drop in commissions, my partner came up with the idea of contacting a cell phone company to offer our services. They quickly gave us the distribution.

We didn't have any salesmen to dispose of there. I decided to remove one of the security product coordinators who claimed to have experience in the field. I asked him how much we could sell. He answered that a thousand postpaid plans a month. I told him that the distributor, who had fifty locations throughout the country, only sold about five hundred.

He insisted that he could sell that number with a reduced sales force of no more than twenty salesmen. I was enthusiastic and supported him in his conviction, which I made my own as well.

When we presented him to the other managers of the company, they smiled; my partner was overcome by a face of doubt when we set the three month deadline for reaching that figure. The rest is history, four hundred and eleven new client contracts in the first month, eight hundred and eight in the second and 1296 in the third month.

Focusing our mind on our dreams is vital; discarding paradigms, fundamental, not looking back and moving forward to conquer our goals.

The real secret is in the visualization of our goals, which consists of feeling sensations, positive emotions that, at the same time, must form those images in your spirit. The subconscious only understands the images and emotions that shape inside.

In our case, it was the excitement and challenge of selling a thousand post paid plans without a single moment's hesitation.
When you visualize and feel emotion, your conscious spirit cannot get in the way. If you visualize the fulfilment of your wish and if you feel an emotion of intense joy, like when you get goose bumps because something has affected you deeply, I assure you that your wish will be fulfilled.

Mind visualization is the key to success, mind visualization is the way with which I can communicate with my subconscious every day and under any circumstances. Focus all your abilities on the realization of your priority desire. When you are visualizing the realization of your deepest dream and aspiration, you will have to feel joy and satisfaction, as if this realization has already come true.

If your priority wish were actually fulfilled, wouldn't you feel happy and joyful?

The subconscious does not understand reason, it understands imagination and emotions.

This is why your visualizations must be accompanied by positive emotions. The outside world is the representation of your thoughts.

Chapter 8: Keys for the Professional Salesperson of a Sales Force Unit

"The less effort you make, the faster and more powerful you will be."

BRUCE LEE

"In a battle between you and the world, side with the world."

FRANK ZAPPA

We must present our mission to our audience and bring it into line with our work philosophy in a second day of training. We must explain some topics to shape the idea of leader and salesman that we intend to form.

In principle, let's start by developing the concept of intelligence; for our approach, we consider that the one who reads all the books and gets the best grades is not the most intelligent, but the one who knows how to take advantage of opportunities and apply his or her knowledge, lead a team, the one who knows the techniques of selling right and wrong.

How many professionals exist today driving a taxi or doing anything else outside of what they studied, frustrating their days, surviving, wasting their strength and their minds in jobs that do not satisfy them and some of them are intoxicated by the spirit. It is a background from which it is difficult to escape, because the time we should have to think is wasted in low paying jobs that leave us no time to develop new opportunities, of which life is full at every step. Time is the greatest added value to our existence, we cannot go to a supermarket and buy time; therefore, we must think at every step if what I am doing satisfies my expectations and my days.

For many, that kind of comfort zone means having a mediocre job; it is a refuge, a cave full of fears where we hide, because we are afraid of escaping from that supposedly full security zone that we think we have. Therefore, we do not want to take a step outside of there for fear of failure or because many times we have family and responsibilities to cover, we suppose; they are just excuses. The harsh reality is that no one taught us where to start, not even in the study rooms.

In these pages we talk about how to develop economically in an exponential way and not about how to survive the circumstances that are presented to us. Everyone is free to choose whether to continue in that world of economic turtles or jump on the side of the successful building dragons.

An opportunity is the capacity to know how to take advantage of the resources and tools that the company gives us to easily achieve the desired success. We must work as a team towards a common goal, where everyone has to commit to what they are doing. You have to look at the forest and not just the tree, old saying, but very true.

A good exercise is for each participant in these trainings to briefly relate their one to one dreams that they have to fulfil in the short and medium term. Then make them see that they must make a commitment to them, and that is the common denominator of successful people, commitment.

Our team must have every day what the main weapon of work will be. Some have their computers, others their diaries and others their phones. Here will be the positive mental attitude. The problems that we all have we must leave them parked in the past, outside the scope of the company; it is useless to bring them to the present, it is useless to walk with the problems on our backs, it is like a very heavy backpack, because you walk depressed and you depress the rest.

People who work sometimes think they are doing the entrepreneur a favour when the only real favour they are doing themselves. The hours when they waste time and stray from their daily goals come out only to their own detriment.

They're not stealing from the company; they're stealing from their families. Every hour that passes and no sale is generated, the seller is fooling himself and no one else. Our company is not going to get richer or poorer because one or more of them stops at a pool hall to play a game, takes two hours for lunch or goes to a casino or a football game.

There's the salesman who says, "I got kicked out of my cashier's job and now I'm taking a job in sales while I get something more stable. Those are the ones who are ruining the sales profession, those are the ones who are passing through while they get a desk.

Stability is in their minds first, not in their jobs. In the U.S., 15% of tax revenue comes from sales. In developed countries, selling is recognized as a career, but our limited vision brings this great profession down to earth. Cell phone salespeople spend a year going from company to company or changing distributors within the same company. Those who are without emotional balance or professional seriousness are themselves, not the companies.

Movement creates emotion. A salesman once talked to me about selling me something. He wanted to sell me, and I let him, he used all the rebuttals or objections to my doubts, I had him try it for fifteen minutes; at the end I asked him to buy questions: "How much is it worth? ». That's a buying question. It was to close right there. I gave him the opportunity and he left, he continued talking without knowing how to listen, which is the first thing we must take into account in a sales conversation, knowing how to capture the needs of the potential customer and knowing how to listen to him.

A salesperson has to be closing all the time and be aggressive, learn to push, talk to as many potential clients as possible, asking them closing questions; getting a "yes" is a goal, then another "yes", and so on until accumulating several to reach the most important one, which is the final yes, the one for closing the sale; the sale is a game of accumulating yeses and constantly trying to close.

The salesman who cannot learn to close must think of another career, and I am serious, very serious.

Let us know that there is no such thing as an interview without a sale; in each interview a closing is made, the seller sells a service or product to his interlocutor or the potential client sells him his reason for not buying. In either case, a sale was made. The only question is: who is going to close it? Is it our salesman or the client? We must be relentless in closing sales.

The clothing that we will have to implement for our company will be a polo shirt with the logos of the company and the position of the person who holds it in the same, accompanied by a cap printed with the position and logo as well and, if it is cold, they will have a windbreaker or raincoats, always with the logos and rank within the structure, besides having pins that identify if they have done some special course or have achieved important goals as the salesman of the month, of the year, the one you choose to reward.

Who likes to deal with salesmen? No one, really. Why? Because they are heavy, they have dense arguments, they attempt against our already stipulated monthly budgets; then, I ask: why look like salesmen if there is so much prejudice against them?

Therefore, the slogan to open a business conversation will be "don't look like a salesman"; always talk about that it is a group of special promotions of the company that only for today presents the product with that determined offer as well. We should always play with the scarcity of the product arguing that there are only two or one left, like in Internet stores, which put a counter to play with the time of the offer pretending that it is limited too.

We will study the best available offers, compare them with our competition and com pact them so that even a child will understand them, that is the idea we must convey.

That is to say, we select a maximum of three devices or products if we are talking about cell phones, two if we are talking about alarms or those that we think are convenient according to the business in which we are involved, but as a maximum we select three.

The reason is simple, we must first make the seller understand the offer in order to explain it correctly to the potential client and, if we have a lot of equipment, rates, options, contract terms, both the seller and the buyer will go for the cheapest and shortest contract term due to the fear of possible rejection by the client, and these options are the ones that generally take the least commission.

Two or three good products, two rates for the service, a single contract term, a single sales conversation that does not go beyond ten minutes.

All of this must be translated into a specific sales script with the technique of approach, presentation, argumentation and closing.

The sales methods that companies have developed over time have been telephone marketing, direct email, attention in public places or shopping malls, stands at fairs or exhibitions, referral work, visits to companies, among others. All of these are relatively effective and are only a complement. Today we add social networks, but their impact is also relative if we want to close daily sales in the heat of the day, unless we implement good sales funnels that we will discuss in a next chapter.

The best approach is to work in the field. Going out to look for clients and not waiting for them to magically appear. Look for them in their workplaces and in their homes. It is the best method to make sales super productions. To show the product, that can prove it, to manipulate it, will be an added value to be able to close the contract. It generates a sense of belonging by having it in your hands.

As a fundamental part, we must explain the sales script we will call success and its objections, implementing filmed sales theatres to detect the failures that arise in them and rewarding the best actors. The colleagues will write down the mistakes of the actors and then comment on them and draw conclusions.

The first five minutes of the presentation will be the concrete foundation with which to build the bridge to success in every sales conversation.

The issue of knowing how to handle "no" in a sales conversation is fundamental.

Who likes to be told no? No" humiliates us, destroys us; our task, in short, is to be told a final "yes" in most cases. The "no" must form conscience in the professional salesman who is paid with the fixed salary he has.

The rest of the rewards will be for the yeses, i.e. commissions, incentives and prizes. They must learn to turn every "no" into a "yes", we need to capitalize on that "no" as it comes.

There are three elements to success: moral strength, organization of time, time is money and sacrifice. Remember that moral strength is the engine that will take us beyond where we ever imagined. He who does not have moral strength is condemned to failure in everything he undertakes. To organize ourselves hour by hour in our day is the basis for the fulfilment of our objectives. Let us know that earning a lot of money is going to take some sacrifice. Giving all of us, one hundred percent, at all times and in all places, is the key.

We must bear in mind and remember that the excitement curve of a salesperson in this special promotion sales force unit scheme lasts about four hours. We must make the most of each of those hours.

If we could get an hourly closing, we would have obtained up to four in a single day; thus we could reach, with just one salesperson, in twenty working days, eighty contracts per month in a group of one supervisor handling four elements in the UFV (sales force unit), and we would be talking about three hundred and twenty contracts per month per sales force unit of one supervisor and four executives. If in this scheme we add four of these units, we will exceed one thousand contracts by far in the month based on our experience.

Chapter 9: Training Manuals and Operating Modes

"We never get what we deserve, but what we bargain for."

CHESTER L. PITCHERS

As for the assembly of a training manual, it should contain and develop fundamental topics to achieve more and better sales. It should be deployed in parts or modules in computer programs such as PowerPoint that allow us to project and train in the mornings to the staff in different topics.

Training must be constant, and this is perhaps the most important point in order to obtain superlative results. It must accompany the whole process. Coaches must convey credibility and energy. They must be based on shoring up a professional sales conversation by giving all the tools and manuals to achieve optimal results.

In order to do so, we must take into account certain aspects regarding the training issue. They must be carried out in a room set up for this purpose, conditioned as described in the part on office installation. We must have money in our pockets for daily incentives. Competition between groups should be implemented, such as practical written exercises to consolidate the concepts taught during training; crosswords or questionnaires may be used.

The screenings should address different topics related to sales and motivation. There should be a substantial collection of films on specific topics that can be downloaded from YouTube. Subsequently, a personalized training coach should be carried out daily with each individual to analyse their day to day evolution and their attitudes.

Our motto must be zero tolerance for attitude problems. Previously, during and after the training, we talk separately with each supervisor and coordinator to monitor weekly goals and motivation levels. Once a month, each supervisor should prepare a training on a specific topic to develop, in order to train future leaders.

As for the training itself, we must divide it into teaching modules so that each morning a different one is dealt with. All of them should be designed for a greater assimilation by the sales staff.

Then we must move on to a competition between groups and set up a jury of team coordinators who will evaluate the results and offer some cash or intangible prize, such as a diploma or just a loud applause and paid lunch.

At the beginning of the morning, after a good breakfast consisting of coffee and sandwiches or something else, it is important to start with a sales technique module, followed by a crossword puzzle to see how much was learned or captured from it; this gives very good results, as you will be attentive to the content of the modules.

Finally, the coach or sales manager or you in person can go on to give the results of the sales rankings or each team or sales force unit and how they are positioned for the awards.

Never tell the end result, but rather talk about the difference in accounts that are kept with each other. This is so that there is no disappointment among the sales elements, since in most cases they believe that they keep more accounts than they are and doubts and thus discouragement may begin. There are times when the accounts will be in process and others will be incomplete, so it is necessary to implement a recovery accounts department. This is essential, because you will find many such accounts for different reasons, including a poorly filled contract, missing a piece of paper, bad credit and rejection, among others that each organization will determine to reject or approve a customer. Although today there are much more modern methods, such as digital, where one sets the print and ready the contract, so simple and modern, or just make a recorded phone call and implement the contract.

Talking about motivation is, among other things, giving the rankings to see how far each one is from reaching the different prizes announced. Very important is to accompany every morning with a daily cash motivation; it can be said that every seller who brings five contracts in the day will get twenty dollars or euros, the one who makes more contracts will be awarded with forty or reward the winning team of the day with a paid lunch, always taking care to put a minimum of daily accounts to get the prizes. As for the weekly or monthly prizes, we can implement cameras, food baskets, etc.

Assemble your own modules easily, too. Go to a bookstore and select the sales and motivational topics that you consider interesting to display and set up your pages as slides for your video projector.

The modules should contain various topics, such as, the closing of a sale, the type of seller we require, the professional business conversation, the objections, the philosophy in sales, personal image and magnetism, goals and dreams, the keys to success, the enemies of the seller fear, selfishness and negativity, the power of thought, self-esteem and self-motivation, self-suggestion and the exercise of affirmations, opening and closing a sale, the sales script, the power of negotiation, the typology of the client, the one who separates a winner from a loser, topics for the training of team leaders, the salesman and his profiles, etc. Good results will be proportional to the readings and practice in daily sales theatres that are executed in teams, that is, more training equals more sales.

There are many topics of interest that we can select to teach our vendors. Unfortunately, we don't have enough space in this book, but they abound in major bookstores and on the Internet; it's a matter of finding, selecting and developing a program to project our sales force every morning.

Pocket manuals for salespeople and group leaders

All manuals should be prepared in such a way that they can be carried daily for consultation and self-motivation. In this one must mark in a simple and amusing way what we must not forget to develop a professional work in the sales area.

We can make it from semihard covers. It must have the logos and some image alluding to the company and the title Pocket Manual for the professional door to door sales executive or, in the case of the manual for leaders, it can be called Manual for super leaders of sales units.

Combine your manual with figures, drawings or photos that identify each topic and, at the bottom of the page, arrange some famous or funny phrase that motivates.

It is important, even if we are not a famous film director, to make a short film of this manual and the script of the sales success in order to train them and let them see the reality of the work to be done. Let's take two or more supervisors and coordinators and film on location a series of conversations with clients. Then we select the best images and put together our own training material.

The objective of the manual will be to compact ideas and concepts delivered during the training, which we must apply and reread every morning, even though it may seem tedious and useless, but it is quite the opposite, since it is the only and most recognized way to fix the concepts in our subconscious in order to make them a habit in our lives or workplace.

We could say that these are proven strategies that, when applied correctly and repeatedly, obtain the optimal results that every salesperson demands for their work: the achievement of their sales goals, which make it possible to realize their dreams in life. Apply them with great enthusiasm. Training is the key to success in this activity and this manual is part of it.

When hiring experienced salespeople, we may find that many of them have vices and bad sales practices, as well as significant negativity. In the end, you will have to invest long hours and resources to change the mindset of these individuals and to eliminate their bad habits, a mission that is almost impossible. Therefore, we maintain that previous experience in sales is not necessary; it is even preferable to avoid bad elements that could intoxicate or contaminate the rest with their baggage of negativity. Lack of experience is made up for by permanent training.

The characteristics we look for in each element of our sales force are good personality, charisma, self-confidence and a warm smile, which denotes a sincere concern for the customer, has good eye contact, knows how to listen to the customer, is confident in speaking, professional and ambitious. A sales executive has goals and is competitive, well dressed and self-motivated. He knows what he sows and then reaps. Convinced of his work and the proposal.

The salesman's manual may contain certain concepts and ways of working so that you can keep in mind, emphasizing the positive attitude, the commitment to your dreams, keeping your smile in the interviews, keeping as mission to provide the best customer service, get the most daily closings to achieve the proposed goals and objectives. The salesperson must have a burning and latent desire, to know that what we project is what we will obtain daily.

Maintain work behaviour, arrive early, train daily, gather all the material before leaving for the zone, concentrate on our goals, which are part of the dreams we want to achieve. Be mentally prepared with the numbers we want to achieve.

Words move, example drags. Emphasize teamwork as a way to achieve objectives. Remember that self motivation is the sum of desire, attitude and responsibility.

No one really knows what they're capable of doing until they do it. Looking in the mirror every day and practicing the best smile is a good thing. Analyse your mistakes and correct them. Take care of your image and speech. Getting to the office early and starting training with your group, reviewing objections and sales scripts is vital.

The optimist sees the flower; the pessimist, the thorns. Never lose the inner strength that drives us to continue until we achieve our daily goals. All virtues are rewarded, but only one is crowned: perseverance.

Using the script of success as we give it to you without adding or taking anything away from it becomes a necessity. The right words are focused on it to achieve closure in a sales conversation.

We must remember that an attitude of indifference towards a client is fundamental. If the attitude is nervous, desperate, expresses fears and asks please to be bought, it will achieve the opposite of a closing before the potential client. Therefore, concentrate on the professional sales script, know how to listen to the client, avoid the fear of closing; 90% of the salespeople suffer from it, position yourself in that 10% and go towards closing every conversation.

It is directly proportional; the more conversations that take place during the day, the more closings you get. They must always keep their work folders very tidy, which always act as a support. Have the objections at hand to evacuate any concerns that may arise immediately.

Know that, if there are doubts, you are the one who sows them in the mind of the client. My favourite phrase was always "have fun and relax", so you get the expected results in sales. Banish the fear of closing a sale from your salespeople.

The leader's manual contains a series of attitudes that you must assume towards the company, the group and your own person, in order to access sales super productions.

The "characteristics" of the leaders we are looking for in our company: they must have closing skills, energy, enthusiasm, motivation, creativity, permanent smile, have incentives for their salespeople, make decisions, feedback their group positively, have an answer for everything, care about their team's dreams and goals, rest only when they have achieved their objectives, know that each referral is a budding closure, trust their work group and themselves, know the sales technique in detail. Motivational messages must be individual, and we must know that they are short lived.

The "traits of success" that a leader must possess are enthusiasm, joy, comradeship. The leader generates confidence, keeps the emotions in his team. He must keep statistics on each of the members of the group to adjust his scheme daily and tighten it where necessary. He must fix the successes of the people by celebrating noisily, stimulating with tangible and intangible incentives.

A leader sets daily objective to be met. It is there that miracles are performed. A person without goals is a zombie who walks aimlessly. Set a daily goal for each one and you will begin to see results immediately.

The leader is planning his departure for the field. He checks that he has all the necessary working material for the number of sales elements he has available. The leader is a born closer, he closes even when customers are hesitant. The leader manages the mood of the team, discovers its ambitions and powers, provides serenity and confidence to each individual. Discipline and determination are essential to ensure that the excitement curve in a salesperson is maintained during those four hours we are talking about. A leader encourages daily competition among his or her own salespeople. A leader always surrounds himself with the best.

Chapter 10: Commercial and motivational management

"If you can dream it, you can do it."

WALT DISNEY

"The only argument you win is the one you avoid."

CARNEGIE

The motivation, in 90%, must be innate and we must detect it in that first line that follows us.

Motivation starts on the day of the interview. We must always emphasize that you were preselected, never tell you that you are already selected, because people interpret it as not being serious enough not to go through several stages of this process. We must implement a second interview and then go on to induction and then to the training sessions

It adds motivation to everything related to the economic perspective and promotions in the structure, administrative policies, salary, commissions, incentives, tangible and in tangible awards, congratulations for achievements, objectives and goals met, stability and continuity of work.

In the motivational area we must ask and question our group leaders constantly in a daily interview. We will then be able to evaluate several aspects related to the management of the company after each talk.

Clarify situations and improve them by implementing a questionnaire containing certain questions that point to the core of the problems we can detect.

An example of questions to implement with our leaders on a daily basis are those listed below: what is the general mood? Is there trust and respect? Are we complying with the defined strategies to retain salespeople? Are we developing the premise of zero tolerance for attitude problems? Are we being effective in selecting and recruiting salespeople? If so, do we verify that the script for success is being correctly stated in the area? Do we know the new vendors well? Are we talking to them? Is there a follow up of the birthdays of each member of the company to create small celebrations? Are you checking that you feel there is an open door policy for dialogue? Is the administrative area fulfilling all its functions correctly? Do we count on communication via cell phone with all the members of the sales groups? Do all the salespeople have their folders up to date with the latest offers, enough contracts and photo IDs, promotional materials, etc.

As far as commercial management is concerned, we must ask ourselves, based on the evaluation we make with our leaders, if we have defined or if the sales strategies, we pro pose from the commercial management are being correctly implemented.

It is essential that these questions are carried out in outcome evaluation meetings. These will be where we analyse strengths and evaluate the achievement of results. We must keep notes and statistics in a notebook to record the strategy on a daily basis and correct any inconsistencies.

We must evaluate the following commercial management policies that we have implemented; investment in human resources, training, personnel selection and corrective actions to avoid rotation, statistics and sales charts per salesperson and supervisor, together with the monitoring of dreams, objectives and goals of each member. The policy of monetary incentives tangible and delivery of diplomas intangible for the fulfilment of weekly and monthly goals.

It implements a policy of corrective measures in the face of negative attitude problems or established minimum yields, managing an anti medium environment. It also has a policy of sales management control, such as quality calls to customers the next day of hire, check of contractual conditions, contracts correctly filled, call to the customer prior to shipment and then upon receipt of the product.

We must always have a compact team or circle of trust made up of the leaders we have selected. This group must possess the same mystique, expectations, common interests, enthusiasm, objectives and high economic goals to form that necessary complicity so that everything flows normally towards the success of the company, which, in short, will be theirs as well. I have seen, in some cases, businessmen who have come to associate or promise to associate in small percentages these elements of our second line.

I have noticed that, when there is no reporting and communication between the owners and management or those in leadership positions, the company is either paralyzed or condemned to a wheelchair and, ultimately, to death.

We must be very aware of a situation that is very common in companies, where there are times when it seems that we have lost control, that decisions are made by certain employees who affect the entire structure, hiding vital information, such as detection of fraud, theft of material, passing from sales structures to competitors or malicious rumours.

It is as if bad management controls everything and they filter the information that is most convenient for them and slowly isolate it from their own company; they manipulate us, they do not control any operational instance, everything is a mess, nothing matters to them, the continuity in time of their job even less, they only live the month of pay and their mediocre world of deceit is so small that they think they have everything controlled with their lies until the snowball of inefficiencies that they inflate and that they think they have controlled explodes in their face.

It's like everyone knows what's going on except those who should know for immediate correction. These are the compromises between employees based on simulated friendships without any basis; rather, they are relationships conspired for evil and to try to destroy what we could have built with so much effort, where bad things are told to the detriment of the company just to discourage the rest and infiltrate the thorn of doubt.

Whoever proceeds in this way believes that he has been defrauded by the company or has some slightly superior offer and decides to take this wrong path of internal psychological warfare.

Another component that we must evaluate in business management is the degree of motivation of the leaders, the degree of commitment and the professional level they contribute. Assess whether they have a long term vision and feeling in the company, whether they want to move up, grow and make a corporate career or are just passing through.

Many times, policies are implemented based on the preferences of the sellers; for example, to sell cheaper or to sell lower quality products. Sellers are afraid of receiving a "no" too often, and that is why they prefer to sell products or services at the lowest possible price.

They think they'll get more sales that way and our reality doesn't go this way. Our experience dictates that whenever we sold contracts at high prices, delivering mid to high range mobile phone equipment, we obtained superlative sales successes.

The sellers had no options, we did not give them options and we were not afraid to sell at higher rates regardless of the competition, because we knew that the most important thing was technique and motivation; furthermore, we knew that offering a higher quality product would give greater satisfaction to the customers and their purchase would last.

We saw many distributors who were bleeding to death selling at very low prices and the costs did not close them.

We earned up to ten times their commission and were able to provide constant security and motivation and take care of high costs and profits in the same way.

Failsafe businessmen are afraid to take on customers and offer something better and more expensive. They are left with little money available, as they do not have enough to encourage and commit their leaders economically because they chose the cheapest pattern to sell for fear of facing a highly competitive market and the customer saying no more than the times planned by manage ment and sales plummet.

The most powerful enemy of the businessman is fear. They believe that customers will look at the competition, and they will not if you provide a service with a capital letter to your customers. The customer buys what we want to sell; as long as they see us reliable, happy, motivated, committed, sure of what we offer and of ourselves in front of them, their attitude will accompany the purchase.

But that joy, confidence, courage, conviction and goals begin with the entrepreneur. In these schemes, it is not the sales force that fails, but the heads, that is, the leaders of the company and, mainly, the entrepreneurs themselves.

Chapter 11: The Sales Success Script

"It is better and more joyful to give than to receive."

JESUS CHRIST

The script is the basis of our argument, it will be our masterful interpretation, as if it were a play and you were the main star. It is the right words, exact words, that lead us to success in closing a sale. The script in question is primarily simple; so, it should be so that it is easily learned by your sales force.

It should be practiced daily in the mornings as if it were a morning prayer that would attract luck. It is necessary to implement theatres of sale for the correct practice of it, and even filmed for later analysis. Once your sales force masters all aspects of it, nothing will stand between you and success.

Their leaders must be the engines of the daily training. In addition to the detailed work that is done prior to the departure to the zone, we must, on the way to the zone, review the objections, the concrete cases and experiences that they have found the day before in their talks.

The script must be adapted to each product and need. It is based on five steps that we must take to reach the signing of a contract. Then we must support the other part of the script, which is the issue of objections, also called rebuttals, which we will take only as questions, doubts or concerns of the customer to our arguments, we must never take them as a rejection of our person.

The rejections in our lives demotivate us, the no's in the sales race are like a previous step to reach the "yes" that will bring us success. Each rejection is imprinted with a new experience that we must write down in our sales career to improve our closures.

The method of learning is, above all, to observe by listening and imitating. We were able to create our own style and develop a constant learning process in our companies based on daily experience.

Being attentive to language is fundamental, every profession uses terms that are its own and ours is no exception. A professional does not speak the same as an aunt or grandmother. A professional who does not train every day is someone who is condemned to failure. You can't go out on the street and improvise. Everything must be rehearsed hundreds of times beforehand, our gestures, what we say, how we say it and the way we dress will say a lot about you when it comes to developing our conversation.

We can make a survey, implement a game with some scratch or roulette of luck or pricking balloons in a corner in which there are envelopes with prizes inside, where you give away something related to your product to attract the attention of passersby and neighbours, but we must attract their full attention to develop this script.

It is very necessary to practice it daily until it becomes flesh in us.

There are five steps on the ladder at the closing of a new contract and will be the sum of each of these steps. The five steps in this script are:

1. The opening. 2. The argumentation. 3. Activating the sense of profit. 4. The promise of service. 5. The closing.

At the opening we introduce ourselves with our name and title and say that we belong to the "special promotions department" and that we will only take two minutes of your time. We also ask for the name of our interlocutor to create empathy and in every argument call him by his name always.

Don't forget the complements of the opening, those first minutes are of vital importance, they are the base where your business conversation will be fixed.

These complements that will give flavour to the mix are the smile, eye contact, show enthusiasm and positive attitude.

In the argument we explain that we are carrying out a special promotion "just for today", which consists of a "commercial exchange" per launch day, and only for that day we are delivering in this area, for example, a cell phone or a security device or the promotion that you stipulate, and in exchange we ask you for two referrals or the exchange that you implement.

It is suggested that you should only make a "small monthly investment" and make him see that every investment is recovered. We divide this monthly investment by thirty days of the month to make you see that that daily amount is diluted by an insignificant amount compared to the services you get.

We also told you that we only have a limited number of equipment or services in that special offer to deliver to you on that day, since the rest were sold, and you only have two left at that time.

We implement a "special promotion certificate", which serves to help us speed up the customer's purchase decision. It is a certificate that makes him/her the recipient of the special promotion we are offering that day only and we always keep only two in our hands.

The "only chance" is a flyer that explains the special promotion. We speak of a unique opportunity showing that it is urgent and will only last that day, since that is precisely what our special promotion and our presence in the area consists of.

There are phrases like: "Surely you know that our company has the best rates in the market, right? ». This conditions the answer, and let's remember that the closing is a sum of accumulating yeses during our exhibition.

Saying "isn't it? "leads us to always answer yes after an argument.

If you have any questions, congratulations, always! It creates empathy.

We replied: "Congratulations! What a good question, you ask something that very few people take into account, I can see that you are very concerned about saving", in communications or in what you offer, and to have a comprehensive, fast, economical and quality service.

We then bring the client's mind favourably disposed towards opening up to an unfavourable situation with their current company or similar service from our competition that the client remembers, if any. We try to encourage scenes in the mind that are familiar to them, asking, for example: "Have you had a bad experience with your current operator", "How much do you spend weekly or monthly? ». Or, if you are concerned about the safety of your family, making it seem priceless to protect them. There are arguments for every product or service, and I am sure you will find yours.

In the third step we activate the senses by putting the product in the hand. This generates the sense of belonging, of possessing a desired good. It allows us to activate the sense of loss if we do not take the offer. By looking at it and manipulating it, it generates the desire to have it. At that moment, we explain the technical benefits and its operation or the virtues of the product and/or service we are offering.

We have to try to generate in the mind of our interlocutor the fear of losing a real opportunity that is presented in the offer as special and unique, only for that day, the last or the only one of the special promotions. We must also note that there is a shortage of product available on that occasion.

Indifference is the key. Make him feel that if he doesn't take it, his neighbours will. To appeal to the sense of status that the product will generate in his environment is a benefit that people hide, but that is latent when we acquire some product that is exclusive. In every sale we should relax and have fun. It is a slogan that we must write with indelible ink.

The sale is relaxed and fun, otherwise it is not a sale, it is quite the opposite, tortuous and does not get results. That security we transmit is what our poten tial client will grasp, and indifference to it transmits security in what we offer.

Influencing the customer's mind with a sense of urgency and scarcity of the product becomes indispensable to achieve closure. Time is money and we must always be in a hurry. By showing ourselves to be active in front of the customer, we generate a sense of urgency in their purchase as well.

In the fourth step we explain the service we will provide and its advantages.

The fifth step is the expected closure, perhaps the most important, as not many sellers dare to take this step for fear of rejection.

The salesman should always smile, because he is having a nice time. We must always look into the eyes. This is done immediately after a promise of service or demonstration of benefits or after answering an objection.

Closure is the natural result of a sales process. The executive can take the closing for granted when he or she has gone through the previous stages. The closing does not end the sale, it is a first step for follow up. A satisfied client recommends.

Most sellers are considered good until this step, but why don't they close? Because of the fear of failure. It's what we call fear of closure in sales. Nine out of ten sellers have it. They are afraid to try because of the fear of not being able to do it, the same thing that happens to those who want to be entrepreneurs and do not take that first step to start walking towards a sure success.

Fear corrodes us inside, paralyzes us, makes us lethargic; we think: "I'd better not try, because from failure it doesn't come back".

From the deepest depression we can advance to the most extensive joy, do the test, start walking and you will see, keep moving, action kills doubts, inaction feeds them.

How to avoid it? It's simple, let's take action and request closure. Rejections are compensated with victories that translate into sales. Our human personality is not designed to withstand continuous rejections. Our fear produces weak management in this process.

The goal is acceptance and commitment to the guidelines of the contract. Remember that basic services, such as electricity, water, gas, are long contracts and one does not take them for a certain period of time, but for a lifetime. Today communication or security are basic and vital services too, and so are other products that we can put in the same basket of basics for our lives today.

Take advantage of the moment when the buyer reveals interest and get on with signing the order without exaggerated pressure, always highlighting the benefit to be derived from obtaining the product. Dramatize the need not to postpone the purchase is a good practice.

Closing requires a lot of tact and diplomacy; therefore, act with serenity and a trusting spirit and as if you were taking for granted what you are dealing with. Accept your success in every conversation. Be convinced of your arguments, you must generate in the listener an excellent state of mind. Don't be arrogant or show superiority to your potential client.

Applying is the watchword for closing a contract. The fear we have talked about is that many sales are diluted in a mere conversation without meaning, because the seller, reaching that point, stops selling. Both parties delay that final decision for different reasons. The customer does not want another ac count or there are many negative thoughts that cross his mind at that moment. The salesperson delays the moment out of panic to be rejected.

He thinks it's his person that's being rejected and not the product. At most, we can speak of a rejection of his poorly outlined arguments or, at other times, they may reject the personal appearance of the salesperson, his gestures or his tone of voice.

Rejection can be contemplated on a personal level, but this is already a mishandling of the leaders, who must advise, guide their salespeople in every way, starting with the care of the personal image. In the end, 90% of the time the order is not requested, that is, the signature, and the closing literally disappears.

Requesting is the basic strategy, so we must always have a request, a pen and self confidence on the table. We must concentrate on one argument, weigh up the pros and cons.

Repeat firmly, with confidence in your gestures and voice the benefits, listing them, one, two, three, etc. And so on, always naming them with forcefulness and gesturing with your hands.

The basis for a closing is to create an appropriate environment, accentuating the positive, using stories that motivate, in an environment without external disturbances, such as noise from children around us, television, radio with high volume, which distract the attention of the client or others.

We will ask ourselves then: when to close? After the argument, when the client has shown his interest. After handling the objections, we must remain attentive throughout the interview.

Let's discover the signs by observing the customer's attitudes to take note of the purchase signals: nodding your head during the argument is a sign, reexamining the proposed advantages, taking up an argument on your own, asking questions to specify something about the service or asking about the value of the product are all purchase signals.

We should expect to close from the beginning. The client picks up his emotions from the first moment of the interview; if you are positive, encouraged, enthusiastic, the client will respond in the same way. If you are positive, encouraged, enthusiastic, the client will respond in the same way. We must not show the slightest doubt, first in his mind, then in his words and finally in his gestures.

What determines a sale is the potential buyer's perception of the competitive advantages that we present to them in our negotiation conversation and no one else. It is a moment where the client forgets all publicity, all offers from the competition, and only relies on the perception that we transmit to him with our speech.

The purchase is not rational, but subjective. Sales should not be delayed in time. They are here and now, or they will never be, that is the reality.

The simpler our arguments, the easier it will be to close the sale. The benefits that the client perceives will be the reason why he will take our offer and not another one.

Our salespeople should sell without rushing, relaxed, without anguish, not showing pressure to close, we should feel as if we are benefiting that person with our proposal, because all those negative energies, as well as the positive ones, are the ones that will capture the potential customer.

Let us know that the client decides based on the trust we inspire in him, the potential client only buys expectations and experiences.

Many buyers put "no" first in order to gain time to better evaluate what we offer. The objections that you put in our way are synonymous with noncommitment. We must convince by advising. Advising is our essential work.

We have to be eloquent in our words, to dramatize them with a certain moderation will give us the certain and expected fruit.

We must have a prompt capacity for analysis so that we can quickly give the right answer to avoid the silences that would cause the conversation to collapse. Patience and perseverance are fundamental in these moments. We must adapt ourselves to any type of conversation that may arise. Let's show a self confidence that can withstand any storm. All these details added up will result in a successful negotiation.

Each ingredient that makes up a closure must be studied in detail and practiced tirelessly, as it is the basis of our profession. Without responsible study there is no success.

Going out into the field and changing words or saying them differently only leads to failure and more failure in every conversation.

Before a case of indifference, we must ask, investigate which detective to detect the areas of need or dissatisfaction, we must put benefits that can get to interest or motivate the

208

client. We must have the ability to obtain information from the client in the right way and at the right time, when we need more data to continue the interview.

We must help the customer to make decisions, because at that moment he is invaded by negativity, doubts to postpone the purchase decision. The role of the salesperson is to be the guide, the reliable advisor. We must constantly expose qualities of an emotional nature.

We must encourage consistency of message at every point to our customers. With these foundations, gaining and maintaining credibility becomes a guiding principle of our behaviour and work ethic.

Teamwork is a detail to be developed within the company. The system to successfully overcome each of the stages presented to you is to assume yourself as a farmer, no longer as a hunter.

The farmer selects the land, plods the soil, fertilizes it, cultivates it and harvests it. In time, he knows that he will have other farmers in his charge and, finally, he knows that he will get a plantation.

The salesperson we aspire to must have some detective skills as well, that is, he must investigate, ask questions to discover the strengths and weaknesses of the client, he must have clear vision in the search for closure, discover expectations, develop the necessary nose to build a sales dialogue based on the well studied script. As a psychologist who also assumes himself to be, he must understand the needs of his clients, clear up fears by resolving incongruities, knowing that the purchase entails conflicting emotions, he must focus on sales closings by sowing his seeds to harvest more clients based on good references.

In the script we must contemplate an item related to the study of the objections that can be raised in a sales conversation.

When the customer does not seem to accept the product, he is likely to object. We must distinguish between objection and condition. The latter is a real reason the customer has for not buying. In contrast, an objection is an apparent reason for not buying that the customer raises. It is always the seller's fault if the customer raises an objection and does not buy.

In order to refute the objections, as a first step, we must put the objection in the form of a question. For example, the customer says: "I don't buy because I think the product is bad". The salesperson answers: "Do you think it is bad?

The reasons for applying this technique are to understand the objection well, minimize it, create doubts and thus gain time. It is a mirror effect so that the client listens to himself and reasons what he said. You have to give the impression that you care about the customer.

In the second instance, if the customer is in doubt, the seller must present an evidentiary argument. If the objection is very difficult, the aim is to minimize it by highlighting other benefits of the product.

The important thing is to make the customer see that there are aspects of the product that he may not be aware of and that fully justify the existence of that aspect that is negative for him. A difficult objection is answered by asking the client the right questions that will lead him to admit that the product has many other positive aspects.

Chapter 12: Organizational and working outline

"Why so much fear, ye of little faith?"

JESUS CHRIST

"Everyone is what they think. If you have positive thoughts, you will be a positive person; if your thoughts are negative, you will be someone full of negativity.

MARCUS AURELIUS

The scheme is based on a work team consisting of coordinators, supervisors and salespeople.

Sellers are divided into levels, according to their category, level of sales closure and knowledge. A star or a diamond, whichever you like to classify them, means that you are trained to only perform openings and sales conversations, while a two or three person salesperson is also an expert in closing sales.

The supervisor should have in charge no more than four salespeople to be able to at tend and motivate each one using the time well. The coordinator should not exceed three supervisors. This organization chart is based on the quality of the sales professionals that we have well trained and motivated and not on an endless number of cobra's salaries that come to pass the time; the one that does not sell in two or three days will not be able to stay in the organization. To avoid spending money on people who come to see our faces, we can establish a period of two days of theoretical training and three days of practice in the area.

Sales staff must be uniformed, which implicitly serves as advertising for the brand.

My partner always told her sales coordinators that they should love their salespeople momentarily, because one has to understand that it is a business and one should never get romantically involved with one's subordinates.

If we give a lot, we'll get a lot. If we belittle the employee, he will not generate results; the employee wants open door management, which does not discriminate against him because of his social or cultural class, which listens to him, contains him and makes him feel part of it.

Every person a salesman talks to must be a conquered territory, a house, a company convinced and confident of what he has acquired. Little by little, you will see that your organization on the streets will be transformed into an unrivalled sales closing machine.

Earning your first million dollars or euros is based on going out to find the customer and not waiting for him sitting in a store, watching your salespeople through the glass as un-watered, dry ferns, mouldy from the negativity they carry from their personal relationships and competitive society.

These desk jockeys that we can see in shopping malls and street shops don't care whether they sell or not. Lack of attitude is the common denominator of all of them. They don't know how to sell because no one has instructed them or given them a direction in sales, much less in their lives. They devote themselves to fly with their ephemeral thoughts, without meaning, to see social networks with their cell phone, to look for a partner or to chat with friends or to attend the calls of their cell phone without stopping, neglecting the work environment and the objectives that nobody drew for them, and much less for themselves decided to draw, because the motivation is nonexistent.

The business is to create a "brotherhood of sellers", like Templar riders, who go out to take the streets and the market ahead, knowing that in every house, in every corner, in every commerce, in every SME there is a closing waiting for them, knowing that in every sales conversation that I have with every potential client there will be a closing.

The seller has stage fright at the closing because he is not clear about the script of the success, which is the only thing that will give him confidence, because he will know what we are talking about. He will step on it strong and firm, as if a magic force were moving him: the magic of the words we knew in the sales script.

That's why we emphasize that the selection of personnel is so important to make up that first group, that first litter hungry to make a lot of money. That is why they must be fresh, spontaneous, jovial, proactive, with or without experience; we will be there to teach them.

We must aim for large sales figures, never settle for small ones, since what we put forward about the subject is what will certainly take our sales force and make our goals its own.

If we propose a sale per day, that's what we'll get for each one, or maybe less. On the other hand, if we talk about five contracts a day being easy to achieve and that is the mini mum goal, that is the chip that will be put in each member's head.

It is a "game of reprogramming the subconscious" that comes with failures in every sense, and that is why we make motivation a turning point without exception in the proposed structure.

They may not get all five contracts, but each one will bring two or three, some will cover all five and others will get maybe six or seven. We have always experienced it, in different countries and continents, economic circumstances, diametrically opposed products and services, different corporations and brands.

However, if we as entrepreneurs do not first become aware that this is an easy and natural part of the investment process in a sales organization, we will not be able to make anyone aware. If we do not believe this previously, much less can we expect anyone to believe in that result and in us.

It's like the saying that we must first find happiness in order to attract money; this is the same, the entrepreneur must first become self motivated to achieve the objectives in his sales groups. Without happiness there are no results.

Let's remember that the generational link between teammates is fundamental, it doesn't work with a mix of, for example, four twenty year old salesmen and one forty year old. There is no chemistry. The same experiences do not exist.

We may have an older coordinator, who will surely pass on his knowledge and experience to a young, wisdom hungry sales force. We have had very good experience in these cases.

One type of leader who is detrimental to the organization is the mythomaniacal character who seeks union leadership rather than leadership focused on success. They are professionals in radio hall assembly. They bring in and out garbage with their words and attitudes. They are friends of the permanent failure in their lives and they spend fleeting moments in a world that overcomes them like a tsunami instead of shining like stars; they are just fireworks that explode, shine and vanish in a matter of seconds, all at the same time. They look like one thing and are another.

Never hire overqualified, i.e. over experienced staff, as this will regularly go against your established procedures. These may be potential elements; if any of them strike us as positive for the organization, we should analyse these cases more carefully.

These potential leaders are usually dissatisfied people; they exhibit higher levels of dissatisfaction than other types of sales employees, as few companies or jobs meet their expectations due to their greater experience. Generally, they are poorly predisposed to new work schemes. There are some that will serve us and others that will hinder the way our organization operates. Therefore, we recommend candidates who fit your way of working. In the United States According to a report by Bloomberg Business Week, 50% of this workforce is unemployed.

Another issue to consider is the type of raking we should do in the area.

In this diagram we see that the meeting point of the intersections of blocks 1234 will serve as a meeting place. Once we have visited, in a clockwise direction, blocks 1234, we jump to the immediate meeting point of blocks 5678 and continue working in the same way until we come across some other limit.

The scheme is as follows:

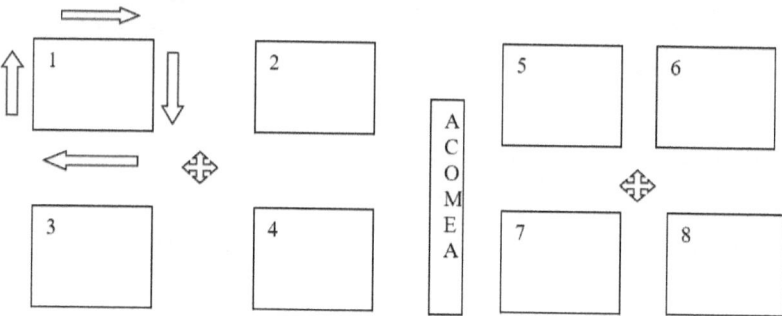

This way, nobody in the area will get lost, because if we follow the direction of the clock and we number the apples in this way, we will know or we will intuit the place where the group that goes ahead is and this way, we will be able to find it easily. It is important that the leaders previously organize and inform their people of the work scheme of the day, and it is a good practice to make photocopies of the map of the area by numbering the apples. We should also identify our salespeople with a kind of photo badge that contains the basic data of the salesperson and the company.

No one is indispensable. Only you.

Let's not be confused if we lose that salesperson, supervisor or manager that we thought was a dream, the ideal of ideals, the one we could trust, let's take it indifferently and quickly see how a better one appears, it was always like that, it always results in this sense. Many times, we become attached to this or that salesperson or supervisor, even manager, and do not realize that he or she may be hindering the progress with respect to capturing new and better elements.

I will now look at the kind of toxic leader that was once even imported by us from another country, based on our belief that it was the solution to have some so called sales guru by our side.

These individuals will always miss their family and customs very much, they will never be ready for the big challenges, their main characteristics are personal instability, arrogance and pride, which are their most terrible enemies.

It is a situation that I have no doubt will happen to many entrepreneurs, to surround themselves and to rely on people thinking with the heart and not with the head.

214

They think they're sales geniuses, he's an overpaid employee, believing that everything depends on him. He thinks no one is good for anything, especially the natives of the country where he is, no one does anything, no one works, just him; he thinks he is a prophet in the land of sales.

It even happens sometimes with a CEO of large companies when they are transferred and are not comfortable with their new situation; they start criticizing everything and everyone. We had this experience, for example, in Panama, with a CEO who did not feel comfortable with the people of the country and secretly did not stop criticizing everything. He asked us how we could sell so much, and we only answered that we thought Panamanians were excellent at selling and managing. If you don't love what you do or the people you work with or the country in which you decided to invest, it will be difficult to achieve success in a context of criticism and discomfort.

We must give what is right, but without getting involved, because local or foreign toxic employees end up believing themselves to be the same or more. They do not respect, they do not recognize their narrowmindedness, their life of failure, and the opportunities they are given are not appreciated.

In your paths you will find qualified employees who believe they are equal to you, or the envy towards your achievements is stronger than the incipient and misinterpreted feeling of friendship that you believe unites you and gives you the right to feel equal, going beyond that hierarchical limit that has to exist between an employer and an employee, even if he is the best collaborator, because the moment will come when he will take the courage to believe he is equal and will betray you.

At a certain point, they only delay the growth that they should really experience in their business projects. This, I think, is the case of many people who believe close to us or give us all our trust and are just waiting for the opportunity or the neglect to give birth to their lowest intentions, fed by envy and the unhealthy ego that drives them.

They are the kind of complicated characters that will only bring misery and trouble to your company. They are those who, with their hysteria, their arrogance, their lack of tact and their darkness, associated with their bad luck, will unbalance their projects. They must be detected in time and eliminated from their environment before it is too late, as happened to us.

Never take the same person you threw out again. Pity is the worst of all feelings; moreover, when you feel sorry for some employee or those weeping employees who with tears in their eyes beg you to forgive their fault in going on in your business, stop for a moment and dismiss them without regard; if you cannot do so because you have a very tender heart, ask for help or you will only have to wait for the moment of disappointment, which will come from the hand of betrayal.

Sit down and wait and see, these are very common symptoms whose timely reading will prevent us from getting a lot of headaches; it never fails, experience it for better or worse as well. Therefore, do not lament or offer extra money to those who think that without them we will be a ship adrift. They are rocks in the neck and not lifelines in the middle of the ocean.

Taking these kinds of hard positions will only propel us forward at a dizzying rate. Get rid of the ballast.

In reality, this kind of person just wants to take advantage of you and is selling you a package full of lies and excuses that are not at all positive for your business. The only important ones in this story are you, your dreams and goals, which you should not lose sight of for a moment.

These management projects end up believing themselves to be something they are not and will not be. Later, they return to their world of poverty and mediocrity, longing for those times when earning four thousand dollars was within reach.

Others steal from under their noses or forge beads, are discovered and, evidently, thrown out, so from earning very well they go on to get jobs where they do not exceed the basic salary, we have seen this.

From these experiences we have an endless list of pitiful people whom we came to appreciate, but who let themselves down without measuring the consequences. Many things that will happen in the company and in its economic future will depend on an intelligent selection of our environment.

Chapter 13: Taking care of details in the organization

"We have been called to the concert of this world to best sound our own instrument."

TAGORE

"There are people who are not loyal to you, they are loyal to what you have or represent, and when their needs change, so easily do their loyalties change.

"If your friends don't motivate and inspire you, you're choosing them wrong."

NEIL PATEL

It has happened very often that, when we neglect the detail of being attentive as detectives to discover the attitudes of each new element, there is some malicious person who shows up in the area and, after having told us everything that he did, does not like the work and infects the rest with his negative opinions, inducing the group to choose to leave the sales area; these individuals are born destroyers, mainly of their own existence, which is full of failure.

He does not tolerate the positive mental attitude of his peers and tries to diminish that positive collective attitude by the envy that mobilizes him.

He will address them with phrases such as: "This is very difficult", "the sale is not for me", he will comment on the inclemency of the sun and the rain and on the fact that the numbers were not well understood; these are the excuses of the eternally anxious ones that are summarized in a "better not to try" where they try to intoxicate the rest with their words.

Therefore, as soon as an element like the one described is detected, we must take it out of the area immediately, without going back, without any pity, because he does not contemplate any pity for the company and his colleagues or ruining a whole serious work that has been developed and that translates into investment of time and money.

Never disperse the new group into different teams already made up of old salesmen; it is not advisable to join old elements with new ones.

It is very important to keep those who demonstrate a more stable profile and who have continuity with work and sales month to month. One month they may be below or above their average, but they will find the breakeven point on their own.

Others will be discarded once they see themselves with good savings, it is as if they are running away from making a lot of money; their north is always to return to their natural state: poverty. I don't believe in the idea that the rich exploit the poor, the poor are poor because no one shows them the way to go.

We just need to choose the sales profession, choose a good product or service and company to back us up and, above all, add a good dose of perseverance, preparation of a professional sales speech and a positive mental attitude. It's a simple equation.

We've had countless cases of young people living in poverty or earning a couple hundred dollars a month in a hamburger company. However, in our company we gave them that passion, that strength, we gave them goals to achieve and the miracle happened, they went from that area of poverty to earning thousands of dollars a month.

This is what has always happened to us in all our undertakings, and I believe that it is one of the secrets of success, to bring love and happiness to our closest business environment and the laws of God's universe will more than pay it back.

My opinion is that the normal state of a society is one of abundance and not poverty, where the latter is a terminal illness suffered by a large part of society and which we must combat from the business world by creating more and better jobs with socially committed entrepreneurs.

There are two types of managers. Those directors of multinationals who en courage and bet from their workplaces on cutting staff and to continue feeding a world of poverty, without caring about those affected by their decisions, while others opt for training and production generated by the world of abundance that humanity claims. The former is transformed into executioners of entire families, brought to that level by the inefficiency and ignorance they display in business and sales organization, attitudes that show their lack of faith and love for the companies they represent.

We all have the same chance, I assure you. Many others have it and lose it because they are not ready for change yet. But it is possible that they will reflect on it later and return to the path.

The basis is honesty and loyalty to a company. The disloyal one is like the unfaithful one in his marriage, sooner or later he is discovered. He ceases to be, then, trustworthy. The disloyal one betrays and never comes to fruition; life gives him back. In our groups we must encourage loyalty to the company, for it will be reflected in the results and in the money that will be safely carried in their pockets.

These are some facts based on our experience of so many years. They are details that

218

we should take note of, we see them as small tropical storms, but they can be transformed into hurricanes. If we detect these facts, let us make the right decision, which is to separate that person from our company. Let's not buy his excuses, which he will probably have by the dozen.

We will be able to observe, sometimes, how in our structures some people look at us badly or with that touch of envy.

They usually ask where we are going, what we are doing, they are aware of whether we are travelling or buying a car or just the model of suit we are wearing, and sometimes they try to sniff out our earnings by asking the accountant. We have to make the right decision, eliminate these elements from our environment. In the face of someone who looks down on us, looks at us badly or does not say hello in the morning, let us implement the shortest and safest route, which is dismissal.

A lurid but fundamental issue is to analyse whether it is positive to have a mixture of both sexes in sales teams. In our years in the field, we consider that it is not recommended. We implemented it again and again and it always failed. We can say that women are excellent salespeople, just like men. But if you are going to choose to have both, do it separately, at separate times and in separate groups. We haven't gone back to the time of the caves, but experience dictates this type of procedure.

When we implement mixed sales groups, distraction occurs in the area and harassment in the office; there is a lot of neglect, remember that these are very young people with whom we work, and that is the issue, they are in the middle of their search for a partner or pleasure. This topic has always brought us conflict over and over again. We did not detect it for years until it was late in Mexico. From then on, we changed our strategy diametrically.

On another occasion, it is the secretaries who make contact with salespeople or supervisors and end up with some furtive encounter.

In the face of the least conflict, and it happened to us on several occasions, they ended up taking an important part of the sales force or, on other occasions, they fall in love with some trusted manager who then leaves us for the supposed love and, at the same time, in the short term, the lover is also abandoned in distant lands. This also happened to us on two occasions, in Mexico and Peru, with two of them. Not to mention the great parties and outings that they organize together.

I repeat again that it is very complicated to handle mixed history; if you are the first time that you are going to develop a sales organization, my recommendation is mixed management in another office of fifty meters away from the salesmen and to which only coordinators can access and have only a male element in the sales field on the one hand and, on the other hand, the female sales personnel taking care of it in another schedule.

Executives without sales experience are more productive than those who have been through many companies. Remember that the work in the area is hard and the motivation curve only lasts four hours to have distractions.

We must arrange for the transfer to the area of the groups of cars or vans owned, rented or owned by the same supervisors or coordinators, which can be negotiated a plus based on the economic wear of the vehicle.

We must provide, as far as we can, equipment or demos of what we are offering.

The uniform is something fundamental to take into account. It must be brightly coloured and have the brand and distributor logos embroidered on it. We must provide a set of two per individual. It would also be advisable for each polo to have the charge embroidered. Do not forget to accompany the polo with a cap embroidered in the same direction.

If it is a place where it rains a lot or it is cold, let's complete the uniform with jackets or pilots in the same direction embroidered, delivering one per seller. It is interesting if we can add to the uniform or on the cap the level that each salesman has in the company; if we measure them by stars, place them embroidered or by means of pins made in metal for the occasion.

It is important not to neglect this aspect because it makes people feel proud of their rank within the company and encourages competition to close more accounts to get more status in the organization and extra money.

Changing the subject, let's always remember that our marketing is twofold: one looks at the inside of our company and the other at the customer. The first is the basis for developing the second. That basis must be very solid. It is an intensive marketing, daily and without space for leisure, unless it is creative. Our sales force is the catalyst for this internal marketing, as are those who make up the administrative apparatus.

We should plan a day or weekend every two months for a meeting at some tourist location of the leaders and management. This will strengthen them and commit them even more to the objectives of the company, its values and vision. They will leave renewed with new strength.

We used to do them once a month in nearby locations, not beyond two hundred kilometres from the office location. We would spend Friday night with comfortable vans in the sales area and then go up there for the training trip and return on Sunday. They were hotels on the beach or by a river or cabins in the mountains. Everything was very inspiring to stop and rethink together strategies and align short and medium term objectives, without forgetting the long term ones as well. Based on these meetings, we can make videos with the technical content and the fun in each of them, which will serve to encourage future salespeople and other executives to access leadership positions.

To access these trainings with travel included, we set monthly goals that had to be met in order to make the monthly trip. Most of the time, those goals were met, and the trip was a fact.

A fundamental issue that we should not overlook in terms of motivation in the area is that we should celebrate loudly at every achievement, because in small steps a salesman becomes big.

It is advisable to implement an anonymous email address where each employee can communicate with management and thus express their concerns without having to resort to possible reprisals from their superiors.

Let us remember that salespeople do not abandon companies, but rather that this is a consequence of poor management by their leaders, who do not motivate, train or allow them to grow.

A bad leader can throw away all our work. When we take on staff, we must remember that people are looking for challenges, so we have to offer opportunities for growth and support, training, motivating and attending to employees' concerns, always taking care of the details.

The company must have as its ultimate goal for its staff the simple fact of involving them in all areas of the company. Its leaders should know as much or more about management than the administrators themselves. Everything in the company is interrelated.

The team coordinator must keep track of each new contract. Every client is a world and we must give them the personal attention they deserve.

We have known administrators who left their bills lying around, as they lacked an electricity bill that corroborated the address or small details in the filling of the same. We had to have two people to deal with these cases because there were hundreds of bills a month that we were losing.

We instructed the group leaders to keep track of everything they delivered in administration on a daily basis, with notes on each contract delivered, and to keep it in a notebook.

One thing we must be on the lookout for is the theft of entrepreneurial talent. We, systematically, have suffered from this in every place and time.

Talent theft usually occurs from not only external competitors, but also from the same distributors of the same brand.

Whether out of envy or lack of knowledge about how to train or select personnel, unscrupulous employers engage in this practice.

Usually this procedure turns against them, we have never seen salesmen who took this path of treachery in our sales force being crowned with success in our competition. They end up comparing, and here we had the advantage all along.

Generally, staff who look for other options in the competition are either tempted direct ly with a higher salary or commission at the door of the offices or offered a position where they are more relaxed, without much work to do. They leave the company influenced by their friends or relatives, they may also opt for this path when there is an absence of career plans or internal disputes between groups or, on other occasions, because of competitions that are lost, although it seems unlikely, this has happened to us.

The theft of talent exists because there are poachers of it. They are businessmen who do not invest in human capital and pretend to steal it, because it is easier for them to do this than to select, train and motivate new staff. We experienced this theft in the eight countries in which we had ventures.

The important thing is the attitude with which we face our days. Happy people treat clients and their coworkers well, happiness leads to creativity, makes every day different, it is a state of mind that leads to nonstop success.

Chapter 14: Goals and Competition

"Reason is a slave to the passions. It is feeling and not reason that moves humans."

DAVID HUME

"What's really valuable is intuition."

ALBERT EINSTEIN

Give a person goals, clear objectives and you will see miracles grow before your eyes. No goals, no sales. Goals and objectives must be very specific and measurable in time and number, daily and weekly, in order to reach the monthly objective; otherwise, the end of the month is in the distance and everything is left for that time in the seller's mind. A weekly flat is stipulated and signed as a commitment with the management.

Goals should be written down and remembered daily by management and team leaders. We must make statistics, bets and encourage internal competition in order to obtain them. Each team will write down their daily and weekly goals on a board to follow up, establishing them individually and as a group in the short and medium term.

Without competition between individuals or groups there is no sales. The competition is followed or graphed in different ways: through a podium or a goose race, where each salesman is the protagonist. Executives compete against executives, supervisors against supervisors and coordinators against coordinators. The best gets diplomas, cash prizes, medals, cups, trips, appliances, dinners, any number of tangible or intangible prizes. This competition helps to point out that people are not a cost, but our most expensive asset, they identify and engage them every day. This work philosophy rewards excellence.

We apply a systemic marketing, that of the interaction between the parties; we talk about a marketing based on people. The strength of a brand is an emergent of what the people of a company do for it. Their attitude and aptitude, their desire and their ability, depend on this. To that sales organization we must demonstrate our commitment so that they feel empathy with our ideas, objectives and way of working.

Of these tangible and intangible prizes, I will give you some examples below:

Podium of winners. It is a system in which we build a pyramid with wood or other malleable material in which we will have a flag per team and per seller. The flags can be of animal figures or symbols that will identify each of the competitors. As they advance in

223

sales, they will occupy different places in the pyramid. We must follow the results every day to achieve the motivation we are looking for. The first three places can be awarded with money and diplomas.

Promotion for stars or diamonds. They will be given to each seller for goals achieved. They are accompanied by a diploma and some increase in commission or salary. When you reach three stars, you will be one step away from being a supervisor and will be trained for the position. They are delivered in the form of metal pins, which is ideal. This pin is engraved with the company's brand.

Ranking. It's a ranking of vendors and a ranking of supervisors. It must be kept on a daily basis.

Diplomas. These are intangible and work very well. They are assembled in PowerPoint and printed on thick coloured paper. They are awarded to the best of the month.

Soccer championship. It's a scheme like the World Cup, where during the first week you play an executive against an executive. In the second week they play against winners of that first week, and so on. In each stage the winners are rewarded with a small compensation and in the last week the champion is consecrated. Having a budget available for this is of utmost importance. I assure you that it is an investment, because the motivation it generates is very high.

Training trip. This type of monthly convention strengthens the group's commitment.
Special training is given, and different topics are discussed.

Daily incentive. Every day, in order to finish the training, it is advisable to give an incentive, such as rewarding those who close five verified contracts, who will be paid in cash. The one who closes the last or the first contract of the day as well. Make up some other daily incentive, a dinner or movie tickets.

Special awards. It was great to buy a forty two inch TV, a high end audio or cell phone and put it on display, setting a monthly goal to cover to win it.

Better elements. Reward the best executive, supervisor and coordinator of the month with cash or another type of prize. We have even given a coordinator in Panama a used Mercedes SsangYong 4x4 truck for exceeding one thousand monthly contracts.

Promotions. It's the most traditional form of reward. Let's remember to play with the stars or diamonds.

A day of sport. We used to do a paintball competition every now and then. During the game, you could see the leadership of some people who had their personalities hidden.

It serves as a game that strengthens the groups of belonging. Usually, in this game the different profiles of each individual, the strategist, the leader, the winner, the loser and the teamwork are evaluated.

Belonging to the club of success. It is a club that will empower the employee for a series of advantages and benefits over the rest of the members of the organization. For example, you will be given a card with which you will get discounts, scheduled outings for members only of this club, advantages such as doubling your commissions if you reach a certain production that suits the interests of the company, among other incentives that we can imagine.

Food basket. It was blunt in Mexico. It's going to a supermarket and we spent about two hundred dollars on food, and we gave out prizes every two weeks.

Many times, with very little, we light a flame that will not be extinguished until we reach a winner. Whatever your reward strategy, don't forget to implement it, it will be a high impact trigger in your daily sales. Make a monthly budget and don't exceed it. Study it carefully.

If we have static points of sale in shopping malls, let's not stop implementing the competition. Let's visit the nearest shopping centre and we will see that the sales attitude is nonexistent. The culture of immobility in the points of sale does not transmit anything, nor enthusiasm, nor energy, nor desire to buy. I have never seen the implementation of games, for example, that attract the attention of passersby. They look like robotic employees who can't wait to go home.

Also intangible motivations have a high psychological impact, an applause from all staff to an employee we want to reward, a handshake, a verbal congratulation to the whole company or alone, take a coffee in the morning with that person ... Everything has a cascade effect if we know how to implement it with method and each member of the sales staff. Let's take action.

Chapter 15: Motivational plans. Your own multilevel from scratch

"I'm looking for men who believe there are no impossible things."

HENRY FORD

"Money is usually attracted, not pursued."

ELY RAMIREZ

Our proposal is based on having a low cost per sale for a structure of about fifty individuals divided into five groups of coordinators.

Earnings should be composed, in the first instance, of a basic salary, the most basic possible depending on the country and the laws that govern it. The minimum stipulated by the Government shall be the correct one. Giving a fixed salary will be synonymous with peace of mind, which our salespeople need. It is giving a base with which to move.

This is the important investment that we must take into account. The happiness of our employees, in the end, will also be ours. Just thinking about it we will get a million dollars the first year and more, I assure you from my own experience.

We then add a small commission according to the amount of the plan sold and per customer activated. We have come to pay between two dollars for a cellular postpaid customer or twenty for an electronic security customer when most paid a hundred.

Here I want to point out a mistake that many businessmen make. For fear, they often pay a very high commission from the first sale.

We've seen commissions to sellers of up to a hundred dollars. This is where a salesperson falls asleep, loses motivation and stops producing, since with three or four sales in a month it is done, that is how the common people think who professionals in the sales area and that are not is 90% of the cases we will deal with.

It is essential to pay large amounts to large productions, never to few sales, because we will generate the opposite of what we intended: conformism.

Another example was in Medellin, Colombia. The distributors received a basic commission for television and the Internet of about USD 250 000 and paid the seller USD 210 000, a real serious mistake; they prostituted the market in a way that I had never seen before.

In our case, we will add up the target bonuses for having reached a predetermined pro duction. These start at one hundred dollars and will increase every so often in number of sales, and so on, always keeping in mind to put high production figures, because if we put low figures, that's what we'll get. It's all about making the goals mental.

If we instil in the subconscious of the sales force low figures, we imply that we are not able to achieve higher figures as an example. Our minimum figure should start, in mobile telephony, at thirty postpaid contracts per month per seller and the bonuses will be extend ed every ten new contracts up to seventy monthly contracts at times.

Many sellers, in our case, obtained fifty, some sixty and the average was around forty activated monthly contracts, although sold without activation, for different reasons, they always shot up twice, which were rejected by the credit part of the multinational for different reasons. To all this we add the series of monthly incentives we have seen to take motivation to the extreme.

In conclusion, there are four parts into which the earnings are divided: salary, commissions, bonuses and daily, weekly and monthly incentives. If we implement a multilevel or network scheme like the one, we will propose, the salary is eliminated and they all become authorized representatives of our company, which, at the same time, is a distributor of the brand.

The goals have to be like the carrot we put in front of the rabbit, but in this case, they should always eat the carrot. It's not by saving a few dollars that we get an unmotivated sales force and end our project in failure by possessing a meaningless and unmeasured greed.

It is necessary to keep in mind that paying a base salary is important because it avoids or decreases the rotation of the personnel, or that of the multilevel that, when buying the membership, becomes of a greater commitment, difficult to break.

The commission, as we said, must be low. It depends on the product we are handling cell phones, alarms, cable TV, Internet, English courses or credit cards. Everything must be framed within these parameters.

The bonuses must be fixed in advance and are one of the carrots that we will put in front, they are fixed and monthly. These have to be at high production per seller. The prizes are modifiable some and others not necessarily. Everything according to the pulse and rhythm of the sale of the day to day, week to week.

An example of commissions can be the following: for the seller, supervisor and coordinator, five dollars per sale to each one, then the seller is made a progressive scheme of prizes, taking into account that at ten accounts will get one hundred dollars/euros, at twenty will be another hundred and at thirty we will add in prizes three hundred, which always results in the same amount in commissions, fifteen dollars per account. This way we will apply it to the other ranges in the same proportion and observing that the net profit of the company does not go down of 35 % discounting the costs as well.

One of the most motivating strategies I know for selling a product is the famous marketing scheme we commonly call multilevel, network or network marketing. About it there are its critics and detractors and also its followers. Let's see, then, what those who know said:

"If I had to do it over again, instead of building a traditional style business, I would choose to build a network marketing business.

DONALD TRUMP

"It's time for people to start caring about their own business.

Having a job means you get paid to care about another people's business. In this new economy, the smart thing to do is to fight for one's business, and network marketing gives you that chance.

ROBERT T. KIYOSAKI

The richest people in the world build networks. Everyone else is trained to look for work.

ROBERT T. KIYOSAKI

"I'd rather have 1% of a hundred than 100% of one. There is no better investment in the world than network marketing business.

WARREN BUFFET

"Network marketing is a new response to a world that is becoming less and less secure at work.

ROBERT T. KIYOSAKI

My first multilevel was in cell phones and electronic security. For this I have set up a system where I merge all types of sales organization I have tried.

It's a completely new network marketing organization scheme that I call NECXUS.

I started in Panama with electronic security and I have repeated it in Colombia with a telephony and television brand in that country.

228

The way to build your distribution network to enhance the sales network will be based on the sales force units, instructing the network on how to shape these structures to project potential sales and not leave them to chance, as in most of these marketing structures, without discarding the classic initial and generational bonuses typical of this way of doing business.

The multilevel, network or network of networks is a marketing strategy that is aimed at those who want to have an independent business with low investment as distributors of products or services of any company in the market or as entrepreneurs who see this system as an alternative to the traditional to market through it some issue itself.

It is based on the recommendation for the sale of the products and the recruitment of potential distributors. The idea is that these distributors are also consumers of the product or service. Recommendations are rewarded with substantial bonuses and commissions.

The distributor's job is basically to create sales volume by incorporating other distributors associated with him who, in turn, create their own structures.

The business becomes interesting when you receive a percentage of the entire sales volume of your partner network. It is not a pyramid, but rather a large network of contacts organized to develop the sale of a product or service.

It has two very interesting features: that it is a turnkey business with residual income. In this type of sales scheme there are four fundamental steps to be taken into account: the recruitment through social networks of our potential partners through a marketing funnel with Facebook and Instagram robots, then make a smart selection of our first line in the organization, where we may have to do a prior screening to find those four that will accompany us in the beginning of our distribution network.

We started by posting ads on a job search portal and we were able to find them there. It's another good way to start, calling on friends or acquaintances in the work environment.

Basically, we propose to them to be owners of a business concept already in operation and with a great potential that, at the same time, look for other people with an entrepreneurial spirit to make the business grow together.

It is a business where the logistics, the marketing plan, the accounting part, among others, are already solved. They are businesses similar to a franchise, but let's agree that to buy one you must have a lot of money; on the other hand, in this type of business, people associate themselves by contributing little capital.

Whoever joins the network must put all their efforts just to sell the products or services and make the organization grow in depth.

Fundamental is the recruitment of new aspiring distributors, an intelligent selection of my four pillars, first generation or my four colonels, to whom I must give permanent training and direct all their energies towards the same objective.

We cannot overlook a strong motivational program of tangible prizes cash awards, travel, etc. and intangible prizes diplomas, pins, courses, etc.

In short, what network marketing offers us is teamwork and a sales and recruitment structure without having to spend a single dollar/euro on salaries, social security contributions or travel expenses, which allows us to organize a company from scratch without having much capital.

I consider it the near perfect way of doing business, as it involves low initial investment, financial freedom, traveling to incredible places, meeting new people, enjoying life without corporate policies, with flexible hours, without the onerous burden of employees, with unlimited income potential, time freedom with residual income and with a lucrative compensation plan.

In our example, we will have different types of daily, weekly, monthly, quarterly and semiannual bonuses and earnings.

In our case, technically speaking, our scheme is known as a business matrix called a forced matrix generational hybrid binary.

There is the multilevel, which is known as unclever or forced matrix, and there is also what we know as the network hybrid binary plan which means that the company pays a certain amount or percentage based on a specific sales volume.

In this search we need to find entrepreneurs who are at the forefront of a working business concept with great growth potential. Basically, we offer a "let's start up together" perfectly applicable to the business plan we have been presenting and as a complement to it.

There are large companies worldwide that diagram the software for any type of multilevel and that we cannot fail to visit to make our support matrix for the calculation of commissions for points and group sales volume of our entire network, among others.

Generalities and concepts

We should always look at the type of product and make small sales kits of the same or initial business packages.

Determine how much the point is worth in order to calculate the qualification

230

volume, where each time the system checks the purchase of a product it adds these qualification points to the upline sales quota to qualify the commission payment. Let's suppose that, in our case, a point is worth ten dollars. That is, if one of my products is worth a hundred dollars, I will accumulate ten points.

We must fundamentally take into account the concept of "group volume", which is that which is calculated on the basis of the commissions of the whole network, that is to say, on the cheque that the whole network underneath me in my organisation cashes.

There are mainly two commission variables: group volume is the commission on the total volume of the check; qualification volume expressed in points, which measures the quota of sales requirements.

As a distributor advances in rank, they move from paying commissions on personal sales volume at each level to commissions paid on group volume. That said, here is the one-to-one analysis of these revolutionary gains for our example, where there will be four types of bonuses, namely: The Enrolment, Residual, Leadership and Competition bonuses.

Types of bonds

The first one we can find is the income from direct sales. They are the foundation of this opportunity. The distributor earns and receives an immediate profit from the sale. Usually paid weekly.

If we want to make a quick and easy profit, retail sales with a significant percentage of profit will be the best option, as our product avoids intermediaries. Its function is like that of a store that offers access to incredible products that satisfy needs. Each distributor must have their own link cloned from our website.

Enrolment bonds

The first of these is the famous fast track, which is the one that invites you to earn money by entrepreneurship. Sponsorship fees compensate for efforts in recruiting new members. The amount of this bonus is based on the level at which your new sponsors enter the plan.

To do this, we must implement a system that recruits for us based on social networking robots.

In our case, we must create permanent recruitment in the so called recruitment days, placing ads on major websites, newspapers, posting advertising pieces and explanatory videos on social networks, where we will apply a recruitment marketing tunnel or funnel where people who arrive will be those who are really interested in participating.

All this to recruit new distributors. Each distributor will pay a membership fee to join. The average is around a thousand dollars and in other latitudes it can be less depending on the weight dollar ratio of each country and its economic circumstances.

For each person who joins the network, you are generally charged between 10% and 20% of the income. This bonus is paid only once.

The investment is easily recovered, usually; the initial membership is supported by the purchase of products and, if they are services, you can be charged for materials, accounting expenses, administrative expenses, weekly training, uniforms, advertising material, virtual offices for meetings, the purchase of the business centres in the software plus a personal website.

Another bonus is the mentoring bonus, where the sponsor has to start a program we call "mentor", where he teaches his new network partner about the product and business scheme. It is to reward whoever makes a certain amount of volume sold in their first thirty days, starting from a minimum of four new members.

The third bonus is super sponsorship, which means that new distributors can receive a large bonus at the beginning of their operations, no matter how long they have been with the company.

1 % of the monthly turnover of the total sales and sponsorships and which will be dis tributed among the three people who promote more sponsorship packages per month. It is to reward the effort in recruiting new distributors.

Also, at the beginning, we can request through social networks or newspapers the incorporation of founding partners if we need initial investment money; it is better than going to a bank, where they are generally reluctant to lend to those who are new entrepreneurs and to whom we sell small packages of shares of the company we have.

Residual bonds

These are bonuses based on the group sales volume of our downline. In our scheme we will develop five very aggressive ones, namely: the generational bonus, the bonus per business centre of the weak side, the compensation bonus on the strong side, the equalisation bonus and the halfway point bonus.

The first of these is the generation bonus, which is the residual. This bonus is earned by each of the generations that have joined directly or indirectly in the recruitment days or by invitation and can be from the first to the seventh generation in our example. This bonus rewards the teamwork of the associates in the long term.

It is based on forming two business centres in which two slopes are inaugurated, right and left. For example, you associate two people in one of the business centres and two in the other; these four will be the first generation. Then two more people enter the team that associate one of those previously associated, so they are the second generation, thus reaching the seventh generation in depth. The founder of this network will only have to lead the four of the first generation in their two business centres and closely monitor their other sixteen in their second line of two business centres.

They are group volume commissions (GV) of the work team up to the seventh generation in their sponsorship tree. Distributors have to generate sales volumes in their downstream organisation, balancing sales between the two sides. When the range of one thou sand points is reached or the ones you have adding the two slopes, a check of 10% up to 50% is accessed, depending on the position or rank in the scheme over the first generation of the GV. And, in addition, you will have access to 5% of the check of the volume of com missions received by the second generation up to the seventh in depth.

Each person I personally associate with, for which I have already received a onetime "quick start" fee, will be part of my first generation.

I can associate without limit the people I want, and no matter their place in the team volume tree or when I associated them, if they were associated by me it will always be my first generation.

The people I associate with my first generation are going to be his first generation and my second generation. The people I associate my second generation with will be my third generation, and so on. For each of my generations, from the second to the seventh, I will charge a percentage of 5% of their group commission volume (GV), that is, of all their checks.

The first generation is four people; the second is sixteen people; the third is sixty four people; the fourth is two hundred and fifty six people; the fifth is 1024 people; the sixth is 4096 people; and the seventh is 16,384 people. Four at a time, it's that simple.

There is a total of 21,844 people in my sponsored generation tree.

Can you imagine the potential of 21,844 people, or better called in this jargon networkers, selling a product?

Two issues we will consider: compression, which is a mechanism to bypass distributors who have not qualified or who are inactive, where they are paid only for active levels of distribution. And spill over, which is when those who sponsor their A and B sides fail to get B to develop or recruit their two sides. Then, the team mentor recruits two new members and places them under B.

The second bonus is per business centre, where each distributor builds these two organizations based on their two business centres. This two organization structure allows you to create depth in your group and ensure you receive excellent support from the line of sponsorship. In this commission you will receive 10% of the monthly GV.

There is no limit to the number of people you can associate, and all the people you associate are placed on the right or left side, always trying to keep the two balanced. Each associate, in turn, will open two more slopes and will associate people who will also associate people in their own two slopes, and so on. What is assembled is a tree that grows exponentially.

Every end of the month, the company will add up the points of the right and left slope plus the two slopes of each associate and will pay me and everyone else 10% of the points accumulated on the weak slope, that is, the one that added the least points.

The third bonus is the compensation bonus. If the volume between the two sides exceeds three thousand points, for example, or those you have in your business plan, you get a compensation of 5% on the total volume of the strong side up to a limit you choose, as well as the amount of points required to compensate this side.

The room is the equalizing room. It compensates with 5% of GV over all its weaker slopes. In the two business centres, only the points of the weak sides of the business are added up. In each business centre, you have two sides, and one side in turn will exceed the other in terms of turnover; for this bonus, you always take the weak side of a business centre, CN1, and the weak side of the other business centre, CN2, add both points and from them you get 5% and multiply it by what each point is worth, which will be stipulated in its value from the beginning one euro is equivalent to ten points, or whichever one fits the most in your calculations.

A minimum point condition must always be applied in order to obtain these bonuses, i.e. all those distributors who have X amount of points can participate.

The fifth bonus is the mega medium bonus. It is applied to the points obtained in the weakest part of my network every six months. Same operation as the previous one. You get, let's say, in those six months 10 000 points. You get 5%, which is equivalent to 500 points, which you multiply by what each point is worth in local currency.

Leadership Bonus

The first bonus is the global common fund, which applies to those who acquire an intermediate plan in the organization and beyond. It is equivalent to 3% of the sales volume commissions of all the distributors; participating with a minimum group quantity of X amount of points of the commission volume, it is divided among all those who have reached that volume.

The second bonus, developing leaders, which is charged for each additional generation line generated and maintained per quarter, with a minimum of one thousand points of GV, and five hundred dollars example are charged for each of the lines we form.

The third bonus is the equalization bonus and applies to the three consecutive months in which a minimum of three thousand points of the group volume (GV) is accumulated, is an example, and 5% of the total GV of the first generation is obtained, that is to say, of all the bonuses and checks of that first generation.

The fourth is the fast bonus, which is for those who form three new distributors with two fifty VG bands in their first month.

The fifth is the fast & furious, which applies every time a distributor generates a fast bonus structure for three months in a row. Its charges double the amount paid in the fast.

The sixth one is the rank advancement. With the compensation plan, team members earn for their achievements in any of the positions within the distribution structure. They are paid from a given rank and each time a level is promoted a onetime check is cashed.

You must have a minimum volume to climb that will be listed in the last column of a requirements table. All positions must specify missions to be accomplished and territories or cities to be conducted in each position, where they must also teach, recruit, organize and sell.

Competition bonds

The championship bonusses. Every month all the groups or business units compete against each other, eliminating each other week by week. They compete in pairs and in different rank groups.

Then the winners of each stage go on to the next week, and so on until the last week of the month, until they get a winner in each category, which takes 1% of the GV of each range of the global business line in which it qualifies.

The pleasure voucher has access to different prizes, such as trips, televisions, cell phones, motorcycles, etc.

How did we manage to develop our scheme? It is only with a burning desire, work behaviour, goal mentality, perseverance, never giving up, constant training, eliminating negativity with 100% positive attitude, knowing how to listen to the advice of your sponsor and teamwork were the engine of success.

We achieved this with a first class brand, but it fits in every sense and place to implement this type of business where ordinary people can invest a small amount of money, join an organization that works and thus achieve economic rewards out of the ordinary. The most daring thing we recommend is to make your own history.

Automated prospecting with robots in social networks

First and foremost, create a brand with your logo and good professional photos, a Face book, a Fan page, a website to capture data, an Instagram and a YouTube channel, and all this to achieve brand virality.

Facebook fan page

Create a group and traffic through interaction, relate the audience and build the group itself. Have a daily budget for a Facebook business manager. Set locations on automatic. Also keep in mind that Facebook charges me when I get "liked".

By publishing on Facebook, I got 50,000 followers on this social network when I had two restaurants in Panama. The truth is that having paid advertising on Facebook does work, and a lot! And then also combine it with Google Ads, without forgetting to have an Instagram business account to generate statistics. My restaurants were always full.

Explore the best markets to sell our products through our Facebook page or Instagram account. We have some tools such as Google Trends, which allows us to observe the trends of the most unique terms or keywords in the Google search engine for the product we are targeting; another very important tool to be able to know for sure the region or city in which to focus our campaigns is the Cross Border Insights Finder, which compares the main opportunities to achieve the best results, and the last one, which is paid, called SEMrush, which is very complete for network SEO.

Create YouTube Channel

By creating an account on Google Ads and our page on YouTube.

We create advertising through YouTube Ads. We make the video with the cell phone if we don't have great means and then we can use platforms like Movavi or so many others to edit it. I take it to my channel and to the data capture website. We continue to budget on Google Ads. Example: one dollar equals one hundred views per day.

How to create a campaign

In Google Ads we have an option to create a specific image and video marketing campaign to capture the attention of the target audience of the campaign, in this case, to enter the network and consume the product.

We must have developed a short thirty second to one minute video, selfie type, where we call to take part of the organization and the benefits, they will acquire in it, and then they contact us by WhatsApp leaving comments.

At that time, we sent our WhatsApp API link. We link all the networks, or another option is to have a link to your website, where they can find a more extensive informative video, explaining in detail the proposal and profit potential without saying the price of membership yet, enter the network and start selling the products.

It is only this stage to prepare them for the call we will have to make to close personally. We send a WhatsApp to find out what state the contact is in, if he has already seen the informative video and to evacuate possible doubts.

To create the WhatsApp API and automatically answer the message we program, we must, using Google, search for "WhatsApp API", read the explanation and arrange a text previously thought, for example, "I want business information".

With respect to Facebook, we must post our posts in groups asking for suggestions according to our business in no more than five groups a day, as we may be blocked.

We can guide interested people directly from Facebook to our WhatsApp and set up an auto response with the WhatsApp robot: "Thank you for your interest in the free conference, to attend the event, please contact us", for example. Always respond with a picture, text, audio and link to the video.

Create a marketing funnel

Use data capture page templates and mount the videos there, there are many on the Internet. People register there with their email, generating a database. They watch the one minute video and then the fifteen or twenty minute news clip and then contact us at WhatsApp.

Facebook Robots

We can use the robots proposed by Facebook or use others, such as the Mega Publish er V3, which shares in thousands of groups at once and makes you get leads automatically and you can program. It has a minimum monthly cost.

Instagram Robots

It's about going on and off people based on hashtags. Send automatic messages to everyone who adds you as a friend on Instagram. There are several software, Next Post, Jarvee, Joolstar, Izzod, with minimum monthly costs or pay to companies, such as www.boostmyfollowers.com, where you buy followers on all platforms.

WhatsApp Robots

There is one called Autoresponder for WA. It is only available for Android. It automatically responds in a personalized way using rules that you create to respond in seconds. You have to combine it with the use of API.

In conclusion, let us know that this method based on recommendation and sale is one of the best schemes to consider when implementing a business if it is done seriously and responsibly

Chapter 16: Administrative Functions

"A person is all the happier the fewer useless desires he has."

BUDDHA

"Imagination is more important than knowledge."

ALBERT EINSTEIN

The team manager is the one who completes a sales group in our scheme. For each sales force unit, we must implement a customized account manager to give greater efficiency and versatility to the correct presentation of contracts.

It is a work coordinated between the administration and the sale. Where there is a mismatch between the two, we will lose a lot of sales. Like the applause, which needs two hands to sound, is how this unit of work should be interpreted. 50% of the sales effectiveness belongs to the administration and the rest to the sales groups.

It is advisable to have bonuses for the quality of the accounts for the administrative department and not for the production in an area where there is the possibility of cancellation of clients.

In the administrative field there are different areas, as we saw in previous paragraphs, that we must cover. One of the important ones is the telephone follow up of clients, either to evacuate concerns or to request referrals. We must take care of the detail in the quality call that we will make after the sale.

It is advisable to draw up an effective sales or customer service dialogue so as not to neglect and leave such an important instance to chance.

We should not trust those who speak softly on phone calls, as they are usually not handling the call properly and are stealing our time, affecting quality customer service.

It is important to avoid elements that spend a lot of time on the Internet; they are harmful, because they spend part of this time surfing and losing hours of our time.

The administration should have a responsible or general coordinator and a team of administrative staff who are in the meticulous and orderly control of the preparation and delivery of invoices, facilities or delivery of equipment, stock control, deposits of money from customers, calls to applicants of the notices, loading data from new customers in the system for the analysis department, be pending an audit and quality call as soon as the seller leaves the closing to corroborate data and the veracity of the information provided, also conduct telephone negotiations with difficult customers.

Already in the area of the relationship with the corporation, we must be in permanent contact, attending to suggestions, technical services or possible failures in the equipment. You must prepare the presentation of forms, photocopies, contracts, and also file the curricula vitae of those who attended training sessions.

We must set up an audit in Excel to be carried out for each account. It facilitates the payment of commissions and shows, in a synthetic way, the operations of the month. It must have the day of the sale, the customer's data, the product he bought, who sold it, supervisor and coordinator, plus who delivered or installed it, the contact and invoicing data. We must also add the status of the account if it is still in process, is low, activated or incomplete, marking the active ones with a yellow color, for example.

For cell phones or similar products that you see fit, it is good practice to have the de livery of the equipment made by an organization separate from the sales environment. It will be a structure that we can put together based on personnel with availability of cars or motorcycles and who know the city very well with GPS tracking.

We will not opt for the delivery of a piece of equipment by the seller, as this will distract attention from the fundamental objective, which is the sale of new clients, and thus avoid possible account fraud as everything will be left in the hands of the seller alone. We were able to observe how distributors fell into innumerable frauds for this reason.

In this organization chart, we will use a home delivery manager who will put together the daily routes to be covered and contact the customers to combine the schedules. He will also control that all the units deliver the equipment on time and form and will request the conformity sheets, which must be signed by the clients to whom they deliver the acquired equipment. They are in charge of collecting deposits, fees or amounts per purchase if any. They will also corroborate address, document of who receives the equipment, preferably taking a photo with the cell phone of the person who receives it.

There will be a credit area or administrative control desk, another customer service area that will call the entire portfolio of users, if it is a service we are selling, once a month to verify the degree of customer satisfaction, solving possible technical services not yet detected by the audit. Dissatisfied customers will be passed on for further attention.

A customer service form is used for these follow-ups, filling out one for each one and filing them month by month for later follow up.

Each executive will be in charge of three months of follow up of the same client. The stock area makes sign numbering that delivers in the corresponding form. Verify that the quality control sheet is signed by the client. Controls the stock of equipment, brochures, uniforms, noting each item on a form.

As for the profile we are looking for in management, we must differentiate between those who have a purely administrative profile and those who have an inclination and empathy for sales. It can even be an accounting assistant or an administrative career, but above all it must be very tidy and with a lot of initiative.

The best elements, in general, are those who do not spend an hour reading and rereading the employment contract, as they are the product of mistrust, fear and negativity, which come from bad experiences where they were misunderstood.

In our offices we can install a telemarketing telephone marketing based on some points that should not be overlooked. First and foremost, we must implement a manual with the coordinates we must have for each case and call. Take into account a sales script that includes objections and a closing manual by phone. Four hour shifts should be taken for those who are fully committed to this task. Each group of operators must be motivated and guided by a supervisor. For each shift there should be two teams working and competing. Implement chimes as a way to start or end certain call times or momentary incentives. Implement a battery of intangible and tangible incentives. Good commissions for redeeming contracts that were withdrawn, accompanied by bonuses and prizes. If there are referrals, we should have some sellers who are ready to go to a closing as the phone deals go out.

Chapter 17: Initial Investment and Fixed Business Costs

"The envy in men shows how miserable they feel, and their constant attention to what others do or don't do shows how bored they are.

ANONYMOUS

Let's talk, then, about how much we need to invest. We must calculate an initial investment that must be extended to support the preopening, the launch and the first three months of fixed costs.

We call preopening the process of making up the commercial company, the renting of the offices, the furniture and everything that involves the preparation of the sales material
uniforms, folders, promotional material, rental vans, plotters, printing, door hangers and stickers.

As for the launch, we refer to the Internet connection, a photocopier, printer, communications, cameras and security alarms, GPS for company related vehicles, money for daily and first month incentives in prizes, money for daily gasoline, advertisements in the newspaper or on the job search website, morning coffee, office cleaning supplies, daily office supplies blackboards, printing paper, pens, etc.

As far as dealing with the first round of fixed costs, it refers to covering those that we cannot avoid until the collection of our first commissions, which corporations usually pay between fifteen and thirty days after the end of the month, while others every fifteen days to maintain a cash flow to their distributors.

This means that we must pay at least three weeks' wages if our brand does not subsidise them.

We have to pay for the second month's rent, electricity, office maintenance, communications payments cellular and fixed telephones, and provide for the payment of all inputs and services.

I comment again that some international corporations invest a lot in their distributors by supporting them with rents or salaries and fixed expenses; therefore, in these cases, their investment really becomes minimal.

We must take into account the months of deposit for rent. To have a minimum computer. The office furniture. A projector to project our trainings, for which we must have a laptop as well. Uniforms, polo shirts and hats. We are talking about approximately fifteen thousand dollars/euros; for in a year or two to earn a million is not bad at all.

Let's remember that this is a business that leaves us 35% to 50% profit at the end of our costs.

What is important, as I have mentioned in this book, is the faith, conviction, strength, perseverance and vision that we determine to have in order to achieve our goals. We do not have enough money to implement all this battery of sales material and incentives up front; we will get it in the first few collections of commissions, and more than that. It will definitely change our life. Let nothing and nobody stop us. Let's close the doors to negative comments and people, isolate ourselves from friends and family if necessary, for a while, above all, so that we can concentrate and not have to listen to the litanies of those who have nothing to contribute.

We were also one of those who began by investing our latest resources and quickly multiplied our investment by one hundred in the first six months. This has always happened to us, and here is the secret, poured out in these pages.

Follow your dreams with faith, mental concentration, action and they will always come true, there is no option for failure, unless you project it yourself or the gentle breeze of negativity enters through a crack.

Chapter 18: Interaction with the Corporation and its Directors

"To be excellent is to do things, not to look for reasons to prove they can't be done."

MICHELANGELO CORNEJO

"The past is history, the future is a mystery, today is a gift, that's why it's called the present.

ANONYMOUS

In communications and electronic security are the business niches with which we develop greater commitment in time and the sales organization that we propose.

The interaction between our company and the corporation is very important; it is the basis on which we must build respect, love for the brand we represent and commitment to its objectives. We must constantly coordinate our actions.

In the least conflictive situation, our experience is that it is not convenient to send an email of complaint to a superior in the chain of command, it is much better to pick up the phone or make a trip to the offices to have a cordial chat and be able to solve the problem. Always bring our best, the consultation should be permanent and if we can give a hand in providing ideas to the corporation, even better.

Sometimes we will see unexpected changes in the driving of these. These changes occur because the commercial management cannot find the way to develop a successful product distribution. They don't know how to run a distributor organization, they don't know their needs, they don't listen, and they don't talk, they just execute policies, and sometimes destructive ones, without assuming the mistakes product of corporate employees without enough experience.

The following is an example of what we can expect, which shows a situation that, although it is not very normal, is an extreme that at some point we may encounter when we are the general management of a multinational with a very poor internal organization.

There were four telecommunications companies in Panama in 2009. According to a note in the newspaper La Prensa of 01/13/2010, the country's largest daily newspaper, in that year, among all these companies they had sold a total of about 42,000 new postpaid contracts throughout the country. We with our distributor in that year sold 15% of that market of the company of which we were distributors. It should also be noted that our organization sold twice as much, but the multinational said it did not have enough staff to handle all our accounts and simply discarded the customers.

As we had not anticipated the flow of sales, the corporation did not have the infrastructure or the ideal personnel for such a flood of contracts in that 20092010, which left out, without processing, that 50% of our production. Added to this was the poor distribution of the invoice to customers, which was only done via the web when all the competition sent it to their homes, as was the usual practice.

Sending the invoice to the customers is an old method and has an added value in the more personalized treatment for the customer, besides being a psychological method of fundamental information for the customer to commit to the payment of the invoice, even a means of communicating news of the company by incorporating an information page attached to the invoice. Not all users access or are aware of their emails or Internet connection, let's agree. It was only possible to pay in the customer service offices, which were few, and not in banks or other very common sites of collection of services in any country or place nowadays.

There were also problems with the overbilling that customers received. All of this greatly limited good service, since it was even in the hands of companies that were intermediaries in the service.

Imagine the employees of these intermediary companies; they don't have the brand's T-shirt on, much less drink from the mystique of belonging to it; in short, the commitment of these employees to the corporation is zero. They only aspired to their meagre salaries and to meet their departure schedules, since in these offices they did not pay commissions or prizes, much less motivate or train.

They launched two products, wireless Internet and fixed line for the home, with major advertising campaigns during those years. They were selling very well, but due to technical problems they were unable to solve, they were taken out of circulation. All this was because the general director had the preconception that the labour element was not of quality in that country, he lived repeating this affirmation, nobody served, nobody did his job well, in short, according to him. Nothing could be further from the truth; he had an easy, shortsighted and limited view of the circumstances surrounding him. He preferred to blame the labour element rather than his blatant ignorance of his business decisions and strategies.

I did not understand at the time how our competitors could do things with much less publicity, and even we, in our company, where we had recruited the right people in all areas. The paradigmatic paralysis in the mind of this CEO was evident, added to the poor selection of personnel that these intermediary companies and the corporate headquarters itself had. It was an implosive cocktail that attempted to develop a significant sale of contracts, resulting in the loss of 50% of production, in our case, in those years.

At the same time, all this became that they only focused on the sale of prepaid, leaving aside the sale of contracts of all kinds cellular, fixed telephony or Internet.

It was easier and more straightforward for him to handle a sale without sending an invoice, without customer service, without support structures, without professional sales forces, without distributors; in short, without any sales or aftersales effort involved in the whole structure of postpaid contracts, whether for mobile phones, landlines, television or the Internet.

Soon, a contract was only sold if the customer had automatic credit card debit, which limited the sale as well. Our company, likewise, sold a very good production in this modality, but at the same time we were informed that they could never give the relevant ACH discount to the clients, so all those invoices were added, about four months, to a debt created by the ineptitude of this general management.

That policy generated a diaspora of executives towards the competition. This is the most extreme case we have ever experienced. We thought that after so many years on our backs in five countries we had seen it all. We achieved our sales and profit objectives, but without any support from the multinational after the arrival of the new policies that were implemented.

This type of director usually imposes a status quo on all aspects of the corporation so as not to complicate his daily routine and enjoy the comfort that his work position implies. To this end, they invent a discourse tailored to the corporations and their highest hierarchies that justifies their inoperativeness without raising too many suspicions. They apply policies that add up to customers who are with one brand today and with another tomorrow, but that do not add up to the profits they should have based on the deployment of advertising and infrastructure they implement. I always found such advertising on TV, newspapers, magazines and public roads just to sell prepaid cards of two dollars or five or twenty phones derisory.

These directorates create downsizing policies in place of not having successful expansionary sales policies due to poor selection of area pipelines and, in conclusion, do not see other options. Not having a north in that commercial area, or rather, not finding someone to lead the sector's expectations, they prefer to cut back on sales jobs. These commercial directions do not know the term "train", much less "motivate".

They change business managers like you change your clothes.

In one year, we saw up to five business managers pass by under our noses, in other times it was three, and so on in all the countries for which we had our company. It is for the same reason that, sometimes, those who lead the multinationals in each country do not find the point of balance that the organization needs in terms of effective commercial management. It is also probable that the general management at some point gets tired of so

246

much trying and decides to take another easier road to travel, such as selling less complicated products that do not need so many trained personnel.

These people, who for a short time held the position of commercial director, never had time to talk to the distributors, never answered an email, much less their cell phones, never trained or motivated, and never set short or medium term goals and objectives. The conclusion: they are fired without any shame or glory.

In Mexico, in 2006, another director of these basics appeared. He was dedicated to lowering the commission to half for distributors and to calling us sales promoters in exchange for distributors or business allies, as he had done until then. Think small and small you will be; that would be the corollary for this character. Instead of encouraging production, he would come to destroy everyone who made honest money investing in the brand's project.

These types of directors are synonymous with the mediocre ones that unfortunately abound in the corporations, who are rising in the ranks not because of merit, but because of friendships that are forged along the way.

Sometimes, it is the corporations that trust in inexperienced hands the selection of their new executives; those talent selection companies often fail and give away any character that knows how to sell in a job interview and has a bulky theoretical resume, but that, in short, has no idea what a corporation's business direction is and how to achieve results in quality sales.

The same company, but this time its subsidiary in Spain, called us to join it again. Here he opted for the opposite; he was starting at the same time a new commercial program called the same as the one in Mexico that was killing the aforementioned director. In Mexico they called it Allied Program and in Spain they called it Alliance.

Same corporation, same name of program; while in Mexico they lowered the commission by half, in Spain they went out to compete with the same amount that Mexico left behind, four hundred euros per contract, and the team delivered it separately for installation. At that time, the euro was quoted at 1.65 to the dollar; therefore, it was about six hundred dollars, the same as what they paid in Mexico on account in that year.

In short, it follows, and it occurs to me in the face of facts that everything depends on the general directions that there are in each country and the trade policies that the CEO of the moment comes up with. Let us know this and make it an integral part of our decision when we choose one country or another, one corporation or another; it is a very important detail to take into account who is leading and where.

If the credit is closed to incorporate customers, it is also an important fact to take into account, because, as happened to us in Colombia, only one out of ten sales passed the credit and the commercial and general manager of the region of Antioquia was conspicuous by his absence; they were those uncommitted characters who are only filling a vacancy for a juicy salary to execute policies that do not make a difference, without motivation, training, or even contact with their agents and distributors, without a project or plan to follow.

It is also added, and we must be careful, that some of the middle management will attempt a chase, with the consequent psychological wear against our company because of our status as a successful foreign company. The bias of discrimination is always felt.

We learned that discrimination is synonymous with ignorance and envy as well, and it is a regrettable fact that they will always have to struggle with when they set up abroad as entrepreneurs. There are places where even as a tourist you are treated badly by the usual discriminators. They are a mediocre and resentful minority, but they make themselves known.

There were times when I had to hear things like, although foreign investment creates jobs, then it steals the country's money and does not allow other local entrepreneurs to grow, when it is quite the opposite, it not only creates jobs, but it pays taxes and that goes directly to the country's infrastructure and benefits everyone, in addition to enriching the strategies of local entrepreneurs with their international experiences.

Definitely, these notable directors, not because of the noble, but because they make themselves known with their bad practices, are moved by inefficiency based on ignorance. They think they are less than an entrepreneur and envy the profits of those of us who invest and undertake.

Their actions are based on their lack of strategy, they are afraid to sell, they do not know how to sell, neither do they train nor motivate, they come from the administrative field or, if they have ever been salesmen, they do not have the money to be leaders, they manage the work groups as they would manage the cattle, they do not govern the corporation by example, but by fear and persecution.

They don't change policies; they send others to do their dirty work for them. They are unstable in their decisions and highly influenced by their inner circle of collaborators, who are of the same mediocrity as their boss.

They think they are smarter than others, they are dismissive, incoherent, changeable, sanguine, brash, they are little authoritarian dwarfs, they have the charisma and the sympathy, but they do not use it correctly, it is only a facade that they adjust to their convenience, they do not respect the work of others and the neighbour is transformed into a passing circumstance.

I don't wish them to cross paths, but if they have that bad experience, they should be treated in a very cordial way, telling them everything that they are and not discussing anything. Try to make them very sympathetic and conciliatory until their almost inevitable departure from the corporation in time.

Changing the subject and taking up again how to get a distribution, we can argue that it is a simple task, following the guidelines we gave in this book, delivering the business plan, arranging a meeting with the commercial manager, deputy commercial director, the manager or coordinator of distributors and presenting their ideas based on these lines, where we have delivered enough material to propose a win win business scheme to the corporation. Show your assembled trainings in PowerPoint. Show conviction in your words and show that you have sales goals to meet with concrete deadlines. Move quickly once distribution is obtained.

There are frequent occasions when these decisions are delayed. The problem will always be some party that opposes our entry as a distributor, or the process requires it. Arm yourself with patience and faith. Generally, it takes up to three months to sign a contract.

The CEOs we talk about very well, and who fortunately abound in these international megacompanies as well, practice open door management and fluid dialogue with the distributors and the entire company they lead.

Generally, our incorporation was effective, as these were times in those countries where the corporation was in need of the type of services, we provided, and the requirements became minimal to obtain distribution.

Similar happened to us in Costa Rica with the entry of two other companies; the first one invited us to participate in the opening of this new operation, an invitation we attended very enthusiastically. Two trips were enough to see the disorganization in this first stage of the company.

I decided to go to the doors of the state owned company, which at that time felt it was losing 50% of the market to these two world class telecommunications companies.

We were very well received, and a unique contract was signed, making us the only postpaid distributors in the country among two hundred companies associated with their brand of cell phones.

These are moments of the historical type where brands need to associate distributors that promote obsolete or depressed structures.

As I mentioned in previous chapters, the same thing happened to us in Mexico when we arrived there, where there were only three distributors out of eighty who had been left out of the company. There are times and places where these large international corporations will need sales schemes like the one, we propose.

Conclusion: everything is negotiable if the project we present is serious and attractive. Let's negotiate and keep negotiating until we reach an agreement.

The most important thing is to have the firm conviction that we will be part of the project of a multinational and that we will bring great quality sales to it; that must be our greatest motivation and goal.

Chapter 19: Implementing a Successful Corporate Policy

"The power of imagination is stronger than the power of reason."

BLAISE PASCAL

Constant improvement must be focused on providing friendly solutions and personalized attention to customers. This is what defines a multinational or company that seeks to obtain total quality in the provision of services.

But they cannot have a management of this kind if they do not start by implementing an intelligent internal marketing directed towards the distributors, who will be the image before the potential clients, since they will carry the brand of the corporation in their uniforms and facilities when they present themselves in the name of the same to the market, a market that is more and more competitive and selective every day. In short, they will be the ones who provide the brand with its sales, follow up and aftersales customer advice. We are talking about the companies associated as distributors to a multinational.

From the commercial and general management of the brand, they must understand this vital concept in order to experience a dizzying ascent to the top and position themselves in a framework of efficiency in obtaining and retaining new customers. We cannot leave this kind of corporate partners to chance. They are the distributors of the product, who have the first contact with the customer and often continue it afterwards.

We cannot try to block the sun with a finger by providing only mediocre and boring product training to their staff and believe that with it the mission is accomplished. Certifications that are of no use without quality motivation and concrete and proven sales techniques on the field, i.e. on the streets and in the points of sale.

These commercial managers must know that they must create the necessary motivation in the entrepreneur and teach him/her how to do things, develop a methodology, show the way, give him/her the necessary material.

Sometimes, CEOs or business managers rely too much on the experience sold to them by inexperienced entrepreneurs, believing their own lies about sales without any method and, therefore, without a certain future of results. Entrepreneurs who lack expertise or are afraid to take too many risks. Conclusion, both end up in an announced failure, the entrepreneur and the commercial director in charge of the corporation, and that is why so many changes in the commercial staff of companies and brands that we have always seen happen.

The only more or less sustainable advantage is service and customer care. The common point in all prestigious companies should be to work tirelessly thinking about how to efficiently satisfy the needs of the customers, covering in the first instance the needs of their distributors so that they can correctly attend to their needs and so that the sale, from the first moment, is of quality and does not fall down at the first blow of wind.

These are needs that range from product training to sales techniques, with the appropriate motivation that must be generated in these ventures in their beginnings, which are babies that are learning to walk in most cases.

To the extent that a distributor feels valued and respected, this transfer of brand culture will be possible.

Corporations should make their distributors aware, make them feel part of it and not enemies or simply consider them occasional partners. Put their shirt on so they can sweat it out together. Without mentalizing the goals and objectives of the corporation in their distributors, there is no roots or path to follow, it is impossible for them to trace them by themselves, with some exceptions. The entrepreneur must be educated in the culture and business philosophy and in what we intend to offer our customers. Quality and service. Efficiency and speed in the solutions we provide. The advice must be constant. Training in the handling of the product. Sincerity and quality in the attention.

So called "successful companies" offer quality services. This excellence in customer satisfaction sought by many corporations should have no ceiling in sight, as customers demand more and better quality at a lower cost every time. Corporations must decode the demands of an increasingly changing, unstable market, with a customer who today moves his company if he does not see his concerns or demands satisfied.

Creativity in business directions is not a constant today in the vast majority, at least that was what we experienced in different countries and years.

Commercial managers must reinvent themselves and put into practice that part of the organization that is open to learning new techniques for motivation and sales.

Many business managers say they bring a wealth of experience to the corporation, but ultimately they don't present work plans or know little about a one on one sales conversation with a customer, much less train a sales force or organize a selection of personnel or the motivation their distributors require on a month to month basis to achieve goals. Their goals end up being confusing and seem like firemen putting out fires rather than organizers of the success the company deserves.

They are hired to provide solutions and more sales, and they only bring their baggage of excuses, because they don't even know where to start. Without a plan or objectives, it's dead management, an empty chair, a nonexistent talent rental. This is what I have seen for years.

Communication, in the end, is what fails; these kinds of directors do not communicate clearly or directly, they hide like an ostrich in their head because they have nothing to say based on their ignorance.

According to the Centre for Financial Studies in Spain, the behaviour of bad leaders or bosses is classified into ten main items: lack of clarity in objectives, failure to motivate, failure to communicate well, failure to listen, failure to lead, failure to teach, failure to train, frequent contradiction, managerial incompetence, failure to manage time well, frequent stress.

These ten points are the ones we have experienced at times when dealing with these types of directors in corporations.

I would add to this qualification that they are only interested in their welfare, salary and armchair, no matter what their collaborators feel or think.

Welfare is based on collecting your salary at the end of the month and having the best time possible without anyone noticing your blunders. They prefer to cover them up with a policy of fear and not of respect and admiration that leadership does bring.

They are characters who block their most talented subordinates from aspiring to take their place. They make other people's work their own. They are usually submissive to their superiors as a way of mimicking their ineffectiveness. He does not produce anything, only criticizes and usually does not even correct the badly done work of the employees. He does not support or promote any training. More than a leader, he assumes the role of foreman of the treasury. He will never be seen to take responsibility or make mistakes in his decisions, blaming his policies for failure and throwing out those who follow him in the chain of command.

It is very difficult to change the mentality of middle managers who do not know or are closed to learning. They end up retired from their jobs because they do not meet expectations. We have always experienced this. It is synonymous with not finding the necessary point of balance for the development of a corporate project.

It is evident that what is not known is frightening and paralyzing; then, better to eliminate it, is an old reaction that some who experience this sensation execute.

They are managers or directors who destroy everything that can bring problems because they do not know how to handle it. It is simpler to blame, to accuse, to look at the straw in someone else's eye and not the beam in one's own, they prefer to eliminate the distribution, because they cannot and do not know how to contain a contract sales overproduction, they fear it and end up losing all the effort and corporate investment.

They base their policy on the panic of casualties and what they attract by law of attraction are lower. They'd rather keep a small farm than conquer the market. They think small and remain small. They're mental midgets.

It is so important to understand these concepts from a business management perspective that there is no other possible way to their success. We can always aspire to a greater degree of efficiency in the management of a chain of distributors, but it will be given by our ability to listen, the flexibility we have at all times and the nature of the good manager in seeking to exceed each objective of each distributor.

The good director assumes as his own that overcoming of each commercial partner and achieves it offering permanent training, frank participation that arises from the interior of the scheme of distributors, giving them the space so that they can contribute solutions to concrete experiences that are translated in learning for the implementation of policies that lead to the efficiency of the organization.

One dissatisfied customer is equivalent to sixty three bad references. If we have a thousand casualties, there will be 63,000 who think badly of us; therefore, our target market is shrinking considerably every day.

In our experience, what the departments that should be in charge of customer containment do is that they deal with the accounting of customer departures without trying to retain them. In short, they are bad elements embedded in corporations that perfectly complement poor management of commercial and general management.

They are only aware of the departure time or lunch hour and what matters least to them are the customers, who fall in a waterfall. They only count them. They immediately find the culprit who, of course, do not consider themselves and their mismanagement, but the fault lies with the distributor.

A bad quality in the attention to the client, a bad calculation in their bill, a claim for signal or installation or flaws of the equipment not attended correctly or a confusion in the sale of a novice salesman transform them into big scandals when they discover one in thousand and flutter like bats to justify their static to pass for the chair that they occupy and they rush to give the discharge and to give the reason to the client, when the only thing that the same one looks for is understanding of their claims and not a discharge of the product in many occasions.

If these "desk tourists" who are hired by many corporations were to take care of proper customer care and retention, I assure you that they could not exceed 5% of casualties in any sales structure. The problem is that no one listens to the customer who complains, let alone provides solutions.

We have known directors of great prestige as well. They were people who knew how to recognize in public and in private the good work of their collaborators or distributors.

They were calm, even under pressure.

They knew the business and applied marketing strategies to position themselves in a competitive market. They motivated the distributors' investment in the business. They contained the distributor and knew how to listen to him; they were open door managers. They made good decisions that advanced the brand. They invested in the training of the distributors and their staff. They convinced everyone to row in the same direction. A manager like this conveys peace, wisdom, confidence and knowledge.

Good commercial management focused on motivation and on the growth of your chain of distributors must implement a series of policies that I set out below as a basic example.

Three aspects must be worked on: the motivational aspect, the organizational aspect and the training aspect.

It is the same as that of the company that acts as a distributor, they are similar schemes because, in short, we are all sellers and suppliers of a service.

Selection of personnel: encourage the distributor to make an intelligent selection.

Sales script: establish a single speech for all distributors through a group of trainers who know the technique perfectly and teach it didactically, with a lot of motivation, based on a sales script to develop in front of the customers.

Unify the distributors: unify a standard of uniforms.

Establish a ranking of companies: following up on the objectives and goals set at the beginning of the month for each distributor, sending out the updated ranking once a week to compare individual and general performance and thus create competition within the organization.

Organize a monthly evaluation meeting: on the first Monday of each month, establish a breakfast meeting with all the distributors to evaluate the performance, give intangible prizes, a diploma or trophy will be enough, to those who achieved the agreed goals, analyse the ranking, give the new goals for the next month, show graphics, statistics, a training talk, make a demonstration of a new product, present a new reward scheme for the most motivated distributors... Everything will be basic.

Implement a weekly breakfast with each distributor to follow up and where day-to-day issues will also be addressed.

Super Saturday: once a month, they will gather all the sales teams from all the organizations in a large room in a hotel or club. There will be a master training of coaches. From there they will go out to rake areas and a competition will be opened for that day among all the participating teams. At an appointed time, they will return to the meeting place and the proposed intangible and tangible prizes will be awarded.

Morning training schedule by corporate training staff, which will be cut once a week. They will be only in the morning so as not to take away useful time from sales. All kinds of topics related to business and sales technique will be addressed, accompanied by a lot of motivation.

Accompany the sales teams to the area once a week to strengthen the technique. The mission will be entrusted to the group of coaches from the headquarters.

Semiannual presentation trips: distributors will be invited to an extraordinary all inclusive training at a beach or mountain hotel where they will be given new and advanced sales techniques. Prestigious personalities or speakers will be called, exercises and sales practices will be done so that they know what their organizations are talking about. In the evenings, there will be special dinners organized by the public relations department. The main objectives for the semester will be outlined. The achievements will be rewarded with distinctions to the distributors who deserve them.

Institutional and technical sales video: one per distributor should be implemented so that they follow the same pattern in their training. It is very motivating for an applicant to know about the corporation he is joining. With the sales technique video, the sales script must be made available step by step so that future salespeople know what the job is all about. We must leave the preparation of the same to professionals in the field so that the video looks and impacts.

If all corporations understood the importance of implementing schemes such as those proposed, and which we also discussed in previous chapters, others would be the results of many directors who pass quickly without leaving any trace in the companies because they cannot achieve the level of organization and results requested by senior management.

Conclusion

**"Be always humble and keep your purity, because these are the two
wings that lift us up to God and almost deify us."**

FATHER ST. PIO DI PIETRELCINA

Statistics tell us that between 90 and 95% of entrepreneurs fail before the fifth year of starting out.

In Spain, for example, some 10 000 companies are dissolved every year, and that is the way the world is, very few know where to go to achieve economic success. They try and fail. Many do not try again, once is enough. Others follow that lifestyle, from failure to failure.

Let us always remember that every failure is a step on the way to final victory. This accumulation of experiences shapes us.

We just have to take note and not make the same mistakes. Now that you have this material, I believe that you will have no major problems finding the path and walking it safely, advancing daily, never going backwards, assuming that each obstacle is a step in the ascent to the top, an experience that will always accompany us, the path to success is zigzagging, never straight and with no stones in the way.

Never give up is the watchword, surrendering is synonymous with cowardice, a choice of the mediocre; it means sinking into the darkest depression, it is forgetting about dreams forever, it is denying oneself dignity and the right to triumph. It is the path that will lead us to a dead end where we will make a hole and from which we will not easily get out.

We must, at all costs, opt for the path of triumph until we exhaust our breath fighting for our dreams. An entrepreneur must know that the world of sales is competitive, tenacious, a world of constant, daily challenges.

He who, when faced with the first fall, problem, betrayal, change of corporate strategies, months of bad sales or resignation of personnel and others, feels anguish, tachycardia, uncontrollable fear, feels unprepared to undertake, then, through the assiduous reading of this material and others, he should fill himself with positive energy inside, mentally and spiritually.

He who does not like sales cannot be an entrepreneur. In the corporate world, the axiom is "I sell, therefore I am". Selling is the origin of business. Without sales there is no company, it is a utopia that feeds on failure.

If you are fearful or negative by nature, you better not try it if you are not willing to make a radical change. Sign up for yoga or a gym, ride a bike, go for a run, play tennis or soccer, or listen to music that puts you in a positive frame of mind. Buy yourself a battery of books from authors that feed your mind and don't stop reading until your spirit is filled with peace and strength.

Do you give up easily? Desist from that attitude, do not allow yourself to be defeated, a skirmish is not losing the war. Adversity will often knock at the door and from that supposedly negative experience will come our inspiration or urge us to take different paths, with other directions, to change our way of thinking and even our way of living.

What better opportunity than today to start a business. Feel the call within that voice that will inspire you to say enough to a life of frustration, it's time for success. Let's start generating those jobs from the creation of battalions of honest entrepreneurs, willing to accompany others to the top of happiness. This is achieved by being full in our jobs and obtaining the results we project to quench the thirst of our dreams.

Our attitude must be humble once we have obtained the money we long for, because pride often leads to losing what we have obtained and, in other cases, we lose more import ant things that we have inside.

There are those who do not want to accept or acknowledge their mistakes or the failures they had in their promotion. Others hide a past of suffering, and all because of the pride that dominates their thoughts, keeping a piece of resentment in the darkness of their interior.

They are those who are always in a hurry or busy or did not want to attend their call, in spite of the years of friendship or kinship that united them; neither will they remember those good times when they shared good moments and counted the coins to pay for the coffee, they are those who changed their feelings for other blacker ones, where ego, pride and greed abound. They are those who, although they swim in millions, would not dare to invite you to a coffee today or, if they were to have dinner, they would eat previously so as not to have to pay the bill.

I speak from experience, but some change for the worse and others do not. At the top, the inner truth of each person is revealed.

Never fall into this category when you make your first million dollars or euros. Stay at the good table with your old friends, share your bread with those in need, help those who ask you, address people cordially, acknowledge your origins; only in this way will you be authentic at heart and not transformed into a sack of pure vanity.

Become a knight of the court of good and not an ally of evil, a multitude of noble businessmen need our society and not rich vainglorious without a soul to show in the twilight of their time in this life under the sun.

How far from reality are those who lie to themselves and to their environment to think they are more powerful. There is no one who has not bitten the dust of defeat on their long road to success. Ask yourself the question that Padre Pio, St. Pius, the Franciscan saint of Italy, asked himself in one of his reflections: "Think about where you were a hundred years ago and where you will be a hundred years from now.

Once at the top, some recognize themselves as arrogant and stubborn, those who believe they know everything and believe they are right, those who do not admit their mis takes for fear that they will discover their inability to know how to listen, due to their stupid arrogance, which is only fed by their empty words, which few convince or delight; after a while, they do not live a reality, but a fantasy in which a series of automatons participate around them that slavishly affirm each speech of its owner, whom they detest.

He alone is convinced, but in reality he is slowly poisoning himself with his life of lies that he holds up to others as if they were a secret code that will one day lead him to a supposed victory or a pedestal, and in reality he is further and further away with every word he utters from the real meaning and destiny that we should give to a part of that accumulated fortune, to share with those who need it most.

Mission number one is to banish pride. In the face of success, to beat the ego. To avoid talking about your work affairs with supposed friends who will appear around you when you see them so changed, in short, to avoid envy, the greatest obstacle to our ambitions and projects and to be able to stay on top.

Most of life consists of making an act of presence, finding the courage, the guts to follow his vision, and starting a new company often depends on being there at the right time, that is the first step, and there, immediately, without any doubt, we must go to action, a fundamental decision to fulfil our dreams, there will be no possible result or form the word "success" in our lives, it will be truncated if we do not take action.

Once we detect an opportunity, we must cultivate the confidence to follow our dreams and bet our money, borrow it if necessary or incorporate a capitalist to our scheme, because the other crucial step is the small economic investment required to start our venture along with the great investment of enthusiasm that is also needed to plant and then harvest the grapes that will give way to good wine. Good ideas are worth more than all the money of an investor; therefore, make yourself worthwhile if you decide to share your project.

Talent is something that we must look for with an intelligent selection like the one we exposed, because it will be the material from which our house will be built, which is the company we will develop.

Always remember not to comment on projects until they are completed, and to avoid the environment of negative people. Try not to be afraid of anything, fear paralyzes and leads to failure, the things we are most afraid of are already happening to us and others will never pass beyond our tortuous thoughts. In the face of the storm, let us remember that eagles fly higher while birds hide.

The world is full of people who have not found their place in it yet, people with truncated careers, abandoned beings, neglected families who break up because of economic issues that burden them, entrepreneurs who fail because they do not know mentors to help them chart their destinies, people who have not had the courage to experience the happiness that God promised us on this earth as well and prefer to sink into a constant depression that leads us, at times, to drugs. Despair does not give us the necessary calm to sit down and project. Dreams, it is a question of state of mind, we will not be successful as long as we do not decide to be successful.

Perseverance will accompany us on this road without rest, as we said, let's treat her like a princess and not make her a heavy burden.

Success in business is not a place that we go through once and it's all over there, it's a constant, continuous, forever way of life. The world is full of opportunities, we just have to discover them, there they are, waiting for some daring, for someone to take the first step, to make the decision to start.

Let us discard the "can't" from our minds, and thus we will always find the path that will lead us to that undiscovered world.

In short, set your mind on the money goal you want to achieve with your project and what service or product you intend to give in return, determine the times to achieve it, make a plan to get there, educate your subconscious and take action. Nothing destroys steel, but its own rust; the same happens with people, only their minds can destroy them.

Faith, happiness and purpose are the axes that we must implement and carry along with our dreams as water for the desert we must cross. I hope that you reach the right decision in your life and take this path that I proposed so that you can leave your mark on this world and not pass like a shadow without anyone noticing your presence. Your time is valuable, do not waste it, give meaning to your life, whatever that meaning is for you; you can float like the leaves in autumn, swayed by the wind in any direction and under any circumstance that you have to live or you can fight for your dreams and convictions and thus write the wonderful story of your life.

Recommended reading that will inspire and complement this, your journey:

- Think and get rich, Napoleon Hill
- Habits of the Rich, Juan Diego Gomez
- Unbroken, Daniel Habif
- The power of now, Eckhart Tolle
- Rich father, poor father, Robert T. Kiyosaki
- The Spirituality of Success, Vincent M. Roazzi
- The total power of the mind, Dr. Donald L. Walson
- Handbook for winners, Suryavan Solar
- Ask and ye shall receive, Esther and Jerry Hicks
- Discover the secret, Janey Bray Attwood and Chris Attwood
- Create your own destiny, Patrick Snow
- Evology, Jaume Banchs López
- Power, Rhonda Byrne
- The law of attraction, Dr. Camilo Cruz
- Discover your unlimited potential, Cynthia Kersey
- Secrets of the Millionaire Mind, Angelica Eberle Wagner
- The guide of the entrepreneur, Hernán Herrera and Daniel Brown
- You can heal your life, Louise L. There are
- Hero, Rhonda Byrne
- Success does not come by chance, Dr. Lair Ribeiro
- **The fish that didn't want to evolve, Paco Muro**
- The power is within you, Louise L. There is
- Motivate to win, Richard Denny
- Change your mind and your life will change, Karen Casey
- **Change your attitudes, change your life, Robert Jeffress**
- Claims, Louise L. There
- How to get rich without worrying, Napoleon Hill
- **To success in five moves, Juan Luis Carratalá**
- Retention Management, Subhash Puri

Sergio Chiti schiti7@gmail.com

261